DEFUND

An Internatio

Chris (

First published in Great Britain in 2023 by

Policy Press, an imprint of
Bristol University Press
University of Bristol
1–9 Old Park Hill
Bristol
BS2 8BB
UK
t: +44 (0)117 374 6645
e: bup-info@bristol.ac.uk

Details of international sales and distribution partners are available at
policy.bristoluniversitypress.co.uk

© Bristol University Press 2023

British Library Cataloguing in Publication Data
A catalogue record for this book is available from the British Library

ISBN 978-1-4473-6166-4 hardcover
ISBN 978-1-4473-6167-1 paperback
ISBN 978-1-4473-6168-8 ePub
ISBN 978-1-4473-6169-5 ePdf

The right of Christopher Cunneen to be identified as author of this work has been
asserted by him in accordance with the Copyright, Designs and Patents Act 1988.

Cover design: Nicky Borowiec
Front cover image: Alamy/Allison Bailey
Bristol University Press and Policy Press use environmentally
responsible print partners
Printed and bound in Great Britain by CPI Group (UK) Ltd,
Croydon, CR0 4YY

FSC
www.fsc.org
MIX
Paper | Supporting
responsible forestry
FSC® C013604

Contents

Contents

List of abbreviations

2SLGBTQQIA	Two-Spirit, lesbian, gay, bisexual, transgender, queer, questioning, intersex, and asexual (Canada)
ABC	Australian Broadcasting Commission
AIM	American Indian Movement
ALS	Aboriginal Legal Service (Australia)
ANROWS	Australia's National Research Organisation for Women's Safety
APHA	American Public Health Association
ATSISJC	Aboriginal and Torres Strait Islander Social Justice Commissioner (Australia)
BAME	Black, Asian, and Minority Ethnic (UK)
BIA	Bureau of Indian Affairs (US)
BLM	Black Lives Matter
CBC	Canadian Broadcasting Commission
CCRB	Civilian Complaint Review Board (New York)
CDC	Center for Disease Control and Prevention (US)
CEDAW	UN Committee for the Elimination of Discrimination against Women
CROC	UN Convention on the Rights of the Child
DIA	Department of Indian Affairs (Canada)
EBP	Evidence-Based Policing
ICC	International Criminal Court
IPCC	Independent Police Complaints Commission (UK)
IPCC	Independent Police Complaints Council (Hong Kong)
IPID	Independent Police Investigative Directorate (South Africa)
IPOA	Independent Policing Oversight Authority (Kenya)

IVAWS	International Violence Against Women Survey
JR	Justice reinvestment
LAPD	Los Angeles Police Department (US)
LGBTQIA+	Lesbian, gay, bisexual, transgender, queer/ questioning, intersex, asexual
M4BL	Movement for Black Lives (US)
NCAT	National Campaign Against Torture (India)
NCHR	National Commission for Human Rights (Pakistan)
NIMMIWG	National Inquiry into Murdered and Missing Indigenous Women and Girls (Canada)
NSW	New South Wales (Australia)
NYPD	New York Police Department (US)
OC	Oleoresin Capsicum (Spray)
PACE	Police and Evidence Act 1984 (England and Wales)
RCADIC	Royal Commission into Aboriginal Deaths in Custody (Australia)
RCMP	Royal Canadian Mounted Police
UN	United Nations
VEOHRC	Victorian Equal Opportunity and Human Rights Commission
ZTP	Zero tolerance policing

About the author

Chris Cunneen is Professor of Criminology at the Jumbunna Institute for Indigenous Education and Research, University of Technology Sydney. He is also an honorary professor at University of NSW and James Cook University. He has published widely on First Nations legal issues, decolonialism, youth justice, policing, penality, and restorative justice. He is a Fellow of the Academy of Social Sciences in Australia, and a Fellow of the ANZ Society of Criminology.

Acknowledgements

Amanda Porter was involved in the initial conceptualisation of the book and her influence remains — especially through her uncompromising critique of policing and her dedication to advancing the rights of First Nations people. Simone Rowe introduced me to the progressive activist literature within disability studies which opened up a new horizon. She also challenged me with her commitment to abolitionism. In addition, Simone provided very helpful and critical comment on the draft chapters of the book. Michael Bryden provided some research assistance and useful discussions on police legitimacy. All my colleagues at the Jumbunna Institute for Indigenous Education and Research are a constant source of inspiration. I am very lucky to work in such a creative, supportive, and politically engaged environment. To all of you, I owe a huge debt of gratitude and many thanks! Of course, it goes without saying, errors and lack of insight are all mine.

1

Time for change

Introduction

The Black Lives Matter movement galvanised protest movements against police and state violence around the globe. A common theme in many protests was the demand to 'defund the police'. One of the motivations for writing this book is the increasing attention the idea of defunding or divesting from police forces is gaining in mainstream politics and media. We need to seriously consider what is required to fundamentally change the way policing operates. The option of divestment opens up this discussion. *Defund the Police* is not another book about police reform. It is an engagement in the contemporary debate on the politics and possibilities of police abolition. To date, the majority of popular and academic literature in policing studies, law reform, and criminology has been preoccupied with conventional ideas related to top-down police reform. These reforms include efforts, for example, to recruit diverse and inclusive police officers, to implement cultural-awareness training, to introduce technical solutions like the use of body cameras, to place limitations on the use of force, and to introduce police-led programmes aimed at cultivating localised or community policing. We have had decades of these types of reforms, and part of the explosion of protest internationally is driven by the profound sense of frustration at the inability of police to reform themselves.[1]

The protests against police violence and demands to defund the police in the US in 2020 were met with various responses from local, city, and state governments – for example, during the course of 2020 the Mayor of New York promised a $1 billion reduction in the NYPD budget; in Minneapolis the City Council voted to disband the Police Department, and several Minneapolis schools rescinded contracts with the Minneapolis police; the LA city council approved a cut to the Los Angeles Police Department (LAPD) budget of $150 million; Portland, Oregon shifted $4.8 million from the police to community safety initiatives. Many of these budgetary changes were later rescinded. Although the organisational structure and funding of the police in the US is different from many other countries – there are more than 17,000 local, state, federal, and specialist law enforcement agencies – the call to defund the police has raised important questions about the nature of policing, including whether police reform is possible, and perhaps more importantly, questions about our social priorities, the values we want to foreground, and the type of communities and society we aspire to create and live in.

Despite the promise of funding cuts, in recent years police forces around the globe have seen record budget increases. In the UK the government announced in January 2020 the biggest increase in police funding in over a decade, as part of the commitment to increase police numbers by 20,000 officers. In New South Wales (NSW), Australia, the state police force was awarded a record $4.4 billion budget for the 2018–2019 financial year, including the recruitment of 1,500 new police recruits – the most substantial increase in 30 years. In Canada, more than $15 billion was spent on the Royal Canadian Mounted Police (RCMP) in the 2017–2018 financial year, a significant increase over the previous year, and this ignores the cost of municipal/ city, provincial and other local police services. Meanwhile, some US cities and states – such as Philadelphia and Virginia – have seen a significant budget growth to their police forces in recent years and in spite of the push towards divestment. In other parts of the US there has been conservative political leverage *against* reducing local police budgets: in January 2021, Texas Governor Greg Abbott threatened various financial and other sanctions against any localities and cities in Texas that reduced their budgets for policing. And in New York City, despite the early promise of reduced funding, police budgets are again being increased after the mayoral election in June 2021.

Against this backdrop, social commentators and political activists have decried the *decades* of failed reform efforts and identified police violence as a public health and social justice issue. Manifestos have been written heralding the 'end of policing' and envisaging a 'world without police'.[2] While the appeal to defund the police appears disarmingly simple, it raises vital concerns covering a range of problems. What are the political, economic, and social reasons for divesting from police? And what does this look like in practice? What is the social and historical background to this movement locally and globally? And what does empirical research say about the merits of police reform and police divestment? These are all key questions explored in this book.

One focus in the divestment discussion has been to contrast police budgets with investment in social, health, education, housing, and other programmes. Community activist organisations in, for example, New York and Los Angeles have challenged the priorities of city spending. In New York, for every $1 spent on the NYPD, 29 cents are spent on homeless services, 25 cents on the Department of Health, 19 cents on housing preservation and development, 12 cents on youth and community development, and 1 cent on workforce investment. Similar examples have been repeated elsewhere.[3] However, simply cutting police budgets does not necessarily signal an end to policing. For example, as the effects of neoliberalism and austerity impacted in England and Wales following the global financial crisis of 2007–2008, police numbers were cut by approximately 14 per cent over the next decade. However, the cuts to social services budgets were even greater, and police took on an *expanded* role despite the cuts. Indeed, the police use of force in England and Wales also grew significantly during this period.[4] It is important to acknowledge the point made by the Movement for Black Lives (M4BL).

> Defunding is not just about cutting city budgets across the board as an austerity measure in the midst of an economic crisis – it is about reinvesting money cut from police departments into community-based services that meet basic needs and advance safety without using methods of policing, surveillance, punishment, and coercion. It is also about investing

in cultural life, arts, recreation, and the things that make and strengthen community and our dreams for our future.[5]

While the #DefundPolice hashtag emphasises the negative, the movement has always advocated to both *divest* from police and *invest* in 'jobs, education, housing, health care – all the elements that are required for a productive and violence-free life', according to leading abolitionist Ruth Wilson Gilmore.[6] The movement is about presence, not absence. It is about building life-affirming institutions; it is about creating the type of society that does not need to rely on force, violence, and mass incarceration.[7]

Not surprisingly, there has been some focus on the pragmatic approaches and solutions that can provide for community safety and replace the police as a state institution of repression. The M4BL has produced a toolkit for activists which outlines political processes and strategies aimed at defunding the police, as well as a range of policies and programmes that can be developed to replace the police. I return to these approaches during the course of the book. The contemporary movement to defund the police has been closely connected to the Black Lives Matter (BLM) movement in the US since its establishment in 2013 after the acquittal of an armed neighbourhood watch captain for the killing of Trayvon Martin, an unarmed Black teenager in Florida. The demands of the BLM and Defund the Police movements have remained prominent in US demonstrations against police killings and deaths in custody since 2013, including, for example, in the deaths of Eric Garner, Michael Brown, Sandra Brand, Breonna Taylor, and George Floyd.[8] However, the contemporary demand to defund the police has its roots in the civil rights period and the ongoing struggle since then against police violence, racism, and over-policing. It has also been prominent among abolitionists for more than two decades, including in the work of Critical Resistance.

A second motivation for writing this book is to explore the connection between policing, abolitionism, and the international movement against state repression. The bulk of the literature on defunding the police and abolition is US-based. However, the challenges to policing also has roots in the struggle to decolonise institutional frameworks of repression – among various poor, marginalised, racialised, and oppressed peoples globally. It is closely connected to the broader abolitionist project which confronts the violence and oppression that are at the heart of how police, prison, and other carceral institutions operate, in both the wealthy liberal democracies of the north and poorer countries of the global south. In both the global north and south, profound class, gender, racial, dis/ablist, and other social divisions and inequalities replicate the targets of police and carceral institutions. Thus, while there is a tendency to see the global north/south divide in geographical terms, it is a relational space ultimately enforced by state institutions of repression. There is an international anti-colonial dimension to the demands for defunding the police that links to the longer histories of imperialism, colonisation, slavery, and settler colonialism – from the development of the 'modern' police in the early 19th century, to the second half of the 20th-century transfer of policing models, training, and hardware as a strategy of imperialism to exert influence and control, to the contemporary role of policing in wielding the direct violence of the colonial state, whether as the Israeli state against Palestinians, or Latin American states against Indigenous peoples, or African states using colonial-style police forces for ruthless internal repression. At one level, strategies to defund the police are local and place-based; however, they also need to simultaneously understand the global intersections of state repression and maintain an internationalist vision.

The demand to defund the police is also linked to decarceral strategies. Again, as the M4BL succinctly states, 'And while #DefundPolice focuses on law enforcement agencies, we are also calling for defunding of jails, prisons, detention centers, immigration enforcement, sites of involuntary commitment and incarceration of disabled people. We are also calling for defunding the military-industrial complex'.

It is a challenge to the punitive and carceral society which embeds a logic that sees state violence, repression, and forced confinement as necessary, morally justified, and of benefit for the protection of citizens. It is a logic that suggests the solution to social problems can always be found in more surveillance, more policing, more prisons, and other carceral institutions. Patrisse Cullors, a cofounder of BLM, recognises that 'we live in a police state, in which the police have become judge, jury and executioner. They've become the social worker ... the mental health clinician ... they've become anything and everything that has to do with everyday life'.[9] Wherever we look, the targets of all this punitiveness remain depressingly familiar: the poor, the marginalised, racial, ethnic and religious minorities, Indigenous peoples, refugees, immigrants, and people with disabilities who fill the police lock-ups, courtrooms, prisons, and other carceral sites in countries around the world.

The global movement against police violence

This book finds its context within a global movement of protest against repressive and violent policing. When George Floyd was killed by police in Minneapolis in May 2020 it was a spark which ignited widespread protests in the US and internationally. Floyd's cry for help, "I can't breathe", became a collective expression of suffocation and rebellion. As Minneapolis police officer Derek Chauvin knelt on the neck of a handcuffed, prostrate George Floyd until he died, for many people a belief in the efficacy of police training on procedural justice, implicit bias, use of force, and other reform initiatives died with him. The nakedness of police brutality was there for the world to see, and the international breadth of the protests sparked by the events in Minneapolis is important to emphasise. However, it is also imperative to understand how these global protests were founded in and strongly reflected specific local concerns with police repression. These localised instances of institutionalised state violence are part of an international struggle. Protests against the police and security forces were local in their grievances but global in their targets of racism, inequality, state violence, and the absence of accountability. In that sense, the struggle against violent state repression which the police and security forces embody are intertwined across time and space. They are struggles for a range of specifically contextual political, economic, and social freedoms. These are the broader underpinnings of the pragmatic demand to defund the police.

During 2020, the global protest movement was impressive. In Africa, protest movements in support of BLM occurred, for example, in Kenya, South Africa, Senegal, Ghana, and Nigeria.

6

However, the protesters were not there only or even primarily in support of the American BLM movement, they were there to express their opposition and outrage at police brutality within these African nations. In South Africa the number of deaths in police custody and during police operations, as well as complaints of police torture, rape, and assaults have continued to grow.[10] In Nairobi, Kenya, protesters drew attention to domestic police violence and extrajudicial killings, while in Lagos, Nigeria, protests against police violence continued throughout 2020, particularly against the Special Anti-Robbery Squad (SARS) police who were responsible for multiple killings of citizens over recent years. Indeed, in late October 2020, army and police forces opened fire on a peaceful demonstration protesting police brutality at the Lekki Toll Gate in Lagos. At least 12 people were killed and hundreds severely injured. A subsequent judicial inquiry described the event as a 'massacre' of 'unarmed, helpless and defenseless protesters'.[11] In addition, violent policing intensified in many African countries during the COVID-19 pandemic where police have enforced curfews in poor neighbourhoods with beatings, tear gas, and shootings – leading to dozens of deaths within the first few weeks of lockdowns.[12] The Nigerian National Human Rights Commission reported more people killed by police than COVID-19 in the first few months of the lockdown. The police in Kenya 'shot and beat people at markets or on the way home from work, even before the daily start of the curfew. Police also broke into homes and shops, extorted money from residents or looted food in locations across the country'.[13]

Emblematic of these killings in various African countries, at the beginning of the Kenyan curfew in March 2020, police shot and killed a 13-year-old boy, Yassin Moyo, while he was standing with his siblings on the third floor balcony of his family's home. Two months later in Lagos, Nigerian police enforcing the curfew, shot and killed 17-year-old Tina Ezekwe while she waited at a bus shelter.[14] Nigerian police were also accused of harassing and extorting health workers as they went about their work responding to the pandemic – the harassment was so extensive it resulted in a 'sit-at-home' strike called by the Nigeria Medical Association. The institutionalised corruption and extortion by police and security forces undermined the nationwide lockdown.[15]

In various parts of Asia, including India, Malaysia, Japan, the Philippines, Korea, Indonesia, Hong Kong, and Taiwan, demonstrators came out in protest after the death of George Floyd. Police violence and racism were dominant themes in these protests. Yet, like African nations, each country had its own history and contemporary experience of police brutality and the use of lethal violence. There was widespread recognition that racism and police violence within the US was not a localised problem, but one which resonated globally. In the Philippines, solidarity with BLM was shown while demonstrating against new restrictive anti-terror laws and the more than 27,000 deaths by police and vigilantes since the government's war on drugs began in 2016. In Taiwan, a BLM solidarity protest was used to highlight the ongoing discrimination against Indigenous peoples of Taiwan who comprise about 3 per cent of the population. In Malaysia, attention was drawn to the longstanding problem of deaths in custody, including those arising from police violence. Official statistics reported 257 deaths in police custody between 2002 and 2016, although independent monitoring claims the figure is much higher. The ethnic Indian population is over-represented among these victims. Police violence and racism were also a focus in Indonesia, in particular, against Papuans who have struggled for the recognition of self-determination in the provinces of West Papua and Papua, which Indonesia annexed in the early 1960s. There are long-standing issues of racism, violence, and the use of imprisonment against Papuan students and activists. Amnesty International recently documented security forces using water cannons and beating peaceful Papuan protesters.[16] Hong Kong had ongoing pro-democracy protests which saw violent police responses, including the indiscriminate use of chemical and other crowd control weapons and firearms, resulting in widespread injuries. Official inquiries exonerated police, despite thousands of complaints.[17] Twelve months before the death of George Floyd, there were demands to disband the Hong Kong police. At later protests in solidarity with the BLM movement, Hong Kong police officers were filmed mocking the "I can't breathe" and other calls used by demonstrators. Opposition to political repression in both Hong Kong and Indonesia are key elements that intersect with protests against police violence.

India has a long history of police torturing and killing people in custody, and various human rights organisations including the Indian National Human Rights Commission have commented on the routine nature of police torture.[18] As in other countries, lockdowns to counter the COVID-19 pandemic exacerbated police brutality against the urban poor, the street vendors, and the tens of thousands of homeless migrant workers who attempted to return to their communities on foot, or by bicycle, rickshaw, bus or lorry – in what the *Economic and Political Weekly* described as a 'sort of dogged civil disobedience' undeterred by police lathis and driven by 'no wages, no food, no savings, no money for rent, no faith [in] the administration ... and great apprehension of disease and death'.[19] As one writer put it, these were the 'unnamed George Floyds of India ... whose voices are easily suppressed'.[20] In mid 2020, the deaths of a father and son, Jeyeraj and Benicks, in Tamil Nadu sparked a broader debate about police killings in India in the context of the BLM movement. The pair were taken into police custody for breaching COVID-19 restrictions on trading and held overnight. Both were tortured and died 2 days later. As is typical in these cases, initially no police were charged with criminal offences, but those thought to be responsible were transferred elsewhere. After mounting public pressure nationally over the deaths, nine police officers were subsequently charged with murder and destruction of evidence.[21]

The death of George Floyd also coincided with protests across Latin America and the Caribbean, stretching from Jamaica, Trinidad and Tobago, to Mexico, Colombia, and Brazil. In Cuba a planned protest for late June 2020 against the police shooting of a young Black man was suppressed by the government. There is a long history of the struggle against police brutality, racism, and class oppression in Latin America. The sheer volume of police killings in the region meant there were ongoing protests against police violence in, for example, Colombia, Mexico, and Brazil, which were independent of the George Floyd murder in the US. These included protests against the killing of a 14-year-old boy in Rio de Janeiro in May 2020 (where police killed on average five people a day in 2019), and the police shooting in early June 2020 of a 16-year-old as he rode his motorcycle with a group of friends in Oaxaca State, one of the poorest areas of

Mexico. Human Rights Watch (HRW) has long been critical of policing in Mexico, including the incidence of torture, arbitrary arrest and detentions, and forced disappearances.[22] Protests against police violence have continued – in April 2021 women demanded justice for Victoria Salazar. Police were filmed killing Ms Salazar. Her neck was broken by a police officer jamming her knee into Salazar's neck. Racism and the targeting of Black and Indigenous people in Latin America has dominated the activism against police violence. In Brazil, for example, police kill nearly six times the number of people compared to the United States, and 75 per cent of the people killed are Black.[23] Similar to the Philippines, much of the police violence in Brazil is related to the war on drugs, increased militarisation and indiscriminate state violence against poor and Black communities. Like the situation in South Asia and Africa, the COVID-19 pandemic increased poverty and inequality, impacted on social unrest and intensified police violence. In Columbia, dozens of people were killed in early 2021 as police and security forces fired into crowds who protested the social and economic policies of the government. Columbian police are within the command of the Defence Ministry and there has been no appetite by government to curb state violence – to the point where escalating protests are targeting police violence, particularly by the riot police ESMAD, as a key focal point of resistance. The Inter-American Commission on Human Rights criticised the Colombian security forces for using excessive, disproportionate, and sometimes lethal force, including the indiscriminate police use of firearms against protestors and bystanders. The use of gender-based and sexual violence against protestors by police has also been highlighted.[24]

Across the global north, the protest movement was equally extensive. In Canada, the death of George Floyd reignited the focus on Black and Indigenous people killed by police. There are no national statistics on race, ethnicity, and deaths in police 'encounters' in Canada, but various sources show that Black and First Nations peoples are especially over-represented. Canadian Broadcasting Commission (CBC) News created a database on people killed by police since 2000 and found that Black people in Toronto made up on average 8.3 per cent of the population, but represented nearly 37 per cent of the victims. In Winnipeg, Indigenous people represented approximately 10 per cent of the population, but accounted for nearly two thirds of victims.[25] The *Globe and Mail* reported that more than one-third of the people shot and killed by RCMP officers between 2007 and 2017 were Indigenous.[26] Similarly, in Australia and Aotearoa New Zealand, there were demonstrations in support of the BLM movement. The protests were used to highlight the deaths in custody of First Nations people in both countries. It was noted in Aotearoa New Zealand that over the past decade, two-thirds of all victims of fatal police shootings have been Māori or Pasifika.[27] Attention in Australia was drawn to [then] more than 400 First Nations deaths in custody since the landmark report of the Royal Commission into Aboriginal Deaths in Custody in 1991 and the fact that not one police or prison officer has been convicted for any criminal offences relating to these deaths.[28]

In the UK and Europe, support for the movement also highlighted racism and policing in the context of existing racial and ethnic inequalities. In Paris and other French cities, protesters drew attention to police violence, deaths in custody, and racism against minorities.[29] In the UK, protestors emphasised the fact that Black people were more likely to die in police custody than other groups and the subsequent lack of police accountability. British protesters carried placards with the names of those who had died in UK police custody, prison or at the borders.[30] In Germany, tens of thousands of protestors marched in cities such as Berlin, Munich, and Hamburg. Like other European protests, these were not simply supporting the movement in the US. Protestors drew attention to police racism and violence within Germany, the lack of police accountability, and in particular, the deaths of refugees and asylum seekers while in police custody.[31] In other parts of Europe, it was noted that Roma were brutalised by police but were no nearer 'their Black Lives Matter moment' in terms of public outcry.[32]

Some common themes

Global protests were sparked by the events in the US, but they were also part of ongoing protest movements within many countries.

In Africa there had been more than 100 popular uprisings led by young people against corruption, violence, and austerity measures between 2005 and 2015.[33] In Australia, First Nations-led protests against Aboriginal deaths in police and prison custody have been a feature of the political landscape for decades. Many of the global protest movements are built on multiple demands from opposition to austerity measures and the ravages of neoliberal capitalism, to demands for racial justice and Indigenous sovereignty. In African nations like South Africa, Kenya, and Nigeria, state officials were held to be hypocritical for comments condemning the death of George Floyd, while consistently ignoring the hundreds of police killings in their own countries over recent years.[34] The same hypocrisy was noted by activists in India where egregious killings by police typically attracted far less outrage than a single death in the US.[35] Similarly, in Australia and Aotearoa New Zealand, First Nations activists drew attention to the apparent lack of popular (non-Indigenous) mobilisation against local Black deaths in custody prior to the events in the US.

There were common themes which united these global outpourings of protest against state violence. The sheer scale of the violence by police against poor, marginalised, Indigenous, and racialised communities is almost incomprehensible, while at the same time the lack of any effective accountability for police violence is legend. One common denominator is that police violence and abuse remain largely unpunished. From the US to Australia, from Brazil to India and Nigeria, the story is repeated: police can kill with apparent impunity. Another set of commonalities is that for many countries in the global north and south, the histories of colonialism, slavery, racism, and dispossession are fundamental to understanding both the targets of policing and police violence, as well as the way that police are organised as a state institution of repression. For example, in Brazil, despite appeals to being a racial democracy there is a long history of racism in the country. It was the last among western countries to abolish slavery in 1888 and had been the largest importer of slaves from Africa, with an estimated ten times more slaves arriving in Brazil than North America.[36] Racial inequality is entrenched, and as noted previously, the vast majority of people killed by police in Brazil are Black. In many Latin American countries, Indigenous peoples also feature prominently among the victims of police violence.

An important part of the critique of policing emerging from the protests has been the call to decolonise policing institutions. In African nations, police were established as repressive arms of colonial powers to conquer, repress, and dominate the population, and have never been there to protect citizens or respect human rights. The widespread use of police violence during the COVID-19 pandemic lockdowns reinforced the view that governments had failed to reform the structures of colonial policing.[37] In Australia and Canada, policing and the criminal law have been instrumental in the colonial dispossession and repression of Indigenous peoples – and First Nations people today are more likely than others to be killed by police.[38] In Israel, the police are at the vanguard of attacking Palestinians and protecting vigilante groups driving Palestinian people from their homes in neighbourhoods like Sheik Jarrah. Globally, police and security forces are at the forefront of contemporary settler colonialism.[39]

In India, the basic structure of the criminal law dates from the time of British colonialism. In May 2020, the Indian Home Ministry established the Committee for Reforms in Criminal Law to update the law and remove its colonial foundations: what was to be ostensibly an exercise in decolonising the criminal law. Yet the Committee did not include any women, Dalit ('untouchable' or 'lower' caste) or Adivasi (tribal and Indigenous) peoples, religious minorities, people from Lesbian, gay, bisexual, transgender, queer/questioning, intersex, asexual (LGBTQIA+) communities, people with disabilities, nor representatives from the south, east, or northeast of India. In other words, as one activist organisation demanding the disbandment of the committee noted, 'No committee member belongs to a group that is under-served and over-policed by the criminal justice system'.[40] Through various mechanisms any democratic participation in the process of reform was stymied.

More recently, in southeast Asia, opposition to the military coup in Myanmar have been met by widespread lethal police violence causing hundreds of deaths; while protesters for democratic reform in Thailand have been met by the use of water cannons, tear gas, and rubber bullets.[41] This is the global landscape in which the plea to defund the police resonates. It stands in stark contrast to the notion of the police as a fundamentally *democratic* institution – established to serve 'the public', to promote community safety, and to enforce the law for the people – a view which continues to dominate narratives about policing. It is obvious from the international record that racism and the targeting of Indigenous, Black, Brown, and minoritised communities is ubiquitous. Further, for many communities globally, challenges to police power are synonymous with an anti-colonialist position against political repression, the failure to ensure community safety, and the state violence inherent to various 'wars' on drugs, terror, and insurgency. Thus, the diverse calls to defund the police, or to abolish the police and carceral institutions, are integral to demands for decolonisation, the eradication of racism, and the development of societies that are built on economic, political, and social justice.

A controversial idea?

Perhaps only a few years ago, the idea of defunding the police and abolition might have been unthinkable – let alone that there might be a broad political movement with practical initiatives to achieve the outcome. However, now is an historic moment characterised by rapidly changing parameters of what are considered contentious and acceptable ideas in relation to policing. The concept of abolition in relation to the police was seen as unacceptable and 'fanciful' by many policing scholars where the focus has been on various aspects of police reform. The breadth and depth of social movements focused on police violence, Defund the Police, and BLM have challenged the political and intellectual comfort zones of many academics and policy makers working in the area of policing. While liberal reformers might continue with various programmes to reform the police, the abolitionist project challenges the very foundations of the institution of police.[42] The challenge has been accepted by many from public health associations to radical social workers who have in common a 'life-affirming' approach to supporting the 'health, self-determination and sustainability of all communities'.[43]

For many people, the thought of defunding the police may seem at best abstract and unrealistic; that we lack alternatives, specific solutions, or policy recommendations; that it is an unachievable utopian vision of the world.[44] Much of this book addresses and responds to these arguments in the various chapters that follow. The goal of defunding the police might be controversial, but it is definitely not new. The institution of policing has been contested since its earliest days. As Chapter 2 demonstrates, there have been debates over the development and role of police dating back to the end of the 18th century in England. Despite mythical origin stories of the democratic foundations of policing, this book focuses on a counter-narrative of police – as military forces of occupation ensuring colonial expansion and control, in maintaining slavery, in safeguarding ruthless economic exploitation in the colonies of Africa, the Americas, and Asia, and their role in the expropriation and genocide of First Nations peoples – the police were fundamental in establishing the foundations of colonial capitalist societies. Police continued in the forefront in subsequent periods of institutionalised violence, racial discrimination, and apartheid. Further, a foundational element of modern police forces was the control of the emerging working class, their radical activists and trade unions in the industrial cities of the global north, and as colonialism developed within the global south. A core argument of the book is established in Chapter 2: a central role of police was not responding to crime, but rather maintaining an unequal and exploitative social, economic, and political order. What we see today are the outcomes of these historical origins, which have been extended and exacerbated through further refinements, including ongoing militarisation and ideologies of risk, zero tolerance, evidence-led policing, and so on.

Community protection is one of the rationales used in arguing the necessity for police: What would we do without them? Who would protect us? Answers to these questions are provided in various chapters throughout the book. Chapter 3 considers the limited role police play in solving crime and the relatively low rates of the public reporting of crime. It reflects on the role of police discretion in reproducing particular social boundaries, using as two examples the use of police discretion to criminalise Black, Brown, and Indigenous young people, while conversely exploring the role of police discretion in not investigating and prosecuting the murders of LGBTQIA+ people. Chapter 4 steps back to consider the role of resistance and oppositional movements to the police from the 1960s through to the current period, especially the role of Black, Indigenous, and people of colour in the US, Australia, and Britain in the struggle against repressive state violence. It concludes with a discussion of the advent of zero tolerance policing and its impact on racial violence.

. In countering the argument that police provide community protection, the book considers the situations where citizens are killed by police. As documented in Chapter 5, so many of these deaths occur after the most minor offence has been detected or there is no offence at all. I consider what we know about police killings through a number of examples in the global north (particularly, the US, England and Wales, Australia, and Canada) and in the global south (Brazil, Philippines, India, Pakistan, and Bangladesh) to draw out commonalities and differences in the experiences of police terror and violence.

Chapter 6 addresses the problem of violence against women and argues that police are not the solution to violence. There has been considerable discussion of the violent nature of policing and its failure to properly investigate and respond to gendered and racialised violence. Indeed, many of the political organisers, activists, and intellectuals that have addressed problems of policing and advocated for abolitionism and divesting from police have been Black, Indigenous, and women of colour. The current Defund the Police and abolitionist movements would not exist without them, and some – like Marielle Franko in Brazil – have paid for their activist opposition to police violence, militarism, and racism with their lives. The chapter draws on international and country-specific evidence to illustrate the failure of police to protect women from violence. Chapter 7 begins from the point that policing has played a central role in defining and controlling disability – police and carceral violence are core to the disabling processes of the state. The chapter recognises that disability activists internationally have provided a compelling voice to the arguments for defunding the police, particularly because people with mental ill-health and cognitive impairments have borne such a heavy toll among those injured, maimed, and killed in police encounters – and often in situations where families have requested positive assistance for their loved one.

As shown in Chapter 8, an integral part of the argument for defunding and abolition of police is the consistent failure of police reform – despite decades of inquiries and reform measures in various countries. Minneapolis, for example, was the site of a major US federal initiative over a number of years prior to George Floyd's murder, designed to improve policing and address distrust between the police and minority and Black communities.[45] Yet we still see the same recommendations for better training, coordination, and so forth. The *New York Times* reviewed more than a dozen evaluations of police responses to protesters after the death of George Floyd. The reports generally blamed poor training, militarisation and lack of preparedness which led to escalations of violence. Yet as the review noted, between 1967 and 1976 there were three federal commissions into protests and riots which reached similar conclusions, while yet another presidential commission after the killing of Michael Brown in Ferguson, Missouri and the subsequent protests in 2015 found that police militarisation exacerbated the situation.[46] The failure of reform adds weight to the argument for shifting funds from police into community sector development. The organisational structure of policing varies across different countries, however the failure of reform and accountability mechanisms in many countries adds a common international resonance to the political call to defund the police.

Defund the Police immediately speaks to a consideration of other approaches to providing community safety and support. Not surprisingly there are many different avenues for thinking through a revisioning or reimagining of life without the institutional structures of violence, repression, and imprisonment. Chapter 9 draws on both a range of practical examples, as well as these broader notions of what life without police might *become*. Practical projects include community safety and community defence initiatives, social reinvestment, and Indigenous and other forms of community governance. However, the chapter also identifies the need for reimagining new possibilities. The BLM and Defund the Police movements are linked back to the broader arguments for carceral abolitionism and decolonialism. Patrisse Cullors, for example, argues for 'new visions, new imaginings of public safety' and draws on the work of long-time abolitionists such as Angela Y. Davis who contends that decarceration and abolitionism are not simply about changing the criminal legal system.[47] Davis's comments on prison also apply to police: the first step is 'to let go of the desire to discover one single alternative system of punishment that would occupy the same footprint as the prison system'.[48] Effective abolitionist strategies would challenge not simply the institution of the police, but the range of relationships that make up the criminal legal system as we know it, as well as other forms of carcerality that, for example, impact on people with disability. There is also a need to bring together abolitionism with the work of decolonial theorists. For example, Mignolo has called upon us to think through 'the many and rich possibilities of governance' that are open to the people outside of the current state which has been forged through the processes of colonialism.[49]

Defunding the police in the context of the carceral state

Much has been written about the long-term increases in imprisonment internationally, the rise of hyper-incarceration and what has come to be known as the carceral or prison state. Considerable attention has been placed on more punitive penal policies: the more frequent use and longer periods of imprisonment, the increasing use of pre-trial detention, and so on.[50] In reflecting on the growth in US imprisonment, Jonathan Simon argued that criminalisation and imprisonment are used as a tool of social policy – a process of 'governing through crime'. Punishment and imprisonment are targeted at those defined as high risk, dangerous, and marginalised, which in practice translates into the targeting of people defined by their race, gender, ableism, class, and their intersections. Furthermore, governing through crime has increased modes of surveillance into a range of state and private institutions including schools, hospitals, workplaces, shopping malls, transport systems, and other public and private spaces. These changes have brought about a transformation in the civil and political order, including fiscal and administrative structures, which are increasingly structured around 'the problem of crime', despite crime rates generally falling in many countries over the past several decades.[51]

A central and perhaps until recently neglected player in this reorientation is the police. Although other functionaries both within and outside the legal system are involved in this criminal/ risk surveillance (including prosecutors, judges, correctional officers, social workers, teachers, and health workers), it is the police who are the frontline troops of this governance structure. They are the presence which makes this political process possible. Thinking about these broader considerations enables us to see why the appeal to defund the police embodies such a challenge – this is not just about bloated police budgets and unaccountable state violence, it is a challenge to the deeper social and political priorities which have underscored penal policy.

A further barrier to progressive change and a pressing reason for its necessity is identified by Bernard Harcourt and Stuart Schrader. Both argue that the hyper-militarised police forces that have taken to the streets of the US in the wake of the protests after the police killings of Michael Brown in Ferguson and more recently George Floyd in Minneapolis are the outcome of 'a new model of government inspired by the theory and practice of counterinsurgency warfare'.[52] This type of policing is not a brief aberration from the rule of law to respond to exceptional circumstances. Rather, it is indicative of an historical and political transformation based on counterinsurgency strategies. These changes have been occurring for decades, first with US military operations in Vietnam and then to Iraq and Afghanistan, and domestically since 9/11 and accelerating during the Trump administration. This change, however, is by no means confined to the US. We can see the same tendencies outside the US – from the policing of favelas in Sao Paulo to the policing of protests in London and Sydney. Thus, the call to defund the police implies confronting and opposing a much larger set of historical processes that are serving to cement the police as a type of domestic military force engaged in a constant process of pacification.

This book argues that what links the vision of Defund the Police with the broader considerations of abolitionism and decolonialism is the demand for reimagining possibilities beyond contemporary state formations and institutions which have produced systems of violence and oppression. Or as Angela Y. Davis has stated, 'alternatives that fail to address racism, male dominance, homophobia, class bias and other structures of domination will not, in the final analysis, lead to decarceration and will not advance the goal of abolition'.[53] There is a simplicity to the concept of defund the police. As several commentators have stated, defund the police means defund the police. It is a plain language political demand without limits or conditions. Saima Desai indicated in an editorial note in *briarpatch*,

> It doesn't mean buying body cameras or any other new technology. It doesn't mean hiring more cops for diversity and inclusion units. It doesn't mean banning choke-holds. It doesn't mean using tasers instead of guns. It doesn't mean 'community policing' that installs more cops in poor and racialized communities. ... It means take the money away from the police. Take the guns and tanks and helicopters away from them. Take away their role as our catch-all hotline for responding to people in crisis. ... Give the money to life affirming Black- and Indigenous-led community projects.[54]

As Mariame Kaba has argued, attempts at liberal reforms have failed for nearly a century. The police cannot be reformed and more of the same type of reforms will not alter the current situation. Police as an institution needs to be made obsolete. However, it is recognised that not all who support a movement to defund the police are also abolitionists. Again, as Kaba notes, irrespective of whether you are an abolitionist or not, 'here's an immediate demand we can all make: cut the number of police in half and cut their budget in half. Fewer police officers equal fewer opportunities for them to brutalize and kill people'.[55] The invitation to defund the police provides a strategic opportunity to build alliances across a range of social groups who understand through their own experience that police do not make us safer.

2

A brief history of policing

We live within institutional arrangements which influence our ways of thinking and responding to the world around us. Those institutions often seem part of the natural order of things – necessary and immovable, defining particular social artefacts as problems and predefining the range of possible responses, reforms, and solutions. The institution of policing is no exception, and its historical weight carries us along well-trodden paths. Instrumental arguments by policymakers, politicians, and police administrators reconfirm the necessity of the police to control crime and to uphold the law, even as a wealth of evidence throws into question the basic claims of these assertions. Indeed, the problems of police violence, ineffectiveness and corruption are as old as the institution of policing itself. And there is a sense of *déjà vu* every time another official inquiry reports on some particularly egregious atrocity that has risen above the normal levels of police violence and mismanagement. The script is time-honoured – it usually begins with the need for upgraded training and improved accountability, followed by more resources, and perhaps something on the requirement for better community engagement and strategies to rally social legitimacy.

What is often ignored is the recognition of policing as a socio-historical process that maintains itself for reasons other than controlling crime. One is reminded of Foucault's discussion of the failure of the prison in *Discipline and Punish*. This failure is recognised in the early 1820s and is constantly re-articulated to the present day – including its failure to rehabilitate and to reduce crime. Yet the institution appears resistant to change and continually re-invents itself to the point where, 200 years later, we are talking about the problem of hyper-incarceration. Foucault poses the questions: What does the prison produce? What interests are served by the prison? I want to shift those questions back to the police. What does the history of policing tell us about the control and maintenance of social divisions including class, race, gender, disability, and their intersections; or about the economic exploitation of labour and political control? What does it tell us of the use of power, both at the local level and more broadly through macro socio-historical movements of colonialism and imperialism? And finally, why is an understanding of this history so important to contemporary calls to defund the police?

The New Police

There is no single history of policing, but there is a myth of origin which tells us a great deal about the need to establish political hegemony, institutional legitimacy, and social consent. The British version emerges as follows: Sir Robert Peel's London Metropolitan Police were established in 1829 to control crime in the rapidly urbanised city and to maintain social order. The new police were a centrally organised, coordinated, and disciplined force drawing their authority from the people.[1] Or so the story goes. There are alternative interpretations, including the role of the new police in controlling an emergent working class across a range of terrains, from industrial disputes and political protest to regulating new notions of public respectability and social order. Opposition to the new police was prominent from a variety of sectors, including those who saw the police as an attack on the 'traditional liberties' of the English, and working-class radicals fearful of repression. Indeed, an early call for police abolition was a handbill printed in London in 1830, entitled 'The New Police', which exhorted others 'to join your Brother Londoners in one heart, one hand, for the Abolition of the New Police!'.[2] Police forces based on the Peel model were introduced in the US, with Boston in 1838, New York in 1845 and other major cities over the following years. Like the situation in Britain, these new urban police forces were focused on policing the organised labour movement, particularly strikes, and enforcing new regulatory regimes among the working-class.[3]

Aside from the Peel police, there were other moves in London towards organised, centrally funded, and prevention focused policing with the establishment of the Thames River Police, with the support of private merchants and manufacturers. As Porter documents, the Thames River Police was important for directly linking the development of policing within the metropolitan centre to the processes of colonialism in the periphery.[4] The Thames River Police patrolled the Port of London. They were initially funded by the West India Committee – a lobby group of English plantation owners in the sugar, rum, cotton, and other industries in the Caribbean who sought to guard their slavery-produced profits. The development of the state police in London owes as much to protecting the economic and political interests of the wealthy plantation owners as it did to Peel's reforms. Further, the development of policing was never simply divided between the metropolitan centre and the colonial periphery – in this case, London and the Caribbean – they were always deeply intertwined in maintaining the stability and profitability of the colonial order.

The establishment of institutional policing in Europe followed a somewhat different path to Britain. The French and Spanish monarchies had founded military police units to control demobilised soldiers and the military with functions that eventually extended into patrolling highways and rural areas. These military police units evolved into the Gendarmerie Nationale and the Guardia Civil. The development of civil police functions grew from the establishment of the office of *lieutenant général de police* in Paris in 1667. From the 1700s the policing function expanded as a 'form of social control which was formal, institutional, and preventative',[5] and predated the Peel Police. After the French Revolution, the Paris model, along with the gendarmerie, was adopted across the country, and under Napoleon, more widely instituted across Europe.

The 19th-century expansion of policing went hand in hand with the rise of state institutions in various areas of social life including education, public health, and social welfare. Police were expected to enforce and maintain a developing notion of social order determined by the state. During the second half of the 19th century and early 20th century, there was a substantial expansion in police and the processes of criminalisation, alongside new regulatory regimes and institutional settings. Developments in the policing of children and families provide insight into these changes. The social construction of juvenile delinquency,[6] and the creation of various institutions including juvenile courts, juvenile industrial schools and reformatories, and a raft of civil and criminal legislation, highlighted the changing historical context of policing. Some of the changes were welfare oriented such as restrictions on child labour, the introduction of compulsory schooling, processes for responding to neglected children, and modified court systems. Others were aimed at controlling public behaviour, popular culture, and leisure activities through a broad range of criminal offences and regulatory requirements covering such issues as 'wandering about', vagrancy, begging and loitering, gambling, drunkenness, malicious mischief, public bathing, dangerous play, animal sports, and discharging fireworks.[7]

Police powers were expansive – going well beyond the policing of what we might consider substantive criminal offences to include the policing of truancy, homelessness, and poverty, and of status offences such as engaging in immoral or depraved behaviour, or being uncontrollable. These police interventions were also gendered in their application with women and girls policed because of their sexuality, and often receiving prolonged institutionalisation, despite being victims of crimes such as rape and incest.[8] The concerns with industrialisation and a rapidly growing urban population were also apparent, and much of the criminalising and regulatory interventions were aimed at working-class children and families. In colonial settings, there was also a strong differential in the treatment of Black, First Nations and other racialised families – which is considered in more detail later. The policing of working-class families directs attention to the expanded monitoring responsibilities of police as 'moral guardians' and welfare agents. The development of police in regulating families sits alongside other expanded activities, such as the policing of public health/hygiene through Contagious Diseases legislation from the later part of the 19th century, and their role in the policing of mental illness. For instance, in the colony and then State of NSW throughout the 19th and early 20th centuries, most people incarcerated in 'lunatic' asylums were there because of police intervention. Indeed, in 1878 police powers to detain 'suspected lunatics' were expanded to include people who were considered neglected, ill-treated, found wandering, or were without means of support.[9] The policing of both public health and mental illness continues to raise questions of the expansive role of policing today, as it did in the past.

There was also continuing resistance within working-class communities to the encroachment of police into people's daily lives, with the prevalence of anti-police riots, protests, assaults on officers, and other forms of day-to-day resistance. Some UK historians have traced the lineage of anti-police activism, protests, and riots from the 19th century to the late 20th century – such as the line drawn from anti-police riots in Liverpool in the 1800s to the Toxteth uprising in Liverpool in 1981,[10] while others have considered the various periods of rising and falling police legitimacy.[11] Public support was always contingent on police behaviour, and the specific nature of police work. The policing of strikes, labour disputes, and political protest were areas historically where policing was heavily contested,[12] but it was also contested in the localised management of public space where the police role was much broader than responding to crime.[13]

Policing in colonial settings

If the Thames River Police brought to the fore the connection between the metropolitan centre and the regional sites of colonial exploitation, these interconnections were equally evident in the developments of the colonial model of policing in Ireland – a militaristic system organised around the use of armed force to govern in the interests of colonial power. The Irish model was exported, influenced, and/or was adapted to the specific conditions in other colonies across the British Empire during the course of the 19th and early 20th centuries in countries as diverse as Egypt, Fiji, Kenya, Canada, Ghana, Nigeria, India, Palestine, New Zealand, Hong Kong, Jamaica, Barbados, and Australia.[14] Local political considerations, the nature of resistance, resources, and other factors determined how the colonial mode was adapted and in some colonies including in Australia, South

Africa, and Canada, both civil and colonial modes of policing were utilised – differentiated between cities and the colonial hinterland or frontier.[15] Somewhat in contrast to the experience of the British Empire, French colonial policing was not centralised or as relatively standardised across the French empire. There was no equivalent of the British Colonial Police Service,[16] nor was any formal colonial police employment scheme deployed throughout the French colonies. However, the police, gendarmes and the military played a key role in maintaining the French Empire, despite the fact that colonial police forces tended to be understaffed and underfunded.[17]

Colonial models of policing were attractive for various reasons: they generally operated with European officers in charge and local people as the lower ranks. However, it was the valorisation of force and violence that was the most obvious attraction. The exercise of colonial power did not involve the consent of the colonised. The racist ideologies underpinning imperialism and the motive of ruthless economic exploitation meant that the idea of political legitimacy and popular consent was largely irrelevant. The aims of policing were to ensure colonial efficiency, stability, and profitability for European capitalists. As Justice Tankebe states, 'to speak of colonial policing and "policing by consent" – and for that matter legitimacy – is therefore a contradiction in terms; it is oxymoronic'.[18]

It was not only the military style uniforms and ranks of the commanding European officers, but more importantly the use of military weaponry and training aimed at the control of colonised peoples' resistance that was fundamental to the colonial model of policing – the ability when required to violently quell social and political resistance to colonial rule. Although the idea of bringing the superior European rule of law to inferior races had been used as a justification for colonialism, in fact arbitrariness, violence, and impunity were prevalent. In discussing policing in Ghana, Killingray demonstrates that there were no legal and disciplinary procedures that controlled the police exercise of power or administered any sanctions for police abuses. The police were 'hated as unaccountable representatives of an alien colonial power imposing a range of new laws and measures of social control which lacked any semblance of popular consent'.[19] Frantz Fanon eloquently confirms that the colonial world was a world cut in two: 'The dividing line, the frontiers are shown by barracks and police stations. In the colonies it is the policeman and the soldier who are the official, instituted go-betweens, the spokesmen of the settler and his rule of oppression.'[20]

Irrespective of whether repressive police violence within colonial settings represented a strong colonial state exerting power, or the resort to violence was emblematic of inefficient policing and a weak colonial state, police violence was a hallmark of colonial control.[21] For example, unrestrained use of violence was apparent during both the height of French colonialism and during the period of decolonisation. French colonial police forces 'were never known to put a strong emphasis on disciplining and educating their personnel' and the 'French empire was marked by the permanence of this logic consisting of slaughtering protesting crowds of colonised people'.[22] Blanchard outlines the magnitude and frequency of these police killings during the period leading to decolonisation. Rather than working towards a transition of power, the police forces became more violent. In Algeria, for example, police units were involved 'in the massive use of torture during the war of independence'.[23] The differential use of violence against the colonised also inflected policing within the metropole. Although police in Paris had stopped using firearms to disperse protestors from the 1930s, the colonised were treated differently with police shooting and killing Algerian demonstrators in Paris in the 1950s and early 1960s. It was the 'racial–political condition of the colonised that determined both the nature and degree of the policing techniques employed' rather than, for example, whether the protestors were peaceful or not.[24]

Although police violence was foundational to the colonial project, the police played other important roles. They were often the key representative of the colonial administration in many areas of the colony and were the agents of colonial rule, for example in parts of Sudan, the Gold Coast, and India, as well as in significant parts of the settler colonies such as the northern frontier in Australia and the Yukon in Canada. Police were the administrative edge of colonial power and were expected to fulfil a range of regulatory and other tasks from veterinary inspections to issuing licences, from delivering mail to determining welfare, as well as reporting on the state of crops, the condition of roads, and so forth.[25] Police were also involved in the political surveillance of anti-colonialist and nationalist activism – both within the colonies and the metropolitan centres.[26] In the late 19th and early 20th centuries, colonial police forces were at the forefront of anthropometric and identification techniques. In French Indochina, for example, thousands of identification records with fingerprints of native and foreign Asian people were collected – and the identification process was imported back into metropolitan France for foreigners and French nationals of colonial origin. In Ghana, a type of criminal profiling was developed through the use of detailed descriptions and photography.[27] In the US-occupied Philippines, the police utilised new communication technologies, finger printing and transportation methods. Indeed, the American police reformer August Volmer based his ideas on police science from his experiences in the Philippines: 'Ever since Spanish-American War days, I've studied military tactics and used them to good effect in rounding up crooks. After all we're conducting a war.'[28] Thus policing in the colonies acted as 'veritable laboratories of modernity'.[29]

From the 19th century the colonial model of policing spread throughout the British Empire through 'the export of training and military ethos' as well as the movement of police and advisors who brought with them ideas about policies, procedures, and so forth.[30] The influence of this model remained well into the 20th century, and continued beyond the period of decolonisation – to be found, for instance, in police training manuals in the 1950s.[31] In India at the time of Independence in 1947, Congress shelved indefinitely the planned overhaul of the British Indian police, and in Malaysia, the post-independence Royal Malaysia Police replicated 'many of the features, functions and failings of the colonial force'.[32] In the former French colonies, continuities in policing models remained. The most 'striking and symbolic legacy' were the national gendarmeries where the decolonisation period acted as a 'second age' for the spread of the gendarmerie model across the Ivory Coast, Mali, Tunisia, Algeria, Syria, and Lebanon, and where these post-independence police forces have, at various times, played their own part in the repression of civilian populations.[33]

Colonial models of policing continued to influence the metropolitan centres. For example, the Chief Police Constables of England and Wales were provided with the details of riot control methods used by the Royal Hong Kong Police.[34] The United States' engagement in colonial war also impacted on the development of policing within the US. The occupation of the Philippines and the establishment of the Philippine Constabulary influenced the development of the Pennsylvania State Police. The Philippine police had been established to control the anti-colonialist movement and its adaptation by Pennsylvania was no accident – coal owners and the state had been in significant conflict with the union movement over the previous decade. The new state police were a paramilitary force that showed little interest in controlling crime, and instead operated as strikebreakers.[35]

Settler colonialism and policing First Nations

Western liberal democratic states define their criminal legal systems as neutral, fair, and universal. Equality before the law and equal protection of the law are regarded as the defining features of the rule of law – which police are said to uphold. However, the policing of First Nations peoples within the developing liberal democracies that were and are simultaneously settler colonial states highlights the violence, genocide and racist regimes – that is the illiberalism – that is at the core of these states. There was a substantial 'gap' in universality and equality when it came to policing in the emerging White settler states of the US, Australia, Canada, and New Zealand. The rule of law was suspended and became a rule of exception in relation to the policing of Indigenous peoples.[36]

Indigenous peoples, even where they were ostensibly equal subjects, often fell outside of the protection of the law. Police involvement in the war against Indigenous people was in some cases genocide. For example, in the Australian context the campaigns undertaken by the Native Police (led by White military officers) against Indigenous nations in Queensland during the second half of the 19th century were genocidal – they were clearly undertaken with the intention of physically destroying a whole group of people. On the other side of the continent, in July 1895, Western Australian senior state officials noted that: 'There can be no doubt from these frequent [police] reports that a war of extermination in effect is being waged against these unfortunate blacks in the Kimberley district.'[37] The Native Police and Mounted Police in Australia conducted the work of an occupying military force. Murderous patrols led by police and 'special constables' still occurred in northern Australia in the 1920s.[38] In Canada, the forerunner of the RCMP was the North West Mounted Police (NWMP) which was required to expand and protect the territorial boundaries of the colony, suppress Indigenous resistance, and criminalise Indigenous social and cultural practices. Former military officers were employed in the NWMP.[39] In various colonial towns in the US, 'Indian constables' were appointed to protect settlers from First Nations peoples in the 18th century. Similar to the Mounted Police of Australia and Canada, in the US, the Texas Rangers protected the interests of White colonisers against First Nations, Mexican, and Spanish peoples. As Vitale noted, they acted first as a type of mercenary force before coming under the authority of the republic and then state of Texas. The Rangers were involved in campaigns of genocide against First Nations people.[40]

As settler colonialism expanded its control over Indigenous lands, open warfare was replaced by extensive government controls. During the 19th and early 20th centuries, settler colonial governments in the US, Canada, Australia, and New Zealand instituted policies and practices to 'civilise' and assimilate Indigenous peoples through the establishment of reservations, forced removal of children and their incarceration in residential schools, the banning of language, cultural and spiritual practices, and the imposition of an alien justice system.[41] Although legislation and policy was couched in the language of protection, the model was based on the institutions of the criminal legal system, through the use of police, civil 'protectors' or Indian agents exercising a range of administrative, policing, and judicial functions. Policing, criminalisation, and punishment were central to the colonial state's governance of Indigenous peoples.

In Canada, the *Indian Act* 1876, and subsequent legislation, shaped various educational, social, and economic policies designed to extinguish Indigenous rights and assimilate Indigenous people. The government made and enforced regulations 'with regard to the full spectrum of public and private life in communities'.[42] The *Indian Act* was deeply gendered: a woman's Indian status was tied to her husband. Non-Indigenous concepts of marriage and parenting were to prevail, with penalties imposed for non-compliance. Indigenous movement was restricted, and participation in cultural ceremonies could be declared as criminal behaviour. Department of Indian Affairs (DIA) agents were given the same powers as magistrates. Their jurisdiction was expanded beyond the *Indian Act* to include certain sexual offences, prostitution, and vagrancy when committed by Indigenous people. DIA agents could lodge a complaint with the police, they could direct that a prosecution be conducted and then sit in judgment of it.[43]

In Australia, protectors and superintendents (often police or ex-police officers) extensively regulated Indigenous peoples' lives: deciding whether children would be removed to an institution, their rations, who they could marry, where they could work and for what salary, access to savings, which areas were prohibited, and where the person would reside.[44] Reserve and mission superintendents administered their own policing, judicial and penal regimes outside, and parallel to, existing formal criminal legal systems. In the US, the Bureau of Indian Affairs (BIA) engaged in similar policing and suppression of Indigenous behaviour that might prevent assimilation. Cultural activities such as feasts and dances, as well as various religious practices, were defined as Indian Offenses.[45]

Colonial regulation had the effect of entrenching and normalising surveillance by police and others exercising police and penal powers over First Nations peoples. Criminalisation, punishment, and carceral institutions (jails, boarding schools, missions, and reservations were all prisons[46]) became deeply woven into the fabric of the settler colonial state. Racialised discourses validated violent and lethal punishments. As the spectacle of physical and public punishments began to disappear for Europeans in the later part of the 19th century, the same did not hold for Indigenous peoples. For example, legislation which banned public executions in Western Australia in 1871 was amended to allow exceptions for Aboriginal people. Public execution was recast as a form of tutelage to broadcast a 'lesson' to tribal groups, as a perverse part of the civilising process. The extended use of physical punishments and restraints (lashings, floggings, chaining) continued for Aboriginal people until well into the 20th century.[47] Similarly, in Canada, the penitentiary was seen as unsuitable for Indigenous peoples, who were subject instead to local jails and corporal punishment.[48]

There is not the space here to document First Nations' resistance to colonialism and the corresponding violence of the colonial state in the US, Canada, Australia, or Aotearoa New Zealand. However, as noted previously, the colonial response to resistance was often genocidal. The introduction of reservations and missions changed the nature of Indigenous resistance, but it did not stop. The elaborate legal frameworks for assimilation had the potential to criminalise virtually any Indigenous activity and installed extensive systems of state surveillance. Many First Nations peoples see current policing as central to the ongoing task of colonial rule.

Policing from slavery to Jim Crow

The history of policing African Americans in the US through slavery, the Black Codes, and later Jim Crow is a story of profound violence and repression. Starting from the 1700s southern colonies began to organise slave patrols, beginning with South Carolina in 1704. These were among the first police forces in the US. Their role was to exercise control over enslaved people, prevent rebellion and escape, and to use physical violence to maintain their domination. In some southern US cities, the slave patrols formed the basis of early professionalised police forces.[49] The slave patrols enforced slave laws and were there 'to enforce a social order based on the theft of Black life and labor'.[50] The slave codes had originated in the British colony of Barbados and defined slaves as the property of their owner (hence, chattel slavery). The codes controlled the activities and movements of slaves – whose body belonged to the slaveowner. Under most slave codes the rape of a Black woman was not a crime, and sexual abuse was systemic. Most 'law enforcement' occurred on the plantations by slaveowners and was marked by extreme brutality – from castration and mutilation to immolation. The same brutality was to carry over into the 'right' of Whites to police, control, and destroy Black bodies through the post-slavery and Jim Crow eras of lynching.

In writing of the way punishment differentiated between Whites and slaves in the US, Davis has noted that the deprivation of White freedom tended to affirm the Whiteness of democratic rights and liberties. White men acquired the privilege to be punished in a way that affirmed 'equality and the racialised universality of liberty, [however] the punishment of black slaves was corporal, concrete and particular'.[51] There are parallels between the way slaves and Indigenous peoples were treated in terms of the extreme physicality and brutality of punishment and its public nature – punishment which was underpinned by the need to maintain economic exploitation and colonial superiority justified by racist ideologies.

After the Civil War, the slave codes were replaced by the Black Codes which continued to control the movement, employment and conduct of freed slaves. Michelle Alexander notes that the codes established both 'systems of peonage resembling slavery', while others foreshadowed Jim Crow laws through segregation.[52] Black men and women were far more likely to be arrested than Whites for public order offences such as vagrancy, offensive language, drunkenness, disorderly conduct, and prostitution-related offences. The laws criminalising vagrancy were used by police to force Black men and women to accept employment or to be subject to convict leasing – where police would receive a kickback from employers.[53] The working conditions were often worse than slavery, as the owners and contractors had less need to preserve their labour force.

Racism, segregation, and discrimination were embedded in the Jim Crow laws, and during this period the policing of Black Americans continued to be intertwined with the maintenance of White supremacy. Lynching, violence, rape, and vigilantism were either ignored, protected, or engaged in by the police. Sherrilyn Ifill's historical work on lynching shows the role of ordinary people in the open, public murder of Black people. However, the complicity of police was also fundamental. Police determined whether a Black person would face a trial or a lynch mob. Lynchers often deliberately sought the grounds outside the courthouse, and in the early 1900s the lynchings were often referred to as 'lynch law'. Lynching a Black person in front of the courthouse was both a physical and symbolic location. Police were also instrumental in legitimating racial murders by the failure to prosecute those who were involved. Ifill notes that, 'there is no record of any white person ever having been convicted of murder for lynching a black person – not in the thousands of instances of white-on-black lynchings in thirty-four states'.[54]

Emblematic of the violence against Blacks and the role of the police was the Tulsa Riot. One of the largest, most extreme acts of racist violence in the US occurred in June 1921 when White rioters destroyed over 1,000 homes and murdered up to 300 Black people in the black neighbourhood of Greenwood in Tulsa, Oklahoma. No-one was ever convicted for the criminal acts of murder and the destruction of property. Police in Tulsa were known for their corruption and had participated previously in lynching and violence against the Black population. The Tulsa riot was sparked by another attempted lynching of a young Black man. Members of the White lynch mob were deputised, armed, and participated along with police and the national guard and other White citizens in the burning, looting and destruction of Greenwood. After the riot, some 70 men who were mostly Black were indicted. However, all the charges were ultimately dismissed. Eighty years after the riot, an Oklahoma Commission of Inquiry into the riots was established. It described the Grand Jury at the time as a whitewash which told 'a laughable story of black culpability for the riot'.[55]

The Tulsa riot was only one example of many other incidents of collective White violence and massacres carried out against Black communities during the latter part of the 19th and first half of the 20th centuries. What they had in common was the goal of ensuring White supremacy. What they also had in common, like lynching, was often the complicity of local police and the legal system in facilitating murder and the destruction of property, of being part of the 'crime problem' and of bringing social disintegration and disorder to Black communities. Policing and the criminal law were fundamental to maintaining racial oppression in the US from slavery to the end of Jim Crow and beyond.

Imperialism, policing, and counter insurgency

For the imperial powers, policing was fundamental to the direct control of colonial possessions and other mandated territories after

34

the First World War. However, the profile of policing changed in the post–1945 period of decolonisation – both during the transition period and post-independence. The British police in the Mandate territory of Palestine had developed their military, political, and counterinsurgency capabilities during the period leading up to the 1948 Israeli assertion of independence and British withdrawal from Palestine. According to historian Georgina Sinclair, after 1948 these police took their counterinsurgency expertise to British colonies elsewhere, to confront the different forms of political agitation and resistance in the colonies that heralded the process of decolonisation. As political and social tensions increased throughout the British empire, so did the development of police intelligence systems and counterinsurgency units, including expanded 'Special Branch' police. Police reverted to semi-military profiles with increased police powers. According to Sinclair, policing by the end of the British Empire resembled the tactics associated with a 'dirty war', and Harcourt has shown in relation to the French, the British, and later the Americans how the independence movements in North Africa, Malaya, and Indochina were used to develop counterinsurgency tactics.[56] We return to the effect of counterinsurgency and police militarisation on domestic policing in the centres of imperialism later in the book. Here, I highlight the developing interconnections of increased 'global' policing, and the role of policing in meeting foreign policy objectives within a neo-colonial environment. Policing during the height of Empire was also 'global' to the extent that metropolitan centres developed and exercised policing across their colonial possessions, and the developments in the colonies had a 'feedback effect' on the imperial centres.[57]

   The US had been influential in establishing police forces in Nicaragua, Haiti, and the Dominican Republic in the early 20th century as part of a nation-building and modernisation programme. However, these US-trained forces engaged in 'brutal repression in the service of US-backed regimes … [and] went on to commit horrific human rights abuses, including torture, extortion, kidnapping, and mass murder'.[58] The latter part of the 20th century saw the expansion of US-based technical and training interventions aimed at police reform across Africa, Asia, and Latin America. The US had developed their own counterinsurgency programmes during the 1960s and it became part of the rationale for training police in various countries of the global south as part of the extension of US global imperialism. According to Schrader, between 1962 and 1974, some 52 countries received 'public safety assistance' within their home country by way of US resident policing advisors, while nearly 9,000 high-ranking police from 77 countries were sent to the US for training.[59] He notes that: 'Among police at home, the experience of coordinating counterinsurgency overseas bolstered their organizational coherence, their reliance of capital-intensive technical wizardry, and their ideological commitment to conflating racial difference with political opposition. Global counterinsurgency was a state-building project, creating new bureaucracies and enlarging security agencies.'[60] The purpose of international training for the US was straightforward – it was designed to quell social unrest and prevent the expansion of communism during the Cold War through the development of so-called 'professionalised' police forces. However, faced with popular opposition the local response often descended into the use of death squads, forced disappearances, and paramilitary vigilantes.[61] The US State Department continues to operate a plethora of police training programmes, police experts, and field offices around the world, and offers assistance in a range of areas including combatting terrorism, border control, and drug enforcement.[62] Sometimes the consequences are devasting. In January 2021 Mexican police killed 19 immigrants near the US border and burned their bodies beyond recognition. The majority of those killed were young men from Indigenous communities in Guatemala. Twelve police were subsequently charged with murder and other offences, three of whom were US-trained.[63] The tragic outcomes of 20 years of US (and German) training of local police in Afghanistan is also noteworthy. Prior to the US and NATO withdrawal in 2021, the local police were referred to in various internal US documentation as 'the most hated institution' in Afghanistan, and a corrupt 'extractive organization' extorting money from the population.[64]

Of equal importance is the simultaneous development *within* the US of counterinsurgency techniques and the use of military refined hardware and software. Hönke and Müller note that contemporary policing has both a global reach, as well as being globally made – it is co-constituted in multiple domestic and international sites.[65] The genealogy of modern policing deepens this insight.

The nature of colonial policing

Why is the historical context of colonial policing so important in understanding contemporary policing? The core element of colonial policing was the defence of the colony. The legal order enforced by the police was the law of a colonial state – a legal system which largely excluded colonised peoples (including slaves, Indigenous, and other colonised peoples) from protection, although they were most certainly the subjects of extensive control. The order that the police maintained was by definition an order aimed at protecting the few, while ensuring the ruthless exploitation of the many. Some 30 years ago, when discussing colonial policing, Maureen Cain commented that 'it is healthy to be reminded that the police are concerned with control of politically, economically, and culturally threatening sections of the populace – sections which sometimes constitute the majority'.[66] The analysis of colonial policing is important because colonised peoples never consented to be governed by colonial power, and particularly in the case of settler colonies have never consented. *Thus, we see in the colonial setting the nature of police power and violence in its most naked form.* The police are central to the maintenance of state power – through the gaze of the colonised we see that power stripped bare of all its niceties, indeed as we do today, for example, with the Israeli settler colonial state's use of police/ military violence against Palestinians.[67] Colonial policing never achieved legitimacy beyond the few who directly benefitted from it – as an exercise of power it remained exogenous.[68] What then can we say about the defining features of colonial policing?

First, colonised peoples were subject to paramilitary policing in a way which was *mostly* outside the experience of White citizens within metropolitan centres. Police actions in the style of military-like operations resembled far more a state of war, than the type of policing expected in rural and urban metropolitan communities where there may have been some degree of social consensus. The intensity of war-like police operations was influenced by the level of resistance; and resistance by colonised peoples was inherent to the colonial relationship. People do not give up everything – their lands, their homes, their families, and their livelihoods – without a fight,[69] and at times the intensity of resistance could threaten the viability and prosperity of the colony. Establishing police legitimacy among the colonised was generally not a motivating factor for colonial power; ensuring governance and stability for the extraction of wealth was.

Second, policing was contextualised within the legal ambiguity surrounding the position of colonised peoples within the colonies. While on the one hand they were seen as subjects of the colonial state, colonised peoples were afforded little protection by the law – and 'suspension' of the rule of law was common. As Justice Tankebe has noted, a distinctive feature of colonial policing was 'the exercise of wide-ranging discretionary powers without accountability'.[70] Further, systems of punishment were racialised and differentiated in their brutality and violence between the colonised and the coloniser. Relatedly, the suspension of the rule of law and the use of terror and violence by police against colonised peoples was contextualised and legitimated by racialised constructions of the colonised as inferior, lesser human beings. Racist ideologies enabled both genocidal interventions and institutional, systemic, and legalised racial discrimination.

Third, police took on the role of managing colonised peoples through administrative tasks which were variously aimed at suppressing, controlling, exploiting, and at times civilising and assimilating colonised peoples. There were extensive regulatory regimes which often sought complete control of the Native and which, when it suited colonial authorities, also effectively criminalised the culture, beliefs and practices of the colonised. In many places, police were the face of colonial power and were expected to fulfil a range of regulatory and other administrative tasks in the interests of a functioning colonial government: some were apparently benign (reporting on the conditions of crops), some were not (removing children from families). In both a symbolic and practical sense, police also embodied the violence of colonial power and the power of White supremacy: from the ruthless suppression of colonial revolts across Asia and Africa to the lynching of Black people in North America.

Fourth, the colonial process and policing in its various forms was gendered and imposed the patriarchal relations of the colonising society. Missionaries and colonial governments challenged the position of colonised women – sometimes expressing a view to 'save' them from the barbarism of inferior cultures. In India, for example, the British vigilantly addressed 'scandalous' forms of gender violence such as sati and those activities that appeared to indicate the backwardness of Indian culture such as child marriage, purdah, and caste-prostitution. However, as Elizabeth Kolsky indicates, 'they were less interested in controlling forms of violence against women with which they were more familiar such as rape, murder and domestic violence', and particularly when committed by European men.[71] Women experienced the double jeopardy of being female and colonial subjects. Colonised women were cast as a threat to White society. Their sexuality was commodified via rape and sexual servitude, and police misconduct (including rape and murder) went relatively unpunished. Sexual violence was integral to colonial violence more generally.[72] Ritchie argues that colonialism (including slavery) lay the foundations for the violent treatment of Black, Indigenous, and women of colour, and follows a continuum through racial segregation and control, the policing of poverty, and contemporary policing approaches to public order, drugs, immigration, and terrorism.[73] There is thus a structured and enduring nature to police violence against racialised women.

Conclusion

The historical role of police in the 19th and 20th centuries raises important considerations for the Defund the Police movement. It has been tempting to argue that police have taken on an *increasing* role over recent years as the stop gap response to all types of problems they were never meant to resolve. However, an historical understanding shows that modern policing since its inception in the early 19th century operated well beyond responding to narrow conceptions of crime. It has been highly regulatory, controlling, and violent. Police were an essential part of the 'great confinement' beginning in the early part of the 19th century – they were a core part of the mechanisms of carceral control – the prisons, the asylums, and various colonial institutions. Therefore, we need to be careful of the tendency to stop asking police to be something they have not always been,[74] that is to assume that they have a role which has at some time not involved widespread, often violent intervention into the social, political, and cultural lives of working-class, colonised, and racialised communities since the early days of modern policing.

The historical analysis reinforces the view that we have a *policing* problem that is grounded within particular structural constraints that are not about or have ever been primarily about crime control. The targets of policing have always been those who for whatever reason threaten systems of political control and economic exploitation and the prosperity of the few. Drawing on the French experience, Blanchard has argued that the origins of policing colonised peoples is a key 'historical operator' in understanding racialised policing today, from the use of deadly force to the routine racial selectivity underlying stop and searches, identity checks, and so on for young non-White males.[75] Furthermore, resistance to these forms of policing are ongoing. In recent decades, for example, in the UK, France, the US, and Australia anti-police uprisings and protests have been mostly associated with police lethal violence and police racism.[76] Furthermore, the colonial legacy of policing has continued within former colonies where police use of lethal violence against the population continues unchecked. Policing has always been intertwined between the metropolitan centres of colonialism and the external colonies. Today these multidirectional flows continue in the interests of political elites and global security corporations: the plantation slaveowners and merchants of London or the American South have transformed into strategic policy advisors in government agencies, interest groups such as the International Association of Chiefs of Police, and a host of corporate entities from big data to military hardware.

If we need to be careful in not expecting the police role to be different to what it has been for the last two centuries, then the historical analysis also highlights the problem of reform. The absence of police accountability has always been a problem, and if the police act in the interests of the powerful, why would we expect it to be any different? The core problem with reform strategies is not simply that they do not work, it is that they have the capacity to actually strengthen the systems of police control. Finally, reading the genealogy of modern policing, the point that looms large is the asymmetrical nature of police power and violence. It is applied largely to the least powerful in society.

3

Don't police solve crime?

Chapter 2 provided an historical setting to contemporary policing. How do police see their role today? If we take the mission statements of several large police departments, there is consistent repetition of a few themes. For example, the Chicago Police Department, 'as part of, and empowered by, the community, is committed to protect the lives, property, and rights of all people, to maintain order, and to enforce the law impartially'. Similarly, the Maharashtra Police Service in India sees its basic duty and purpose as 'to uphold and maintain the law fairly and firmly, to detect and prevent crime, to protect, help and reassure the community, [and enforce] the various laws of the land', while the London Metropolitan Police's mission 'is to keep London safe for everyone'.[1] Police define themselves primarily by their functions, including preventing, detecting, and investigating criminal activities, enforcing the law, maintaining public order, and ensuring community safety. In the spirit of Peel's 'New Police', the mission statements in some form or another see police legitimacy as deriving from an amorphous and undefined community.

A limitation of seeing police work through what the police say they do is that the variety of situations in which police intervene is much greater than law enforcement, solving crime or even simply maintaining order. As we saw in the Chapter 2, the role of the police has always been expansive, in both colonial settings (for example, removing children from families, undertaking summary justice, banning ceremonies, and undertaking political surveillance) and in the metropole (from controlling the labour movement to apprehending 'lunatics', controlling the homeless, and policing school truancy). An argument we often hear is that the role of police has expanded significantly, and they are now required to respond to an increasing number of social problems. However, this argument needs to be read within the broader historical context. Part of the reading of this issue is that 'crime' and the necessity for a police response is contingent on the power to define the activities that constitute crime, disorder, and the social activities that necessitate police intervention. For example, in the 1990s and since, the international appeal of the 'broken windows' approach to crime and the concomitant rise of zero tolerance policing has seen a focus on the aggressive policing of people who are the contemporary equivalents of the 19th-century vagrants, beggars, undeserving poor, the disreputable, and those living with disability or mental ill-health.

A second limitation of defining police by their end goals such as solving crime and ensuring public safety is that it draws attention away from the features that define how police conduct their work. Two irreducible elements of policing are the legal authority to use (lethal) violence and coercion to resolve situations; and the ability to use discretion, so that it is not law enforcement *per se*, but the ability to decide which laws to enforce, and how and when to enforce them that is important. The elements of police violence and police use of discretion are explored further as the book progresses. For the moment, I want to pick up on a point made by Stuart Schrader that the messages about police solving crime, preventing violence, and being answerable to the community are part of the sustaining myths of policing. More importantly, these messages are political arguments as well: 'They are instrumental, a means toward an end. Police attempt to achieve legitimacy through the stories they tell about themselves. Police legitimacy means public compliance. It means power. The core of policing is not safety. It is social control.'[2] Thus, it is worth returning to the foundational political arguments for the existence of police and their assumed necessity and legitimacy.

Danger

Many of the arguments for *not* defunding the police include in some form that police are indispensable because of their crime-solving abilities, that they are highly trained and are required by the public to respond to dangerous situations. However, in England and Wales, the College of Policing reported that non-crime related incidents account for 83 per cent of all calls to police Command and Control Centres.[3] In the US, an analysis of police calls for service show that most calls for service are for non-violent problems. A *New York Times* investigation into calls for service for ten police departments (including cities such as New Orleans, Baltimore, Phoenix, Cincinnati, and Seattle) found that the percentage of calls relating to serious violent crime was around 1 per cent. The research showed that the amount of time officers devoted to handling serious violent crime was about 4 per cent, while more than 30 per cent was devoted to responding to non-criminal calls.[4] Similarly, Michelle Brown and colleagues analysed 2 years of call data in Knoxville, Tennessee. Some 44 per cent of the calls were property-related, 18 per cent of calls were for responses to motor vehicle accidents, calls relating to 'interpersonal conflict and violence' were 12 per cent, and officer-initiated calls relating to activities on patrol, assisting citizens, location checks, etc were 7 per cent of the total. In addition, there was a high number of hang-up calls.[5]

At least two related issues arise from the research on calls for service: the extent to which police are *necessary* for effective responses to public requirements for assistance, and second, whether they are *appropriate* responders. As noted in a paper from the Brookings Institute: 'Police officers' skillset and training are often out of sync with the social interactions that they have. Police officers are mostly trained in use-of-force tactics and worst-case scenarios to reduce potential threats.'[6] Further, Brown and colleagues have argued that the call for service, while foregrounding public demand and need, also evokes and legitimates the expansive power of police. Irrespective of whether the call is crime-related or not, the police are established institutionally to dictate the social responses they determine to be appropriate – for example to matters involving homelessness or disability. Research on calls to police relating to homelessness show that most do not concern criminal behaviour, yet they generate a high volume of arrests for minor offences.[7] Analysis of calls for service have been important for progressing the Defund the Police movement and for abolitionists more generally. It provides a pragmatic opportunity to shrink the criminal legal system by reducing the scope and funding of police. It also requires us to think through other ways of responding to citizens' demands for assistance which do not reproduce new forms of carcerality, so that it is not just about the absence of police, but also *the presence of well-resourced communities* that can respond to their own social needs – a point that was acknowledged by activist and revolutionary groups opposing police brutality and lethal violence in the 1960s and early 1970s.[8]

The argument that the police are the 'thin blue line' between the community and violent anarchy also begs the question of how dangerous policing is as an occupation. According to the US Bureau of Labor Statistics data for 2019, police officers do not rank in the top ten most dangerous occupations as measured by workplace fatalities. Forestry workers, construction workers, iron and steel workers, sales drivers and truck drivers, refuse collectors, agricultural workers, farmers, pilots, and grounds maintenance workers all have more dangerous jobs than police officers.[9] In Australia, workers in the public administration and safety industry (which includes police, emergency services, prison officers, and other public administration workers) were at the mid-point in terms of the fatality rate of all industries (that is, of the 19 industry categories they ranked number 10 for fatalities).[10] Although there are variations between countries, where there is data, we know that around 75 per cent of police deaths in the line of duty are accidental and that the majority of these are related to traffic accidents. A minority of police deaths are caused by an offender. For example, Allard and Prenzler found that over the 60-year period from 1948 to 2007, some 80 per cent of Australian police officer's line of duty deaths were due to accidents.[11] Longer-term improvements in police procedures and technology have resulted in reductions in the rate of police fatalities. Typically, in Australia there are one or two deaths on duty per year.[12] In the UK the rate is similar: in 2020, five officers died in the line of duty – three were the result of motor vehicle accidents, one from being accidentally struck by a vehicle, and one officer died in a shooting.[13]

The US is anomalous to the extent that, taking into account different population sizes, there are a large number of police deaths compared to nations such as the UK or Australia, and a greater proportion of these police deaths arise from shootings. According to the Federal Bureau of Investigation (FBI), a total of 93 law enforcement officers were killed in the line of duty in 2020. Of these, just over half the officers died in accidents (47) and the remainder of officers (46) died because of the actions of offenders. Just on 90 per cent of the officer deaths caused by offenders involved the use of firearms (41 out of 46). Of those who died in accidents, more than half (26) were killed in motor vehicle crashes and a further 12 were struck by vehicles. Five were killed in firearm-related accidents.[14] There is a significant disparity in the shooting deaths of police in the US compared to other countries in the global north, which is itself partly related to the availability and use of firearms within the broader society.

We might also compare the number of police killed by firearms in the US with the number of civilians killed by police in fatal shootings – there were over 1,000 civilian deaths from police shootings in 2020.[15] Again, these civilian killings are high compared to other countries in the global north. The Prison Policy Institute compared the rate of police killings per 10 million of the population across ten countries. It found that the rate in the US was 33.5 per 10 million of the population. It was 9.8 in Canada, 8.5 in Australia, 2.3 in the Netherlands, 2 in New Zealand, 1.3 in Germany, 0.5 in England and Wales, 0.2 in Japan, and zero in Iceland and Norway.[16] Comparing the number of civilians killed by police to the number of police killed by civilians opens consideration of the epidemiology of gun killings involving police. According to public health research, one in 15 firearm deaths in the US is at the hands of police; among Black Americans it is approximately one in 10.[17] While policing may be a relatively safe occupation compared to many others, its negative impact on community safety is clearly problematic. Further, the vast majority of these police killings are defined as 'lawful' and thus do not appear in reported crime statistics. Policing is dangerous – not necessarily to the police – but certainly to the community.

Solving crime

Given the strongly promoted image of police as 'crime fighters', it is legitimate to question how effective they are in solving crime. Most standard books on criminology or policing will tell us unequivocally that police do not do a very good job at solving many types of crime – that their rates for 'clearing' crime are quite low. Taken together with low reporting rates, this raises serious questions concerning the competency of police in what are seen to be one of their core roles. For example, according to the Pew Research Centre, in the US less than half of crimes are reported and less than half of those are solved.[18]

Although there are some definitional variations internationally, police clearance rates for crime are usually based on the calculation of cases that end with an arrest or the identification of a suspect who cannot be apprehended. They are not a measure of convictions. In 2019 in the US, more than 38 per cent of murders were not solved, as were nearly half of aggravated assaults. Two thirds of all reported rapes were not solved, nor were nearly 70 per cent of reported robberies. The clearance rates for burglary and motor vehicle theft are even worse, where approximately 86 per cent of reported offences are not solved.[19] The low police clear-up rates for robbery and property offences in the US are common across many countries. For example, in England and Wales less than 10 per cent of robbery and criminal damage result in a person being charged with an offence.[20] In NSW, Australia, the clear-up rate for robbery, burglary, and motor vehicle theft is low – almost 70 per cent of robberies and more than 90 per cent of burglaries and motor vehicle thefts are not solved.[21]

The US clearance figures for murder cited earlier are nationwide. However, in large cities such as Chicago, more than half of reported homicides remain unsolved, and in cities with majority Black populations like Baltimore, the situation is even worse, where two thirds of homicides were not cleared in 2019.[22] In countries not afflicted by excessive levels of gun violence and murder rates,[23] the clearance rate for homicide is much higher. For example, in Australia, the clearance rate was 94 per cent in 2019, and has been consistently above 85 per cent since 1990. In Europe, homicide clearance rates are typically 80 per cent or significantly higher.[24] In these contexts, police are more likely to solve murders because of the high proportion of murder victims killed by someone known to the victim, including family members, current or former intimate partners, or acquaintances and where, among other factors, the number of suspects is relatively limited.[25] Not surprisingly, in cases where the offender is known to the victim and there is less use of guns as the murder weapon, the more likely police will successfully solve the crime.[26] However, homicides with victims from racialised and marginalised communities (including the homeless, sex workers, people living with disabilities) are more likely to remain unsolved, not investigated, or undetected. Although homicide is something of an exception for the reasons outlined previously, the bottom line is that the majority of many types of crime reported to police are not cleared. The argument that police are indispensable because of their crime solving abilities simply does not fit the evidence.

Reporting and recording crime

The role of the police in solving crime is only one part of the story. Another is the willingness by the community, or more accurately, multiple different communities to report crimes to the police in the first instance. Social divisions based on class, gender, age, race, ethnicity, Indigeneity, disability, sexual orientation, type of work, citizenship status, prior experience with police and legal institutions, and their multiple intersections, all impact on the likelihood of whether a person will report an offence to the police. Crime victim surveys generally measure whether a person has been a victim of crime, whether they have reported the offence to police or others, and the reasons for reporting (or not). Many countries conduct regular surveys, and the United Nations Interregional Crime and Justice Research Institute (UNICRI) has conducted various international surveys. There are limitations to these surveys including who is surveyed and who is excluded, how they are surveyed, and what types of crime are included and excluded by the surveys. These limitations are further compounded in international comparative surveys where differences in cultural, legal, and administrative factors come into play. However, having said that, they do provide a window on the reporting of crime. What stands out in the analysis of this data is that many offences, and in some cases the majority, are not reported to police. For example, in the US only about half of violent crimes and a third of property crimes are reported by victims to police each year.[27]

Between the late 1980s and 2005, UNICRI and associated national organisations conducted a number of International Crime Victims Surveys (ICVS). Of the reports generated from this research, one in particular focuses on crime victimisation in 30 countries and 33 large cities, mostly from the global north.[28] In general, the reporting levels of crime to police (across a range of offences) is higher in wealthier countries, yet even here in the highest reporting countries of Europe, there is significant unreported crime ranging between 30–40 per cent in Austria, Belgium, Sweden, and Switzerland. In contrast, in the cities of Sao Paulo, Phnom Penh, Lima, and Maputo, more than 80 per cent of offences are not reported.[29] In a survey of 13 African countries,[30] slightly more than half the victims of burglary reported the offence to police. However, of those who did report, nearly 70 per cent were not satisfied with the police response. In relation to robbery offences, only one third of victims reported the offence to police, and of these more than 60 per cent were not satisfied with the police response; in the cases of assault less than a quarter of victims reported the offence to police, and of these, two thirds were dissatisfied with the police response.

Significant rates of corruption by police and other government officials were also identified by victims in some of the African countries which were surveyed. The highest rates were in Uganda, Nigeria, and Mozambique, where one in three people, and Tanzania, where one in five people, identified being a victim of corruption. Perhaps not surprisingly, the reporting of corruption to police was negligible in these countries, ranging from 1.4 per cent in Uganda to 5.6 per cent in Nigeria. One of the most serious offences which is frequently not reported to police is rape/sexual assault. In the African survey, women were asked about sexual victimisation – which was broadly defined – and very few victims reported these offences (14.5 per cent). The issue of policing and sexual violence is discussed more extensively in Chapter 6.

The relatively low reporting of crime to police raises questions of why people decide not to report. Responses to this question depend on the type of crime and where the survey was conducted. However, major reasons are the belief that police could not or would not do anything about the offence, or that the offence was not serious enough. The ICVS study of mostly wealthy countries referred to previously, found that more than 40 per cent of people did not report an offence because they thought police could not or would not do anything. This particular reason for not reporting is often more common in the global south. For example, in Latin America, the lack of police effectiveness is the most common reason for not reporting crime. In general, these types of responses are not surprising when we consider that of the offences *reported* to police, most will not be *solved*. To return to the US data, 47 per cent of violent offences and 35 per cent of property crime are reported to police; 46 per cent of the violent crimes and 19 per cent of the property crimes reported to police were cleared. Thus, broadly speaking, for every 100 violent crimes in the community, police solve a little over 20; and for every 100 property crimes, police solve seven.[31] In this context, Schrader's point that the stories police tell about themselves as crime fighters and the 'thin blue line' are clearly politically instrumental for maintaining legitimacy in the public sphere, especially in a situation where the factual information on reporting by the community and solving crimes by police tells a quite different story.

As noted previously, the likelihood of reporting crime to police is mediated by a range of social and political factors. For example, we know in the LGBTQIA+ community, there are lower rates of reporting offences to police than the general population. Research across various countries has indicated numerous reasons for this, including the belief that police are homophobic, that police will not take violence and harassment against LGBTQIA+ people seriously, that they will be subject to abuse when reporting, and that experiences of persecution and discrimination from a range of institutions means that many members of the LGBTQIA+ community will avoid the police.[32] Similarly, people living with mental ill-health and disability also face problems reporting offences to police, despite the frequency with which they may be victims of crime, including within institutional settings. For example, analysis drawn from US National Crime Victimization Survey estimated that only 5 per cent of crimes against people with disabilities were reported to the police compared to an average of 44 per cent for the general population.[33] In Australia, various research has shown that prejudice and discrimination mark the interaction between people with disabilities and police, and victims of crime consistently report fearing that police will not protect them, that they will not be believed, or they will be viewed as lacking credibility.[34]

This question of credibility also raises the concern that even when offences are reported to police, they may not be *recorded* as crimes – depending on who the police see as credible or worthy victims. More extensively, these police practices become institutionalised corruption, where the manipulation of crime statistics is carried out in the interests of demonstrating police efficiency and falling crimes rates. For instance, in the UK in 2014, the government's Statistics Authority removed its approval of police recorded crime statistics because of recording malpractices and inaccuracies. Her Majesty's Inspectorate of Constabulary estimated that as many as one in five offences reported to police were not being recorded – including serious offences such as rape.[35]

Who do we trust?

The argument which is often advanced is that efficacy of the police is dependent on their relationship with the people in the communities they police – hence the constant reformist measures that seek to improve community/police relationships. Yet this avoids the type of structural relationships of oppression that underpin relationships with police – the history of which was outlined in Chapter 2. The widespread international protests against police during 2020 showed the serious absence of police legitimacy in many countries, particularly among racial and other minoritised groups. As McManus and her colleagues have written regarding the US:

> Since the 1960s, studies have observed consistently racial disparities in Americans' attitudes toward police. Black Americans are consistently found to report lower levels of confidence and trust in and/or satisfaction with police. Additionally, research finds Black Americans are more likely to perceive the police as racially biased, less courteous, and to perceive police

use of force as more of a problem. A national survey
... [found] only 40% of Black respondents reported
favorable views of the police, compared to 68% of
White respondents.[36]

A recent survey by the Pew Research Centre found that only 9
per cent of Black respondents believed that police treated racial
and ethnic groups equally, compared to 42 per cent of Whites.
There was also widespread divergence on the view as to whether
police were doing a good job protecting people from crime;
only 28 per cent of Black Americans believed this to be the case,
compared to more than two thirds of White Americans. Besides
the difference between various groups, it is also relevant that the
majority of White, Hispanic, and Black respondents believed that
the police treated racial and ethnic groups unequally. Similarly,
a majority of all groups believed that police were not using the
right amount of force, nor doing a good job in holding police
officers accountable for misconduct. A majority also believed
that civilians should have the power to sue police officers who
use excessive force.[37]

Of particular interest is research by the Urban Institute
conducted in heavily disadvantaged, high crime communities in
six US cities. Residents questioned 'the intent, effectiveness and
equity of the criminal justice system' in their communities where
they experienced an intensive police presence, and high rates of
incarceration and community supervision.

Indeed, police may carry out aggressive strategies that
target quality-of-life infractions and drug-, gun-, and
gang-related violence in ways that undermine public
confidence. Perhaps not surprisingly, areas with high
levels of mistrust tend to be those that are heavily
policed, where police use tactics such as pretextual
stops that damage their relationship with the people
they are charged to protect. The results can be far-
reaching: a distrust of the criminal justice system,
an unwillingness to cooperate with the police, and
a cynical view of the law that can perpetuate crime
and victimization.[38]

Two-thirds of the people interviewed in the six communities identified themselves as Black, 12 per cent as White, and 11 per cent as Latinx. The research showed that 'respondents' perceptions of police across measures of legitimacy, procedural justice, racial bias, relatability to police, and applied principles of community policing, on average, are extremely negative'.[39] Police often acted in ways that were inconsistent with people's ideas about what is right and wrong. For example, only one in four people believed that police made fair and impartial decisions, or that the police were honest. Less than one in three people believed that police:

- treated people with dignity and respect;
- behaved according to the law;
- were responsive to community concerns, or prioritised community problems.

Despite these highly negative views of the police, a majority also indicated that they would still report crime to the police and would attend a community meeting with police to discuss neighbourhood crime. One reading of these apparently anomalous results is that people in these highly disadvantaged communities have a genuine concern for public safety – they want to live in a safe environment for themselves and their families. Although they demonstrably do not trust the police, they seemingly have no other available social or institutional responses they can call on – a situation which has been exacerbated in many communities by years of neglect, unemployment, and withdrawal of social services.

Chris Hayes's book *A Colony in a Nation* makes the case that the criminal legal system in the US is not simply a single system with massive racial disparities, but rather two distinct systems. 'One (the Nation) is the kind of policing regime you expect in democracy; the other (the Colony) is the kind you expect in an occupied land'.[40] In an argument reminiscent of Frantz Fanon, Hayes maintains that in the Colony, police violence looms constantly, and any non-compliance can be fatal: 'In the Nation there is law, in the Colony, there is only a concern for order. In the Nation, you have rights; in the Colony you have commands.'[41] The racial composition of the Colony is primarily made-up of Black and people of colour. However, as a result of neoliberalism, deindustrialisation, and wage stagnation, 'the tendencies and systems of control developed in the Colony have been deployed over wider and wider swathes of working-class white America'.[42] Ultimately though, there is no single experience of crime and punishment in the US, the experiential differences mean there are two different countries separated by the intersections of race and class. This issue is not particular to the US, and can be seen from the policing of young people of colour in the *banlieues* of Paris to the youth prisons of the Northern Territory in Australia, where it is not unusual for Aboriginal children to comprise the total incarcerated youth population. It can be seen in the UK, where reportedly 85 per cent of Black people do not believe they would be treated the same as a White person by the police.[43]

Of course, the 'colony' and its aftermath is not simply a metaphor. As Justice Tankebe notes in his work on the Ghana police, successive postcolonial governments failed to shift policing from its colonial foundations, and contemporary human rights violations, police violence and corruption, and the absence of accountability can be traced to these colonial roots. In the aftermath of colonial independence, police reform was aimed at Africanisation and expanding the operational capacity of the police. The 'ideological orientation of the police and how they carried out their functions were left largely untouched ... [and] police were used by successive governments to suppress liberties and political freedoms'.[44] If unaccountable police power had been a feature of colonial policing systems, it continued largely unabated in the postcolonial period. Indeed, if anything, it worsened. While Tankebe is specifically discussing Ghana, the lessons can be seen elsewhere in police forces carrying on the tasks of colonial control through summary arrests, detention, imprisonment, extra-legal executions of suspects, and political opponents, and so on – now being done for the new local elites that replaced the former European colonialists.[45]

Police discretion

One of the defining features of police is broad discretion – the ability of police to decide whether, when, and how to act in enforcing the law and maintaining order. Police are sometimes referred to as 'street-level bureaucracies' to capture the idea that police exercise wide discretionary decision-making in their interactions with the public. The question of discretion is connected to matters of accountability and legitimation. If discretion defines how police act, then we need to be concerned with whether police are accountable for their actions – police actions occur with 'low visibility' in terms of review and accountability. A further concern is whether police discretionary actions are seen as legitimate by the community being policed and the broader public. Moreover, police discretionary decisions define the types of people, behaviour and events that come to be seen as criminal and crime – and that knowledge is mirrored back to public in their understanding of danger, risk, and criminality.

The use of discretion is bounded and influenced by a range of factors, including peer group pressure, elements of police culture more generally (such as loyalty, machismo, individualism), and police training, which inculcates a heightened sense of danger and the resort to violence. Various official inquiries and royal commissions[46] over the years in many countries have identified endemic problems within police culture including a high tolerance of dishonesty, lying under oath, falsifying information and evidence, the view that inconvenient legal rules can be ignored, and systemic or institutional racism. At the more extreme level, police utilise discretion in whether to use violence (euphemistically referred to in policing literature as force), and the 'appropriate' level of violence. Coercive and sometimes lethal violence is used more frequently in interactions with Black, Indigenous, and people of colour. The use of individual police discretion is often mundane in the day-to-day decisions of who to stop, who to search, what subsequent actions to take, and whether and how these interactions are mediated by the individual attributes of the public including race, class, age, mental health/disability, sexual orientation, and gender. In other words, the use of police discretion is socially patterned. Other factors that may place limits around how police act include whether the boundaries of the law are seen to apply, systems of accountability, and the social visibility and location of encounters with the public. The events at protests after the death of George Floyd were an example of the absence of these limiting factors – from indiscriminate police violence against protesters and bystanders to the selective targeting of journalists.

Police do not (and could not) enforce all the laws all of the time, and it is through selective enforcement that police choose who is funnelled into the criminal legal system.[47] The law itself may invite discretion through, for example, the use of diversionary options for young people, or the decision to proceed against an alleged offender by way of arrest or by court summons. Although these decisions may appear mundane from a policing perspective, the legal and social effects on those who are the subject of these decisions are far from mundane (for example, bail, court, pre-trail detention, fines, jail, criminal record, loss of employment, loss of housing). Discretion exists at all levels of the organisation, from the police commissioner to the officer on the beat. At the organisational level, it exists in the development of policing policies, in the setting of targets to police certain types of crimes, offenders, and locations, and in the allocation of policing resources. At a local level, it exists in the interpretation of these policies by local police commanders: how seriously they take diversion, where they place resources, whether they target particular neighbourhoods or housing estates, and so forth. If local police are being kitted-out with military weapons, hardware, tactics, and technologies to respond to public demonstrations, we need to ask what message that provides to police on the ground. What are they being encouraged to do? How are they being invited to utilise their discretion? These institutional and organisational imperatives define matters such as task orientations and policy priorities and affect the use of discretion at the individual level. They directly impact on the definitions of and reactions to events and situations defined as 'crime'. In the following sections, I briefly consider two examples of how police discretion influences the broader problems of both criminalisation and solving crime: the policing of children and young people, and the policing of violence against people from LGBTQIA+ communities.

Policing young people

The social patterning of police discretion and the way it negatively impacts on Black, First Nations, and other racialised groups is particularly apparent if we look at the policing of young people. There is evidence over many decades that police powers are applied disproportionately in accordance with racialised views of youth crime and disorder. Comparative work between England and Wales and Australia illustrates the problem.[48] In Australia the adverse use of police powers has targeted primarily First Nations children, and various refugee and immigrant children, including from Indochina and more recently from Africa, and Arabic-speaking children in line with periods of Islamophobia. For example, over the last decade there have been consistent complaints by African–Australian young people of police racial profiling, harassment, and violence in many Australian cities. In one case a racial discrimination complaint ended in a Federal Court settlement between the Victorian police and six young people of African background.[49] Similarly, in England and Wales there is comparable long-term evidence that minority ethnic young peoples' experiences of policing are often characterised by hostility, lack of confidence, and a general mistrust of authority, and that particular racialised groups are most at risk of disproportionate police attention including African Caribbean and Muslim young people. We see the problem manifested in both Australia and England and Wales with the disproportionate and routine use of stop and searches, knife searches, strip searches, and move-on powers. In the majority of these cases, nothing illegal is located – which compounds young people's feelings of being subjected to targeted police harassment.[50] Crudely racialised constructions of youth 'gangs' have further extended discriminatory policing. In 2014, the London Metropolitan Police reported that nearly 80 per cent of the people included in its Gang Matrix database were classified as Black and a further 9 per cent were from other minority ethnic communities. Comparable biases are found in other police gang databases in England. As Bridges explains:

> The ethnic composition of the Gangs Matrix and similar databases is not simply an issue of bias in the way such instruments are compiled. As the police themselves turn increasingly to so-called 'intelligence-led' operations ... these databases feed directly into

the ways in which policing policies and priorities are being targeted on particular groups. In other words, the racial bias in the databases becomes institutionalised in police practice.[51]

Generally-speaking, youth justice has developed historically with a greater emphasis on diversion from formal criminal proceedings than has been the case with adults – in recognition of the need to prevent unnecessary criminalisation and stigmatisation of children. The preference for using diversionary options for children in conflict with the law is prioritised in the UN Convention on the Rights of the Child. In most cases, police are the access point to diversion from formal criminal proceedings. However, it is clear that police discretionary decisions are differentially applied along racialised boundaries – which leads to greater criminalisation and more punitive outcomes for some groups of children. In Australia, First Nations children are significantly less likely than other young people to receive a police diversionary option (such as a warning or caution) and, conversely, they are more likely than other children to be arrested, to have bail refused and to have their cases referred to court for determination. In England and Wales, police can opt to either charge a child with a crime, or divert them from the legal system by way of 'no further action' or by issuing a reprimand or a final warning. Various research has shown that police are less likely to issue a reprimand or final warning to Black and 'mixed race' young people, and less likely to divert them through no further action, compared to White offenders. The outcomes of these police decisions influence and cumulatively compound through the legal system with the greater use of police custody, more extensive criminal records and more punitive sentencing outcomes, including a greater likelihood of imprisonment.[52] Discretion and the policing of young people highlights the discriminatory nature of many police interventions, and in particular how racialisation becomes embedded in police practice. It goes to the heart of the argument that contemporary policing is more about maintaining systemic inequalities than solving crime *per se*. It also speaks to how, in popular discourse, we come to see crime as being perpetrated by Black, Indigenous and minority young people – both male and female – rather than seeing the role of police decision-making in creating a racialised 'juvenile criminal'.

Investigating violence and murder of LGBTQIA+ people

Police violence against the LGBTQIA+ community has a long history and continues today – openly in many places. For example, in Turkey the annual Gay Pride parade has been banned since 2014. The LGBTQIA+ community continues to gather for the procession in Istanbul to be met by police repression. In June 2021, battalions of Turkish police in riot gear fired tear gas and rubber bullets at the crowds attempting to take part in the parade. In June 2022 police began arresting people before the march started, raiding cafes and bars in the area, and detaining nearly 400 people.[53] Other Pride rallies internationally have challenged the participation of police in Pride parades, and some groups such as the No Pride in Policing Coalition in Toronto have called for the defunding of the police. It was noted earlier in this chapter that the LGBTQIA+ community is a group who is less likely to report criminal offences to police. The 2015 US Transgender Survey found that of the survey respondents who had contact with the police, more than half (58 per cent) experienced some form of mistreatment. Police often assumed that transgender people – particularly transgender women of colour – were sex workers. More than half (57 per cent) of respondents said they would feel uncomfortable asking the police for help if they needed it.[54]

Police responses to anti-homosexual/transgender murders provide a window on how police discretion impacts on investigations, and how at a deeper level the structures of heteronormativity are policed. On the surface, we might expect the investigation of a murder is an area where police discretion is limited. Yet research into police responses to the deaths of people in the LGBTQIA+ community shows otherwise. For example, researchers have considered the dozens of killings of gay men and transgender women which occurred in NSW (particularly Sydney) during the 1980s and 1990s. They have raised the question of whether the unsolved homicides which were dismissed as accidents, suicides, or low priority killings by police, reflected the view by police of LGBTQIA+ people as 'unworthy' victims. Over the last decade, a number of subsequent coronial re-investigations of these deaths (particularly into the murders of gay men in Bondi, Sydney) have been highly critical of the original police investigations, including ineptitude, poor practices, stereotypes of the murder victims as 'paedophiles' and the potential impact of police corruption.[55] An NSW Parliamentary Committee conducted its own inquiry into violent crimes committed against LGBTQIA+ people between 1970 and 2010. The Committee reported in May 2021 and found that the police force had failed in its responsibility to properly investigate cases of historical gay and transgender hate crime. As recommended by the Committee, a judicial inquiry has been established to inquire into unsolved cases of suspected gay and transgender hate crime murders.[56]

These issues are not particular to Australia. In many countries, including the UK, Canada, and the US, violence against LGBTQIA+ communities is on the rise. Reflecting the problem of police discretion, a recent UK report from Her Majesty's Inspectorate of Constabulary found that victims of hate crimes faced a 'postcode lottery' in terms of the effectiveness or otherwise of police responses.[57] The US also provides a graphic example of the exercise of police institutional discretion at the highest levels, which minimises the importance of violence against LGBTQIA+ communities. Reporting hate crimes to the FBI is not mandatory, and the number of police departments making these annual reports has been declining. In 2019, some 71 US cities with populations greater than 100,000 either did not report data to the FBI or reported zero hate crimes. According to the Human Rights Campaign, a report of zero incidence is clearly not credible: 'The lack of mandatory reporting means that the FBI data, while helpful, paints an incomplete picture of hate crimes against the LGBTQ and other communities'.[58]

The failure of police to properly investigate violence, harassment, and murder of people on the basis of sexual orientation reflects particular use of police discretion on many levels and reinforces the structures of heteronormativity. Obviously, not all police officers are heterosexual, and there are police who as individuals treat violence against gay, lesbian, and transgender people as a genuine issue. However, it is also the case that failing to take violence against the LGBTQIA+ community seriously is a systemic problem that establishes and legitimises the structural boundaries of acceptability. Those who fall outside those boundaries are ineligible for protection, and those who commit harm are ignored or excused.

Conclusion

The chapter has provided an outline of why we need to be sceptical of the ability of police to solve crime. We know that rates of reporting crime to police are low and the ability of police to solve crime is limited – as shown in the rates of crimes that are cleared. A distrust of police and the criminal legal system, an unwillingness to cooperate with the police, and various forms of racism and discrimination by police, impact on whether people will report and whether they will be believed. Localised increases in crime are often used as propaganda tools to argue for more police resources. However, we need to acknowledge the significant limitations of crime data particularly in relation to what is reported, measured, and ignored, as well as the more fundamental question of whether police are necessary and appropriate for effective responses to the type of assistance which communities require.

There are also questions which run much deeper, including the broader functions of police in the process of criminalisation. Hayes's argument that the criminal legal system is in fact two distinct systems divided and experienced along primarily the line of race, needs to be expanded to include other social divisions such as sexuality, ableism, and age. Driving through these categories are race and class – thus we know, for example, that children and young people that end up in the juvenile legal system are drawn from the most disadvantaged and oppressed neighbourhoods and communities. They have biographies scarred by combinations of low income, disrupted education, and welfare and child protection involvement, that compounds further through police intervention.[59] Similarly, we know that both class and race mediate which people living with mental ill-health and disability will come to police attention – it is particularly those who are poor and homeless.[60] Policing creates the boundaries of legitimacy and acceptability, of those that remain outside the legal system and those that become 'police property'.

Through the use of discretion, policing reproduces the social boundaries of who is problematic and who is not. It is a power utilised at an organisational and individual level that is one of the core attributes of policing. It enables police power to be exercised in a targeted and economical way – it is the filter device of criminalisation. Occasionally it is misdirected – the White middle class woman is shot dead by police on the lawn of her home after calling for police assistance, or the Harvard University professor who is Black is arrested in his leafy upmarket home for a suspected break-in – but mostly it works the way it is supposed to.[61] The two examples drawn on is this chapter, the policing of children and young people, and the policing of violence against people from LGBTQIA+ communities, illustrate these issues. Discretion and the policing of young people highlights the discriminatory nature of many police interventions, and in particular, how racialisation becomes embedded in police practice – pushing racialised young people into the furthest reaches of the juvenile legal system. Police discretion also impacts on murder investigations. The research into police responses to the killings of people within the LGBTQIA+ community strongly suggests a situation where negative perceptions of victim status reproduce heteronormative assumptions and normalise violence. These examples go to the heart of the argument that contemporary policing is more about maintaining systemic inequalities than solving crime.

Moreover, the question of police discretion is symbiotically connected to the utilisation of violence – police violence, carceral violence, state violence – the discretion to kill, maim, and imprison. It links the historical discussion in Chapter 2 on the history of the role of the police in enforcing colonial exploitation and control with Chapter 4, which picks up on the contemporary background to the movement to defund the police – movements that were forged in the direct challenge to the use of violence by police.

4

The protest movement never stopped: from Black Power to zero tolerance

The demonstrations, protests, and uprisings against police internationally, and the rise of the BLM movement, are inextricably connected to police violence and deaths in custody, and especially the deaths of Indigenous, Black, and people of colour. While there is a long history to policing as the violent arm of colonialism and slavery as discussed in Chapter 2, the more recent history of the struggle against police violence arises in the global revolutionary movements of the 1960s and 1970s. The anti-imperialist struggles against the US war in Vietnam and opposition to its interventions and support for dictatorships in Latin America and elsewhere, the anti-apartheid movement, the civil rights movements, the rise of worker's and student's militancy, and the women's rights and gay rights movements, brought a generation of people into direct contact with the ferocity of state power. Police in various countries were at the forefront of often violent repression of these popular movements. The other important lesson from the resistance to police violence is that the popular movements were not simply oppositional – they were concerned with responding to the needs of communities in areas such as access to health, education, legal services, and housing, and in building solidarity across groups.

Intertwining stories

Taking Australia and the US as examples, the struggle against police and state violence was central to the radical politics of the Black Panther and Indigenous liberation movements. The formation of the American Indian Movement (AIM) in Minneapolis, the Black Power movement and the Aboriginal Legal Service (ALS) in Sydney, and the Black Panther Party for Self-Defense in Oakland are central examples of First Nations and Black movements for autonomy, self-defence, and self-determination which emerged alongside protecting local communities from police violence. Reflections on First Nations and Black history since the late 1960s bring to light parallels which bear directly on understanding the current BLM protests and the demands to defund the police. In short, the struggle against police violence and racism has been one of the defining features of modern First Nations and Black radical political movements in both Australia and the US, and it began at similar moments in both countries.

The movements clearly understood that colonialism was a core structure that underpinned police violence. The Black Panther Party for Social Defense was formed in 1966 and the initial strategy involved direct resistance to policing. Activists like Stokely Carmichael and Bobby Seale linked the contemporary position of Black people in the US with the history of domestic colonialism and the war of US imperialism in Vietnam. The work of Frantz Fanon was used as a point of analysis in the Panther' writings, and police violence and killings were constant themes. According to Seale, 'the racist military police force occupies our community just like the foreign American troops in Vietnam'.[1] The Black Panthers' Ten Point Program called for an end to 'police brutality and murder of Black people, other people of color, and all oppressed people inside the United States'. They called for an 'end to all wars of aggression' by the US. The Black Panthers were also abolitionists.

> We want freedom for all Black and oppressed people now held in U.S. federal, state, county, city and military prisons and jails. ... We believe that the many Black

and poor oppressed people … have not received fair and impartial trials under a racist and fascist judicial system and should be free from incarceration. We believe in the ultimate elimination of all wretched, inhuman penal institutions, because the masses of men and women imprisoned … are the victims of oppressive conditions which are the real cause of their imprisonment.[2]

In the late 1960s and early 1970s First Nations political activists in Australia understood the contemporary position of Aboriginal people as created by colonial oppression. They had connections with Maori activists in Aotearoa New Zealand, the Polynesian Panthers in the Pacific, both the American Indian Movement and the Black Panthers in the US, First Nations people in Canada, and the Caribbean Black Power movement. They were also involved in the opposition to apartheid in South Africa and Australia's involvement in the American war in Vietnam. The more radical activists were influenced by a range of international writers, from Frantz Fanon and Sartre to Stokely Carmichael, Malcolm X, and James Baldwin. They saw their position within the context of colonialism and imperialism and as part of the international Black Power movement.

In late 1971, Black Power activists established the Black Panther Party of Australia. Key members included Denis Walker, Sam Watson, Gary Foley, Paul Coe, Gary Williams, and Billie Craigie. Their platform and programme had some similarities to the US Party, except that it contained some important and specifically Indigenous provisions for land rights, restitution, and a United Nations supervised plebiscite for Aboriginal people to determine 'the will of black people as to their national identity'. In relation to the police, the Black Panthers of Australia demanded 'an immediate end to police brutality, murder and rape of black people'. This could be achieved by giving 'communities the control of the police'.[3] Aboriginal activists such as Bruce McGuinness saw the establishment of the Black Panther Party in Australia not as a copy of the US but rather as part of an international movement and an international philosophy – it was akin to what Fanon had advocated for – a Third World movement.[4]

The Black Power movement in Australia and the Black Panther Party and AIM in the US were subject to covert surveillance, monitoring, active intervention, and violence by law enforcement and security agencies. The FBI's Counter-Intelligence Program COINTELPRO targeted the Panthers and AIM as well as other groups, and aimed to 'expose, disrupt, misdirect, discredit or otherwise neutralize' their activities. It led to the killing of the chairman of the Chicago chapter of the Black Panthers, Fred Hampton.[5] In Australia, the federal Australian Security Intelligence Organisation (ASIO) and state police Special Branch operatives monitored the rise of the Black Power movement throughout Australia during the late 1960s through the 1970s.

The Indigenous and Black movements were never merely negative protests. Like the BLM movement and the calls to defund the police today, they were quintessentially about positive interventions for community protection, advocacy, and the building of community-led initiatives to support Black, Indigenous, and oppressed peoples. Huey Newton recognised the necessity to connect with communities and their needs. Thus began the provision of the Panther's many survival programmes, including free breakfasts for children, food packages, schooling, legal and social security advice, free ambulances, free clothing, free bus transport for prison visits, housing, and medical treatment.[6] So while the Black Panther Party set out to protect the community from police violence, they also provided community services and support that could not be otherwise accessed. They developed a wide-ranging commitment to addressing social need. As Mary Bassett writes, 'the Black Panther Party evolved from an organisation focused on armed self-defense against police brutality to one that framed police violence as part of broader social violence'.[7] The provision of community-based health care is an example of addressing social need. Utilising the assistance of health activists, the Panthers set up free community-based medical clinics beginning in Chicago in 1969. In the early 1970s, there were free health clinics established by the Panthers in 13 American cities and a national sickle cell screening programme.[8] By 1972, the Ten Point Program of the Black Panthers called for 'completely free health care for all Black and oppressed people'.

We believe that the government must provide, free of charge, for the people, health facilities which will not only treat our illnesses, most of which have come about as a result of our oppression, but which will also develop preventive medical programmes to guarantee our future survival. We believe that mass health education and research programs must be developed to give all Black and oppressed people access to advanced scientific and medical information, so we may provide ourselves with proper medical attention and care.[9]

The Panthers pursued a community healthcare model. They linked ill-health with poverty and racism and had a holistic approach to healthcare – health and social justice were intertwined – and racism was a core determinant of ill-health. A similar model was developed by AIM in the US and Black Power activists in Australia. It has had a lasting legacy on the provision of community health care to poor and oppressed peoples ever since.

The American Indian Movement began in Minneapolis in the summer of 1968. A group of First Nations activists led by George Mitchell, Dennis Banks, and Clyde Bellecourt called a community meeting to address the issue of extensive police violence, brutality, and racism experienced by First Nations people in the city – as a result AIM was formed. It was 'born out of the dark violence of police brutality and the voiceless despair of Indian people'.[10] It established the Minneapolis AIM Patrol to actively monitor police violence and brutality against First Nations people, particularly around public housing projects. A national network of AIM patrols was established in 16 cities and communities facing similar problems across the country. The following year AIM established the Indian Health Board of Minneapolis which was the first First Nations urban-based health care provider in the US. In 1970, the Legal Rights Center opened in Minneapolis through the activism and support of AIM, Black activists and attorneys committed to addressing the overrepresentation of First Nations, Black and people of colour in the criminal legal system.[11] The Legal Rights Centre still operates today and continues its fight against police violence and racial and culturally-based oppression.[12] AIM continued with its activism, advocacy and demands for self-determination, participating in the 19-month occupation of Alcatraz Island, the establishment of Indian Survival Schools to provide culturally-based education for First Nations children, and the Trail of Broken Treaties march on Washington DC in 1972, which resulted in the occupation of the Bureau of Indian Affairs. It engaged in a range of other community-based and national initiatives, from local food and employment programmes to strategies for fighting racism in sport and media nationally. The AIM was instrumental in establishing the International Indian Treaty Council (IITC) in 1974. Today, the IITC has membership of Indigenous peoples from the Americas, the Caribbean, and the Pacific. It is recognised by the United Nations and supports Indigenous struggles against colonialism and for Indigenous rights and environmental justice.

In Sydney, Australia concern over deaths in police custody and constant police violence, brutality, harassment, and racially discriminatory arrests of Aboriginal people led to the establishment of the first ALS. During the 1960s, the Aboriginal-Australian Fellowship and the NSW Council for Civil Liberties were involved in a number of important legal cases over police killings, assaults, and the abuse of police powers. However, a group of young Black activists took more direct action. In 1969, Gary Foley, Paul Coe, Gary Williams, Bill and Lyn Craigie and others decided to establish a patrol to observe and collect information on police violence and harassment in the Redfern area. The group was aware of the Black Panther's establishment of the pig patrol in Oakland, California to counteract police violence and intimidation, and similar pig patrols were also established in Brisbane by Aboriginal activists.[13] Developing from the pig patrol and with support from volunteer lawyers, in early 1970, the ALS opened its doors as the first free shopfront legal assistance service in Australia. It still operates today.

The Black Power movement in Australia was committed to community empowerment. As Black activist Roberta Sykes stated, 'concerted effort on behalf of the entire community, and with the assistance of the entire community, creates a force and a power in itself … which will propel the people towards a better way of life'.[14] Gary Foley affirmed that 'the establishment of the Redfern Aboriginal Legal Service was to create a resurgence of pan-Aboriginal nationalism'.[15] In July 1971, the Redfern Aboriginal Medical Service was established based on the same model of community control as the ALS. Around the same time, the Aboriginal Housing Company was established as a community housing provider in Redfern. A breakfast programme was established for local Aboriginal children in Redfern in 1972, which later became a community-run childcare centre, Murawina. The National Black Theatre was also established. Over subsequent years, Aboriginal-controlled legal, medical, housing, and childcare services were to spread throughout Australia. The model of community-run legal and medical services was to influence the establishment of similar service delivery initiatives in the broader society. Today, the peak bodies for First Nations' legal and medical services, the National Aboriginal and Torres Strait Islander Legal Service Secretariat (NATSILS) and the National Aboriginal Community Controlled Health Organisation (NACCHO), are two of the most influential bodies representing the interests of First Nations peoples in Australia.

In Minneapolis, Redfern and Oakland, First Nations and Black organisations, born from the struggle against police violence, were fundamentally concerned with fighting for sovereignty, self-determination and community control. In 1972, both the AIM's march on Washington and the establishment of an Aboriginal Tent Embassy in Canberra were powerful symbols of Indigenous nationhood within colonial states. The struggle against police brutality and the use of the prison system against Black, Indigenous, and other oppressed peoples were at the forefront, however it was always part of the development of broader strategic political platforms, including sovereignty, self-determination, restitution/reparations, and land rights.

Furthermore, while organising and fighting against police violence was an immediate response to the need for survival, First Nations and Black organisations pushed those demands further through the provision of mutual aid projects in areas of health, education, housing, legal assistance, community safety, and other forms of support. Mutual aid was not charity. It was and is part of the process of meeting community needs, building solidarity across groups, and deepening the political understanding of the causes of racism, poverty, and oppression.[16]

The struggle against police violence and repression has continued through the late 1970s into the new millennium. The contemporary protest movement by First Nations, Black, and people of colour against police violence and racism is the continuation of an ongoing struggle.

Shock troops of the law and order society: Britain

One of the most important books published in the later 20th century on policing, race, and the politics of law and order in the global north was *Policing the Crisis*. Stuart Hall and his colleagues showed how crime and policing were used to reconstruct hegemony at a time of crisis in state authority.[17] The promise of 'law and order' was the slogan for the counterrevolution against the social dissent of the late 1960s and early 1970s. Racism, authoritarianism, and state violence were enabled through the tropes of dangerous young Black men and the crime of 'mugging'. The dog whistle of black youth and crime heralded the 'problem' of Black and Asian immigration and more strident levels of racism. Policing and the maintenance of law and order became attached to an appeal to the 'British Nation' and the policing of Britain's internal colonies (to use Hall's term) increasingly involved arbitrariness and brutality. Racist violence and Black and Asian resistance to police harassment and abuse were evident throughout the 1970s in places like Notting Hill, Stockwell, Southall, and Brixton in London, and elsewhere in England including Manchester and Birmingham.[18] As another key Left intellectual, Sivanandan recognised, 'the story of black struggles in the 1970s has almost always been the story of confrontations with the police'.[19]

Paramilitary police units began to play a greater role during the 1970s. The Special Patrol Group (SPG) was formed in the early 1960s and came under notice for differentially policing particularly Black communities. From 1973, the Police Support Units (PSUs) were also introduced into the majority of the country's police forces. According to Gordon, the PSU 'cut its teeth on operations directed against black and anti-racist mobilisations'.[20] Both the SPG and PSU were active in policing anti-racist and anti-fascist demonstrations such as Rock Against Racism and Anti-Nazi

League protests during the 1970s. Anti-racist demonstrator Kevin Gately died in an SPG baton charge in London in 1974, and an SPG officer killed Blair Peach in 1979 at a demonstration in Southall against the neo-nazi National Front.[21] It took 31 years to release a contemporaneous internal police report which had found that Peach was 'almost certainly' killed by an SPG officer. Forty years later, in 2019 there were renewed calls for a public investigation into his killing and why it had been covered up for so long.[22]

Another Black British academic and activist, Paul Gilroy, articulated at the beginning of the 1980s a key understanding of contemporary defund the police advocates: it is 'fruitless to search for programmatic solutions to "discriminatory police behaviour" in amendments to [police] training'.[23] For Gilroy, part of the problem was the tendency to see racism as a product of individual bias rather than a structural condition in which policing played a significant role. Similarly, in its 1978 report *Police Against Black People*, the Institute of Race Relations had raised the challenge of institutionalised racism. Gilroy also noted that the war in Northern Ireland had affected policing in the rest of the UK through the adaptation of operational techniques and methods of surveillance. Policing was changing through the influence of counter-insurgency planning and growing militarisation. Likewise, 'community policing' was never more than a complementary strategy to militaristic police interventions.[24]

In 1980, Stuart Hall followed up the themes of *Policing the Crisis* in a short piece for the Cobden Trust entitled *Drifting into a Law and Order Society*. He wrote: 'We are now in the middle of a deep and decisive movement towards a more disciplinary, authoritarian kind of society. ... This drift into a "Law and Order" society is no temporary affair.'[25] While generated by several factors, Hall identified the role of social anxieties, polarisations and tensions which had become forged into a disciplinary 'commonsense' which demonised the poor and powerless. Controlling the 'ungovernable', the 'scroungers', or the 'enemy within' (to use Margaret Thatcher's phrases) demanded a strong authoritarian response. This authoritarian state was the corollary to the reformulated capitalist 'free market' and the retraction of the welfare state which was inevitably and simultaneously driving social conflict and class polarisation.

For Hall, police had become 'the disciplinary arm, the shock troops of the Law and Order society'. He noted the highly visible role of policing in industrial disputes, and in the policing of racial conflict which he referred to as the 'war of attrition' between the police and Black people. Hall also identified the militarisation of the police, particularly evident in the saturation policing of Black areas and use of discriminatory stop and searches. For Hall, the SPG showed the claim that the British police were an unarmed force was largely a 'semantic quibble': the British police were 'now in effect an armed and fully equipped technical force' which had been transformed to take on a wider disciplinary and law and order role.[26] His analysis was prescient to the events of the 1981 and 1985 uprisings and the policing of the British Miners' Strike in 1984.

The summer of 1981 saw anti-police riots across many English cities involving mostly Black youth, sparked by aggressive policing, discriminatory stop and searches, and saturation policing in predominantly Black neighbourhoods. The most intense clashes were in Brixton (London), Toxteth (Liverpool), Handsworth (Birmingham), Moss Side (Manchester), and Chapeltown (Leeds).[27] As a result of the riots, police received more riot training and more equipment, including CS gas and plastic bullets. Meanwhile, the public face of policing continued with a community policing profile – multiagency initiatives, racial awareness training, neighbourhood watch, and so on.[28] The British miner's strike began in March 1984 after the Thatcher Government chose to close collieries they regarded as uneconomical. The ensuing strike over the next 12 months was reportedly the longest in British history. It was met by a massive and violent police response – with police often outnumbering striking miners two or three to one. Arthur Scargill, the president of the National Union of Mineworkers, described the outcome of the policing of the miners' strike:

We had 11,000 people arrested during the course of the dispute, including myself. We had 7,000 people injured, many of them hospitalised, including myself.

We also had in the region of 200 jailed. We also had, tragically, eleven people killed during the miner's strike … this involved four who were killed on picket lines and the rest killed in incidents associated with the dispute. The police also did something that was more blatant than we'd ever seen before. They fabricated evidence, they deliberately lied in the witness boxes, they forged documents.[29]

Riot police and their tactics had made the miners' strike more violent, particularly when combined with broader government support for more 'aggressive' policing.[30] Comparing the experience the miners had with unrestrained state violence to that of racialised policing, Arthur Scargill commented, "police tactics in this dispute have revealed clearly to us what black and Asian communities throughout Britain mean by 'police harassment'".[31] In September and October 1985 there were further violent confrontations between young people and police in Brixton and Tottenham (London) and Handsworth (Birmingham). All of these were sparked by police violence and brutality: the police beating of a Black woman in Handsworth, the police shooting of a Black woman in her home in Brixton, and the death of a Black woman in her home in Tottenham after a police raid. Sivanandan noted at the time that this was life in Britain's Gulags.[32]

The confrontations with police through the 1970s and 1980s gave rise to new forms of community-based organisations and resistance. Some of these interventions used the legal system to advance political struggle through, for example, using criminal trials as a political platform, while at the same time mobilising community support and protest outside the legal system. As Paul Gilroy explained, 'this combination of tactics and the synchronisation of protest inside and outside the law provided a model which was to become central to the political repertoire of black activism up and down this country'.[33] The campaigns and struggles included self-defence groups against racist violence, defence and support groups for particular people victimised by police and the justice system, and local groups established to monitor police.[34] There was also the use of independent, community driven inquiries after serious confrontations and

deaths had occurred at the hands of the police. This was a direct
response to the limitations of official inquiries or the refusal by
the state to hold any inquiry. After the SPG killing of Blair Peach,
the National Council for Civil Liberties established an inquiry
into his death and the policing of Southall during the anti-fascist
demonstration of April 1979. As Sim et al note: 'The Inquiry
documented a chilling picture of uncontrolled state violence
towards legitimate demonstrators whose primary motivation
was to protect their community from a racist presence on
their streets.'[35] During the 1980s, local councils also established
independent inquiries into policing, for example, in London and
Birmingham. These Inquiries documented people's experiences
with the police. In Tottenham: 'Witness after witness to our
Inquiry spoke of the indignities which they suffered at the hands
of the police officers for no other reason that they were Black.
The bitterness of their experience was shared by old and young,
men and women, professional people and unemployed.'[36] In
discussing the period of the 1990s, a key moment was the racist
murder of Black teenager Stephen Lawrence in London in April
1993. He was killed by a White racist gang that were known for
other attacks in the area. The events following Stephen's murder
included the establishment of the Stephen Lawrence Campaign
and the subsequent Macpherson Inquiry which reported in
1999.[37] Macpherson concluded that there were fundamental
police errors in the murder investigation which was 'marred by
a combination of professional incompetence, institutional racism
and a failure of leadership by senior officers'.[38] The Inquiry
echoed the words of the evidence of Black Church Leaders, 'the
experiences of black people over the last 30 years has been that we
have been over-policed and to a large extent under-protected'.[39]

The aftermath of police corruption, incompetence, and racism
in responding to the racist killing of Stephen Lawrence was to
reverberate for decades. It was not until 2012 that two of the five
perpetrators were convicted for murder. The legacy of Stephen
Lawrence's death lived on in other ways. In 2013 Peter Francis,
a former police officer with the 'Special Demonstration Squad',
revealed that while working undercover in an anti-racist campaign
group, his superiors constantly pressured him to find 'dirt' and
'disinformation' that could be used to smear the reputations of

the Lawrence family and supporters, and to undermine their campaign. Senior officers also withheld information from the Macpherson Inquiry about his undercover role.[40] In the longer term, the importance of the Stephen Lawrence Campaign was critical. Adam Elliot-Cooper acknowledges that the campaign was both a search for justice by the family, and 'also a movement of resistance which took on the most powerful state institutions, forcing London's Metropolitan Police to concede publicly their own institutional racism in the face of irrefutable evidence and widespread community support'.[41] The Campaign resulted in a range of community outcomes, including the Stephen Lawrence Centre in south London; the Stephen Lawrence Trust focused on education, and a Stephen Lawrence Research Centre at De Montfort University. Doreen Lawrence, Stephen's mother, was made a Peer and sits in the House of Lords. She continues her work on social justice. In 2018, the government announced that 22 April would be recognised annually as Stephen Lawrence Day – although as shown in Chapter 5, police violence and racism continues.

There are two final points in this discussion on the recent history of policing in Britain. One is the debate which emerged (especially in the 1980s) among the Left on questions of reformism and abolitionism which, while bound by its historical milieu, is still relevant today in the discussions of Defund the Police. Those who adopted a liberal, reformist position on police and the state, emphasised that crime was a problem for working class communities which needed to be addressed, and further, that reform of the police and criminal justice system was capable of achieving that outcome. Those on the Left who understood the limitations of reform were disparagingly described as abolitionists and 'idealists'.[42] Yet the reformist position failed to address the profound impact of institutional racism and the intersections of class and race. Despite the weight of historical evidence, the extreme state violence evident in Britain during the 1980s and the social and political authoritarianism of the Thatcher Conservative government, reformists argued that the police could be made accountable to the community, that increasing militarisation could be stopped, and public confidence restored. History was not kind to the reformist position. New Labour came to power in 1997 with a 'Tough on Crime, Tough on the Causes of Crime' slogan, and a further strengthening of the law and order agenda.

The second point concerns community activism and is drawn from the analysis of the Stephen Lawrence Campaign by Elliot-Cooper and his observation that 'almost every campaign calling for justice following a Black death at the hands of the police is led by a woman', a mother, a partner, a sister.[43] He makes the point that Doreen Lawrence and her campaign for justice for her son was to influence how subsequent campaigns approached grassroots community building, protest, the court system, and the mainstream media. In addition, he acknowledges the role of Black feminism in seeing the family as a potential source of strength, as a space or site of resistance against racism, rather than primarily as a site of oppression.[44] We see something akin to this in the role First Nations families played in the public campaigns over police killings in Australia from the 1980s onwards and the role of Black and First Nations women in the BLM movement in the US. It is also a demonstration of the strength of Black, Indigenous, people of colour, and working-class familial relations which runs counter to the dominant racialised discourses (media, academic, political) of dysfunction, violence, and criminality.

Aboriginal deaths in custody: Australia

In Australia during the 1980s, there was renewed concern over First Nations deaths in prison, and particularly in police custody. One of the most notorious killings was 16-year-old John Pat who was beaten to death by police in Roebourne, Western Australia in 1983. Five police officers were charged, stood trial, and were acquitted by an all-White jury. Other Aboriginal deaths which captured media attention included Eddie Murray, Charlie Michael, Dixon Green, and Robert Walker. The number of Indigenous deaths in custody appeared to be increasing (although no-one was sure at the time of the exact number), many in suspicious circumstances, including the deaths of Mark Quayle and Lloyd Boney in police cells in NSW. The community-based Committee to Defend Black Rights (CDBR) estimated in 1987 that one Aboriginal person was dying in custody in Australia every 11 days.

Key Aboriginal organisations including the ALS and the CDBR, along with the families of those who had died in custody and supporters, pressured the Australian government both domestically and internationally to establish an inquiry. The CDBR was especially important: it was a national organisation comprised of family members of Aboriginal people who had died in custody. It organised three national conferences of family members which focused on political action, as well as cultural expressions of family who had died in custody through poetry, artwork, and music. Like the involvement of Black women noted previously in Britain, Aboriginal women were key activists in the struggle. The CDBR organised a national speaking tour of family members, and also continued with direct political lobbying.

International pressure on the Australian federal government to establish an inquiry into deaths in custody also mounted. From the mid-1980s, Amnesty International began to critically comment on Australia's record on Aboriginal custodial deaths. Then in August 1987, foreshadowing the language of the BLM movement, the chairperson of the CDBR, Yawaru and Bibbleman woman Helen Corbett, addressed the United Nations Working Group on Indigenous Populations in Geneva:

> The Australian Government must implement a federal Royal Commission to inquire into these deaths, to show that it strongly believes that Aboriginal lives are worth the same as the rest of the Australian population … these deaths of Indigenous people in custody show that our rights are not respected, that racism exists with disastrous effects on our families and that we cannot trust Australia's justice system.[45]

In the weeks following Helen Corbett's address in Geneva, the Australian government announced the Royal Commission into Aboriginal Deaths in Custody (RCADIC). The Royal Commission investigated 99 Aboriginal deaths and made 339 recommendations. It reported in 1991. Most deaths occurred in police custody and most of these involved people held for minor public order offences. Those who died had early and repeated contact with the criminal legal system: in almost half of the deaths the person had been removed as a child from their families by welfare authorities, and a similar proportion had been criminalised before they were 15 years old.[46] Broadly speaking, the recommendations focused on three areas: reducing the number of Aboriginal people in police and prison custody through various reforms to law, policy, and practice; addressing the social and economic underlying issues that brought Aboriginal people into contact with the justice system; and putting into effect the principle of Indigenous self-determination.

The RCADIC identified the institutionalised and systemic racism by police directed against Aboriginal people. The Commission recommended prosecutors consider criminal charges arising from some deaths, however no-one was ever charged with a criminal offence. The absence of prosecutions led to a profound disappointment in the outcomes of the RCADIC. There were cases such as the death of David Gundy who was shot dead in his bedroom by SWOS police in an unlawful police raid. The Director of Public Prosecutions declined to prosecute officers – although NSW Police did make an ex-gratia payment to his widow and young son. The Commission found that many deaths occurred because custodial authorities failed in their responsibility to exercise a duty of care, such as checking cells regularly, ensuring prescribed medicines were available, and facilitating proper medical treatment. There were some successful civil claims made by the families of the deceased against police, but there were no state criminal prosecutions.

During the 1980s and into the 1990s, there were regular reports in Aboriginal communities of civil unrest generated by police violence and discrimination. This conflict was exacerbated through the establishment of paramilitary police groups – the Tactical Response Group (TRG) in NSW and Western Australia and similar groups in other states. These paramilitary police squads grew in size and expanded operational duties particularly in the policing of Aboriginal communities. For example, a significant paramilitary operation occurred in early 1990 with 135 police in a pre-dawn raid on a number of Aboriginal houses in the inner Sydney suburb of Redfern. Although the search for drugs was the official justification for the raid, no drugs were ever located. Senior police officers also provided racist justifications for the use of paramilitary police – describing the community as 'all one breed' where normal policing operations were ineffective. The Federal Race Discrimination Commissioner described the police raid as 'a significant act of racist violence'.[47] In 1991, the Australian Human Rights Commission reported on its inquiry into racist violence. The Commission found that 'Aboriginal-police relations had reached a critical point due to widespread involvement of police in acts of racist violence, intimidation and harassment'.[48]

During the 1990s there were several independent reviews of the post-RCADIC situation. One review found that in more recent Indigenous deaths in custody were numerous ongoing breaches of Royal Commission recommendations.[49] Another review found a failure on the part of governments to adequately address recommendations to reform the criminal legal system, and many recommendations were being undermined by the political shift during the 1990s to a more punitive approach to law and order.[50] Several reviews noted the ongoing and widespread complaints about violent, racist, and inappropriate police behaviour, the prevalence of racist attitudes and institutional racism in the police.[51]

Amnesty International also continued with its criticisms of Australia during the 1990s. In 1993 it found, among other things, that conditions in certain police and prison facilities amounted to cruel, inhumane, or degrading treatment. For example, that Aboriginal men had been forced, through lack of water, to drink from toilet bowls while they were held in police cells. It also found that the families of Aboriginal people who had died in custody, and who were engaged in public activism over these deaths, were subject to police harassment.[52] A further Amnesty report in 1997 confirmed systemic discrimination and ill-treatment by police and sometimes serious deficiencies in the standard of custodial care.[53]

During the early years of the new millennium, political activism and collective anger continued over the ongoing high incarceration rates and deaths in custody of First Nations peoples, and lack of movement in implementing the recommendations from the RCADIC. Deaths in Custody Watch Committees had grown out of the earlier work of the CDBR in the late 1980s and early 1990s. In addition, Indigenous Social Justice Associations were established in Sydney and Melbourne. These groups continued with their support, activism, and advocacy work, often led by family members of those who had died in custody. The anger and frustration at the lack of accountability were vented through protests and sometimes riots and uprisings. For example, the uprising on Palm Island (Queensland) reflected the depth of Indigenous community anger at police violence and injustice.

In November 2004, Cameron Doomadgee died in police custody on Palm Island after being arrested for a minor public order offence. Post-mortem results revealed that he had been violently assaulted by police, suffering four broken ribs, a ruptured spleen, and his liver almost cleaved in two. A protest riot occurred after Doomadgee's death, and the local police station and courthouse were set on fire and extensively damaged. Dozens of riot police were flown to the Island. The White police officer responsible for the death was charged, tried, and acquitted of manslaughter. Aboriginal people involved in the subsequent uprising were charged, convicted, and some received substantial terms of imprisonment. After a long activist campaign and legal battle against the police and state government relating to racial discrimination, in May 2018 the Queensland government settled a class action with 447 claimants from the Palm Island community for $30 million.[54] It was not justice, but it was some vindication of the community's struggle.

Penal abolition and mass imprisonment: North America

During the 1980s and 1990s, First Nations political pressure within Canada led to the establishment of various inquiries into Aboriginal justice issues and particularly police treatment of First Nations peoples. These included the Nova Scotia Royal Commission on the Donald Marshall, Jr., Prosecution (1989), the Aboriginal Justice Inquiry of Manitoba (1991), and the Canadian Royal Commission on Aboriginal Peoples (1996). These inquiries recognised the importance of Indigenous self-determination. Further, all the inquiries made findings in relation to the problem of systemic discrimination or institutional racism in the treatment of First Nations people by the criminal legal system. Activists in Canada also played a significant role in building the global abolitionist movement. In the early 1980s, the Canadian

Quaker Committee on Jails and Justice promoted the idea of an international forum on abolitionist praxis, which resulted in the ICOPA (the International Conference on Prison Abolition). The first conference was held in 1983 in Toronto. Subsequently, ICOPA has continued to meet every couple of years in locations across the world. Black communities in Canada also organised against police violence during the 1980s and 1990s. In Toronto, the Black Action Defence Committee was formed after a number of police killings. As was the case in other countries, the family members of those killed were subjected to police surveillance and harassment.[55]

The burgeoning US carceral state resulted by the end of the 1990s and early 2000s in millions of people jailed and the highest national imprisonment rate in the world. Critiques of policing in the US were part of the social movements that developed to challenge Reagan's and George Bush Snr's war on drugs and the associated racially discriminatory legislation that led to massive imprisonment of racialised peoples. The Clinton and G.W. Bush periods of neo-liberalism and the war on terror furthered these trends of punitive law and order policies. Opposition to police violence, violence against women and against the LGBTQIA+ community, racism, and Islamophobia were foundational to the critiques of policing. Barbara Ransby in her discussion of the contemporary rise of the BLM movement and the M4BL in the US shows that there has been a continuity in community organising and activism from the 1970s to the present – led by a Black feminist politics which has been 'the intellectual lifeblood of this movement and its practices'.[56]

Robin D.G. Kelley nominates many of the key activist organisations in the US that have maintained the struggle against police violence and promoted abolitionism for more than two decades, including (to name only some) SistaIISista (established 1996), Critical Resistance (established 1997), and INCITE! Women of Color Against Violence (established 2000).[57] These movements laid the foundations for current ideas on abolition and defunding the police. Critical Resistance was formed by activists challenging the idea that policing and imprisonment was a solution for social, political, and economic problems. In 1998, Critical Resistance organised a conference which brought together over

3,500 activists, academics, former and current prisoners, labor and religious leaders, feminists, and LGBTQIA+ activists from across the US and internationally. Women played a foundational role in Critical Resistance.[58] In 2001, Critical Resistance and INCITE! jointly called on 'social justice movements to develop strategies and analysis that address both state and interpersonal violence, particularly violence against women' and to 'develop responses to gender violence that do not depend on a sexist, racist, classist, and homophobic criminal justice system'.[59] In 2008 they published an organiser's resource and tool kit on police brutality and other forms of law enforcement violence. It contained strategies and ideas for documenting and organising against police violence and 'for building responses to violence in our communities that don't rely on law enforcement'.[60] SistaIISista was formed in Brooklyn in the context of the rise of zero tolerance policing. In the early 2000s, their work increasingly focused on racialised and gendered state and interpersonal violence. After the murder and rape, as well as police shootings of young women of colour in Brooklyn, the organisation created Sistas Liberated Ground as a place where 'violence against women would not be tolerated'.[61]

Zero tolerance policing: reasserting the legitimacy of state violence

The focus in this chapter thus far has been on community activism against police violence and the changing nature of policing in the post-1960s period. In drawing the discussion towards a conclusion, it is important to identify the nature and spread of zero tolerance policing (ZTP). Its origin and most immediate impact was in New York City. As Nicole Burrowes from SistaIISista recognised:

In 1994, Rudolph Guiliani was the mayor, and we were watching the city transform beneath our feet. 'Broken windows' policing and 'law-and-order' policies made the city less liveable for many of us as it meant an increase in arrests, surveillance, racial profiling, and harassment in communities of color but did not lead to a corresponding increase in safety or justice.[62]

ZTP impacted heavily as a strategy and *de facto* justification for the use of police harassment and violence against poor and marginalised communities – not only in New York City where it was aggressively adopted by Mayor Giuliani and Police Commissioner Bratton, but also in other US states and internationally. It became a beacon for police commissioners and politicians from around the world including other parts of the Americas, Britain, Australia, South Africa, and Europe. The idea behind ZTP was that a strong law enforcement approach to minor crime (in particular public order offences) would prevent more serious crime from occurring and ultimately lead to falling crime rates. The approach relied on an analogy drawn by Wilson and Kelling regarding 'broken windows'. If one broken window is not repaired in a building, others will be broken and the building vandalised, followed by other buildings, then the street, the neighbourhood, and so on. An unrepaired window is a sign that no-one cares and therefore more damage will occur.[63] Similarly, if disorderly behaviour is not dealt with, then more serious crime will result. Small 'incivilities' such as public drunkenness, vandalism, begging, and so forth create an atmosphere where more serious crime can flourish.

In the decades after Wilson and Kelling articulated the 'broken windows' approach, the ZTP philosophy moved towards a more punitive approach to maintaining public order. The idea of negotiating acceptable public behaviour at the local level – which was in the original Wilson and Kelling proposition – was dropped, and instead ZTP emerged as a strategy aimed at increasing the use of stop and searches, targeted 'street sweeping', and increased arrest rates for disorder – or so-called 'quality of life' offences.[64] This aggressive vision was captured in Giuliani's electoral campaign in 1993 of 'reclaiming the streets'. ZTP locked into the idea that tough policing can work if police are allowed unfettered power to do their job, with minimum oversight by external bodies and maximum legislative discretion to police the streets. It distanced itself from perceived permissive attitudes to crime; it distinguished itself from welfarist explanations of offending behaviour and from notions of community-based policing. ZTP also aligned with the requirements of neo-liberal managerialism: the demand for performance indicators, targeted use of resources, and measurable outcomes. Zero tolerance strategies were geared to performance indicators that were immediately measurable and perfectly understandable to government: arresting people for targeted offences.[65]

During the 1990s, under ZTP, police numbers rose in New York and arrest rates increased for minor offences: misdemeanour arrests rose by 40 per cent and misdemeanour drug offence arrests rose by 97 per cent between 1993 and 1996. The period also saw a much harder police response to public processions, marches, and rallies – permits were regularly refused and there were complaints of police violence, provocation, widespread arrests, and a refusal to negotiate with organisers. More aggressive public order policing, the routine use of violence,[66] and the targeting of minority groups were all indicative of the problems associated with ZTP. Complaints against the police registered with the Civilian Complaint Review Board (CCRB) rose sharply after 1993. Meanwhile, the Mollen Commission of Inquiry into corruption in the NYPD in 1994 found police officers were involved in drug dealing, robberies, assaults, perjury, and falsification of records. It also found a failure by the NYPD to discipline officers accused of violence. A 1996 investigation into the NYPD by Amnesty International revealed that more than two thirds of the cases of police brutality involved Black or Latinx complainants. Most of the police officers involved were White. In the cases of deaths in custody reviewed by Amnesty, nearly all of the victims were members of racial minorities. Human Rights Watch noted in a 1998 report that there was 'continuing impunity for many officers who commit human rights violations' and that 'there is often a racial or ethnic component to police abuse cases in New York City'.[67]

ZTP is a simple proactive crime control strategy: arrest more people to reduce crime. It locked into a powerful populist rhetoric of tougher approaches to law and order and legitimated heavy handed policing strategies against minorities. It provided a bridge between old style 'machismo' police crackdowns on racialised and other groups, with the demands of a managerialism besotted with easily measurable performance indicators. It combined with 'hot spot' and saturation policing to make a 'science' of repressive policing strategies. Indeed, internationally, ZTP fitted with growing xenophobia and racism in a range of countries. In parts of Europe, zero tolerance approaches were linked by both the far-Right and more moderates with strategies to control asylum seekers and 'foreigners'.[68] In Australia, zero tolerance was seen as most attractive in states with large Indigenous populations and in major cities with racialised and criminalised minorities such as Arabic and Vietnamese communities. Zero tolerance policing signalled a revalorisation of the politics of *intolerance* – and not just in New York and the US.

Conclusion

The contemporary calls to defund the police reflect the generational struggles against police violence and racism, from the late 1960s through to the present. Fighting against police violence was foundational – hence Sivanandan's reflection that the history of Black struggles in the 1970s is the story of struggle against police. His observation applies beyond Britain and that particular decade. These movements were often internationalist in their outlook, while simultaneously committed to local community empowerment and meeting community needs.

The struggle against police violence gave rise to new forms of community-based organisations and resistance against police violence and racism – these often involved the families of people killed by police and/or White racists and were often led by Indigenous, Black, and women of colour. Some of these interventions used the formal system in calling for criminal prosecutions, and/or the establishment of royal commissions and other types of formal inquiries. Outside the justice system, there was systematic political lobbying, the use of media, public protest, and the mobilisation of community support. There was the use of the cultural expressions of the people who had been killed by the state through poetry, artwork, and music, and there were the larger intersections of music, youth culture, and political protest quintessentially captured in *Rock Against Racism*.

At the same time, policing was changing with the adoption of new more heavily armed and equipped paramilitary police units. There was renewed ideological justification through ZTP for heavy-handed policing of minor public order offences which also reinforced and justified racially discriminatory use of saturation policing and stop and searches. Underpinning this was the constant outrage at ongoing police killings, particularly of Black, Indigenous, and people of colour. Finally, we might ponder another continuity: in 2017, the FBI developed the term 'Black Identity Extremism' (BIE) to describe the BLM movement and Black activism. It was grouped with White Supremacy Extremism as an equivalent threat of racially motivated violent extremism. According to Kimberlé Crenshaw, 'these allegedly equivalent tendencies were treated as a threat on par with ISIS, justifying a major programme of surveillance, investigation, and infiltration'.[69]

5

Police violence is the pandemic

Widespread outrage at police violence, fatal shootings, and deaths in police custody created the current international protest movements and calls to defund the police. However, as shown in previous chapters, there is a long history to protests against police violence, and there are multiple movements to change policing globally which draw on localised contexts. Police violence is experienced at a local level, however, it has global reach and is pervasive to the institution. It directly costs the lives of tens of thousands of people annually – and many more if we include the numbers of forced disappearances – and leaves incalculable numbers of people with permanent injuries and disabilities. The victims are overwhelmingly from the most marginalised communities whether defined by race, religion, class, Indigeneity, gender, sexual orientation, disability, citizenship or immigration status, and their various and compounding intersections.

One of the main causes of death, disability, and injury for people deprived of their liberty are the acts of violence and use of force by police and other state agents.[1] This chapter sets out what we know about the nature and context of police violence, shootings, and deaths in police custody – including overt violence and the violence of neglect – and it attempts to do so with reference to contexts of both the global north and south. It considers some of the wider drivers which are international but impact on domestic policing such as expanded militarisation, the impact of the war on drugs and the intersection of policing with security forces, border control, and other law enforcement bodies.

Police killings and deaths in police custody

A defining feature of policing is state-sanctioned legitimacy for the use of force and violence, including lethal violence, against citizens. The importance of police discretion was discussed previously in Chapter 3. Police discretion extends to the use and intensity of violence. Notwithstanding the fundamental importance of a state-sanctioned decision to end someone's life or seriously maim them, it is difficult to get a handle on the overall size of the problem of police violence, killings, or police custodial deaths. Most countries do not publish comprehensive national information, so the estimates are left to media, human rights, and other non-government organisations. A further problem is that even where governments do provide data, there are widely inconsistent reporting requirements and definitions that make international comparisons difficult.[2] Dylan Rodriguez has argued that the absence of 'accessible, coordinated data about the casualties of police violence composes an *infrastructure of official ignorance*'. The absence of information is not a failure of states but rather part of the infrastructure of police power that obscures 'the evidence of everyday police terror and its various forms of atrocity'.[3] It enables plausible deniability.

The US government fails to publish reliable national data on police violence, killings, and deaths in custody. In 2015, the *Washington Post* started to count every fatal shooting by an on-duty police officer. The newspaper began the Fatal Force database when it became clear there was no consistent national information after the fatal police shooting of Michael Brown. The FBI data is based on self-reports of justifiable homicides by police and is voluntarily provided by some law enforcement agencies in the US. It undercounts the number of police fatal shootings by more than 50 per cent. According to the *Washington Post* data, police shootings remain steady at around 1,000 per year (1,055 in 2021). The database shows that more than half the people fatally shot by police are White. However, given their population size, Black Americans are fatally shot more than twice the rate and Latinx at slightly less than twice the rate of White Americans.[4] Similar undercounting (by 55 per cent over a 40-year period) has been estimated from the Center for Disease Control and Prevention

(CDC) data on reported deaths by law enforcement, including non-firearm related deaths. The burden of these deaths falls on Black, First Nations, and Hispanic peoples – the rate of deaths for Black Americans was found to be 3.5 times higher than Whites.[5] The rate of police killings also varies across the country and by race/ethnicity. In the Chicago metropolitan area for example, Black people were killed at 6.5 times the rate of White people.[6] Despite the CDC estimates, little is known about deaths in police custody which arise in other situations – such as untreated medical conditions, trauma-related injuries, or suicide.

In England and Wales, the community-based organisation INQUEST maintains a database on deaths in police custody. In 2020 it recorded 39 deaths, of which three were the result of police shootings, two occurred in road traffic incidents, 14 during a police pursuit, and a further 20 while in custody. INQUEST's analysis of 20 years of data found that 'Black, Asian and Minoritised Ethnicities (BAME) die disproportionately as a result of use of force or restraint by the police, raising serious questions of institutional racism as a contributory factor in their deaths'.[7] In 2017 a government-commissioned review of deaths and serious incidents in police custody found that 'the disproportionately high number of deaths of black men in restraint-related deaths, often in contentious circumstances, is a serious issue'.[8] Similarly in Aotearoa New Zealand, a review of the period 2000–2010 found that almost half the deaths in police custody involved Māori (who comprise about 15 per cent of the general population). Thirty per cent of Māori deaths occurred while being restrained by police, which was three times higher than the proportion of deaths of people from a 'European' background.[9]

In Australia, government data shows 24 deaths in police custody for the 12 months ending June 2020. Of the 24 deaths, 16 were fatal police shootings – they are obviously a significant cause of deaths in police custody. Further, First Nations people are more than five times more likely to die in police custody than non-Indigenous people.[10] *The Guardian* newspaper established the Dying Inside database which covers First Nations deaths in police and prison custody from 2008 to the present and provides far more detail of the person and their death than official accounts.[11] The Canadian Broadcasting Commission has established a Deadly

Force database to overcome the absence of official data on police killings and 'fatal encounters' where police used force. It does not include in-custody deaths, self-inflicted wounds as a result of suicide or attempts to evade police, or accidental police-caused deaths (such as traffic accidents). It currently covers the period from 2000 to mid 2020. The database shows that the rate of deaths has continued to rise over the past 20 years. Furthermore, Black and Indigenous people are disproportionately represented among the fatalities. Based on their population, Indigenous people are nearly four times and Black people nearly three times more likely to die in police fatal encounters. In 2019 there were 34 fatal encounters with police.[12] An analysis of the database between 2000 and 2017 showed 70 per cent of fatal encounters involved a police shooting.[13]

The data is unequivocal in showing that Black, Indigenous, and people of colour are over-represented in police shootings, restraints, and other deaths in the countries just discussed. As discussed in Chapter 3, the Prison Policy Initiative has drawn some comparisons on police killings (primarily based on fatal shootings) across ten countries of the global north.[14] The US is an outlier for police killing civilians with a rate more than three times higher than Canada and four times higher than Australia. However, Canadian and Australian police (who routinely carry firearms) have higher rates than other countries in the Prison Policy Initiative comparative group. Other research shows there is no clear evidence 'that arming police automatically or necessarily makes them or the community safer'.[15] The differences raise many questions, not the least of which is the relationship between routinely armed police and the level of police fatal shootings, as well as the use of community-based and public health alternatives to police custody.

The war on drugs in the global south: Brazil and the Philippines

The incidence of police killing of civilians can take on qualitatively different dimensions when we consider the experiences of parts of the global south. As noted in Chapter 1, Brazilian police killed nearly six times the number of civilians compared to the US – despite having a national population only two thirds the size of the US – and Brazil is by no means the worst in Latin America.[16] Outside of Latin America and compared to Brazil, the problem of police killings has a similar, if not greater, magnitude in the Philippines. Both the Philippines and Brazil provide a window on the effect of the war on drugs on policing and violence. Further, both the Philippines and Brazil highlight the problem of where we place the role of police acting as vigilantes in conducting state condoned and/or encouraged extrajudicial killings – seeing them as 'off duty' and acting in their individual capacity seems disingenuous.

In the Philippines, then President Duterte launched the 'war on drugs' in 2016, and publicly encouraged the extrajudicial killing of drug users. The Philippines Commission on Human Rights estimated in late 2018 that the number of drug-war killings could be as high as 27,000 and there were reports of local police forces being given targets to meet in terms of deaths.[17] In September 2021 the International Criminal Court (ICC) ordered an investigation into the killings associated with Duterte's war. The ICC said the initial evidence indicated that killings were not the result of legitimate law enforcement operations and that a widespread and systematic attack against the civilian population took place. The prosecutor's preliminary investigation found a reasonable basis to believe that the crime against humanity of murder has been committed in the Philippines between July 2016 and March 2019 when the Philippines withdrew from the ICC.[18]

Like the Philippines, the broader context for police killings in Brazil is the 'war on drugs' – which itself has led to a distorting, if not collapsing, of distinctions between police and military roles. In Rio de Janeiro in early May 2021, some 200 heavily armed police, supported by helicopters, moved into a poor, densely populated favela and engaged in a firefight with alleged drug traffickers that killed at least 25 people. The United Nations High Commissioner for Human Rights called for an independent investigation of the incident.[19] Similar police massacres in Rio's favelas have continued through 2022.[20] The use of helicopters armed with snipers have been a feature of policing in Rio since at least 2018 when the city's security was given to military commanders, 'who assumed operational control of the police and also deployed troops in the favelas'.[21] In recent years, the State Governor as well as then President Bolsonaro have both openly promoted deadly violence against "criminals" who, according to the President, would "die like cockroaches". The number of people killed by police in Rio has been rising steadily from around 1,000 deaths in 2016 to 1,800 annually by 2019. Across Brazil, police killings have also been going up, jumping by 20 per cent in 2018 to 6,220, then increasing to 6,357 in 2019. By the first half of 2020 they had risen a further 6 per cent.[22] These figures do not include extrajudicial killings by death squads. Police killings have sparked various movements since the late 1970s including the Unified Black Movement Against Racial Discrimination (MNU-CDR, later the MNU), and the Reaja ou Será Mortx (React or Die) which has been active over the last decade fighting against police violence and the genocide of Black people, and shares similar messages to the BLM movement.

The 'war on drugs' was introduced into Latin America because of international pressure, and more specifically in many countries in the region as a condition for US economic assistance and trade. Highly punitive drug laws, more heavily militarised policing, and growing prison numbers were the result. The 'war' has fallen most heavily on poor Black and Indigenous communities.[23] Drug-related policing focuses on drug users and small drug dealers and has had little impact on the drug trafficking chains. Police also exercise substantial discretionary power over whether a person is prosecuted for drug use or drug trafficking.[24] Like the comparisons that can be drawn within the global north, there is essentially a parallel system of law enforcement operating based on class and race: 'Though recreational drug use is in effect already decriminalised in wealthy, white-majority enclaves of Brazil, going about your business in a black-majority neighborhood during a raid can get you killed.'[25]

Torture, extrajudicial killings, enforced disappearances: India, Bangladesh, and Pakistan

The use of torture by police to extract confessions and bribes and to impose summary punishment is commonplace in many countries, and provides another consideration in understanding the problems of police violence and deaths in custody. The major South Asian countries of India, Bangladesh, and Pakistan provide examples.[26] HRW identified 591 deaths in police custody in

India between 2010 and 2015, the National Campaign Against Torture (NCAT) reported 125 deaths in police custody in 2019, while the National Human Rights Commission reported 77 deaths in police custody and 62 alleged extrajudicial killings by police in the first 10 months of 2020.[27] The torture of people in custody by police is recognised as a major problem in India. In 2016, HRW found that 'police still often torture suspects to punish them, gather information, or coerce confessions' and do so with continuing impunity.[28] More recently, the National Human Rights Commission noted that 'custodial violence and torture is so rampant in India that it has become almost routine', while the NCAT found that the police practice of torturing suspects constituted the primary cause of deaths in police custody.[29] India has not ratified the UN Convention Against Torture.

NCAT indicated in relation to the 125 deaths it reported in 2019, that 74 per cent of people died during police custody due to 'alleged torture/foul play', while a further 19 per cent died under suspicious circumstances. In addition, the NCAT indicated that the armed forces (the Indian Army and the Central Armed Police Forces) who are deployed in insurgency affected areas and border areas, and have the power to take persons into custody, were the subject of many reported cases of torture and sexual violence.[30] Further, Forest Department officials were also responsible for torture, sexual violence, and killing, particularly of Adivasi (tribal) peoples.[31]

Irrespective of whether they are the victims of police, security forces, or other government agencies, the majority of torture victims come from poor and marginalised communities, including Dalit, Adivasi, and Muslim minorities. It is not uncommon for police to destroy incriminating evidence of torture by not conducting mandatory post-mortem examinations and quickly cremating the bodies of torture victims.[32] Women continued to be tortured or targeted for sexual violence in custody, and children, because of poor implementation of juvenile justice legislation, continue to be illegally detained in police stations and subjected to torture. The NCAT documented the deaths of four children arising from police torture in 2019. In addition, the NCAT identified multiple cases of police torture of men, women, and children where the victims survived, and also the police rape of women and children (including a child with a disability, and the sexual assault of a 7-year-old boy).[33] The Chief Justice of India, Nuthalapati Ramana, publicly called out the nation's police stations as the most significant threat to human rights and bodily integrity. According to the Chief Justice, 'custodial torture and other police atrocities … still prevail' and fall disproportionately on the poor.[34] A recent survey of over 12,000 police personnel in 21 Indian states indicated some commonly held police views which justified the use of violence. The survey reported that:

- four in every five police believed 'there was nothing wrong with beating up criminals to extract a confession';
- three in every four police felt that 'police violence towards criminals was justified';
- one in five police felt that 'killing dangerous criminals was better than a legal trial'; and
- one in five police would not advise their own daughter to attend a police station alone to report a crime.

In addition, two in five police thought that 'common people' were hesitant to approach police even when there was a need.[35]

In neighbouring Bangladesh, deaths in police custody from torture, the frequency of extrajudicial killings, and enforced disappearances by police have been criticised by the UN Committee against Torture, HRW, and Bangladeshi policing scholars. The UN Committee recognised the allegations of widespread and routine use of torture and ill-treatment by police for the purpose of obtaining confessions or soliciting bribes. The Committee also noted the 'numerous, consistent reports' that law enforcement agencies have 'arbitrarily deprived persons of their liberty, subsequently killed many of them and failed to disclose their whereabouts or fate'.[36] The Committee particularly drew attention to the Rapid Action Battalion, which is comprised of police and military personnel, and has been responsible for committing torture, arbitrary arrests, undocumented detention, disappearances, and extrajudicial killings of people in their custody. Despite their reputation, the Battalion has received training from British police.[37]

According to HRW, and supported by other observers, extrajudicial killings and disappearances are committed 'with near complete impunity' in Bangladesh.[38] In addition, the frequency of forced disappearances has been increasing in recent years.[39] Mistreatment and torture is not confined to adults. Children interviewed in youth detention revealed they were subjected to physical torture by police including electric shocks and beatings, as well as threats of violence and the production of false statements and confessions.[40]

In Pakistan there are numerous reports by human rights groups of police extrajudicial killings, forced disappearances, detention without charge, torture of detainees to obtain confessions, biased investigations, failure to investigate crimes, corruption, harassment and extortion of individuals, incompetence, and lack of professionalism.[41] Despite its obligation under the UN Convention against Torture, Pakistan has failed to enact legislation criminalising torture. HRW noted that:

> Several police officers who spoke to Human Rights Watch openly admitted to the practice of false or faked 'encounter killings' in which police stage an armed exchange to kill an individual already in custody. ... Police are rarely held accountable for these killings and families of victims are deterred from filing complaints against police out of fear of harassment or being accused of false charges.[42]

The National Commission on Human Rights (NCHR) acknowledged the broad estimates of forced disappearances in Pakistan: Defence of Human Rights reported more than 5,000 cases of disappearances that were not resolved, while the Voice of Baloch Missing Persons identified that since 2001, some 18,000 people have been forcibly disappeared from Balochistan (the poorest province in Pakistan where there is also a separatist movement). The NCHR observed that not a single perpetrator has been held criminally accountable for an enforced disappearance in Pakistan and that the appeal to 'national security', although not defined in law, has been used 'as a cover on many occasions to cover for unlawful acts committed by the personnel of law enforcement agencies'.[43] In addition, HRW and the US State Department, among others, have noted that the government has used draconian sedition and counterterrorism laws to stifle dissent, and harassed and at times prosecuted human rights activists, lawyers, journalists, and civil society groups for criticising government officials and policies.[44] The US State Department Country Report on Pakistan found that: 'Kidnappings and forced disappearances of persons took place in nearly all areas of the country. … Human rights organizations reported some authorities disappeared or arrested Pashtun, Sindhi, and Baloch human rights activists, as well as Sindhi and Baloch nationalists without cause or warrant.'[45] Public surveys and reports show that the police are among the most feared, complained against, and 'least trusted government institutions in Pakistan', lacking accountability and 'plagued by corruption at the highest levels'. Local police are 'often under the control of powerful politicians, wealthy landowners, and other influential members of society'.[46] Victims of crime, especially women and those from vulnerable groups, fear approaching a police station because of harassment and poverty – the NCHR has previously indicated that there is a common perception that police will demand bribes before accepting a crime report, subject complainants to abuse, and falsely accuse the complainant of committing the crime.[47]

Policing scholar Zoha Waseem notes that police violence, excesses, and corruption have led to 'social movements and civil society resistance borne out of public grievances with publicly punitive and authoritarian styles of policing'.[48] An example is the Pashtun Tahafuz Movement (PTM) that has grown out of opposition to the violence of law enforcement and security forces against the Pashtun and has been fuelled by extrajudicial killings of leading figures including Naqibullah Mehsud in 2018 in a staged counter-terror operation and Arif Wazir shot by unidentified persons in 2020, and the imprisonment of other activists.

If we look more broadly across the policing examples referred to in this section, the nature and intensity of the problem of police violence and killings depends on a range of factors including:

- the influence of 'war on drugs' policies and the militarisation of police;
- the collapsing of police and military functions in the name of protecting internal (or national) security and fighting crime;

- the extent to which specialist police squads conduct disappearances and state-sanctioned extrajudicial killings either in the interests of a crime control enforcement policy or as a direct political tool of authoritarian regimes;
- the extent to which police torture is routinised; and
- the extent to which police play a direct role in dispossessing or controlling local landholders, villagers, and communities who, for whatever reasons, threaten capitalist economic development and its projects.

The list is not exhaustive. Perhaps apart from political repression and the 'disappearing' of political opponents, journalists, and activists, the targets of all this violence and corruption are inevitably poor and marginalised communities – whether by way of class, caste, race, Indigeneity, gender, religion and ethnicity, or other status, such as police involvement in the abuse of LGBTQIA+ communities in Bangladesh and Pakistan.

Finally, in this discussion on state violence, we must consider the example of a settler colonial state at war with a colonised, largely dispossessed, and racialised minority. I refer here to the Israeli state's war against Palestinians which utilises a combination of military, police, and settler terror. The killing of thousands of Palestinian civilians (including children) over the last decade alone has kept Palestinians 'in a permanent state of terror'.[49] The recent state terror in May 2021 showed that military and police violence goes unchecked, while settler vigilante violence against Palestinians receives police protection. As has occurred previously, the use of criminalisation and mass arrests plays an important part of colonial control. It has been noted that a dual process of suppression entails 'the securitization of crime (treating crime as a security issue) and the criminalization of resistance (treating political mobilization as a criminal issue)', coupled with enhanced punishments for Palestinians and the use of indefinite administrative detention.[50]

Deaths arising from police interventions for minor offences

Notwithstanding the systematic use of violence against groups of people discussed in the previous section, one of the features of police killings and deaths in police custody is that in many cases, the deaths occur where the initial police intervention is for a seemingly trivial matter – such as Eric Garner in New York (arrested for selling single cigarettes); the so-called Saskatoon 'freezing deaths' in Canada during the 1990s and early 2000s when First Nations young people were apprehended for minor public order offences, driven from the city and left by police to die in freezing conditions[51]; or First Nations deaths in Australia such Cameron Doomadgee (detained for offensive behaviour), Ms Julieka Dhu (detained for unpaid fines), or Adama Traoré in Paris (detained for not having ID).

Research over many years strongly supports this finding. A review of deaths in police custody in England and Wales between 1998–1999 and 2008–2009 found that more than half of the 333 deaths involved custody for public order, public drunkenness, driving, and theft offences. Similar results have been found in later studies.[52] As noted previously, the RCADIC in Australia found that the majority of deaths of Aboriginal people in police custody involved people held for minor public order offences (such as offensive language or public drunkenness) or being unable to pay fines.[53] A review of police fatal shootings of 135 unarmed Black men and women in the US found many of the deaths arose from police interventions for minor offences or from interventions where there was no legal reason for arrest. More than two dozen of the police involved had previous citizen complaints with some relating to the use of force. Some police had also been involved in previous shootings. Of the 135 fatal shootings of unarmed citizens, two police were found guilty of murder, and two were found guilty of manslaughter.[54]

The apparent senselessness of these deaths adds to the public outrage globally. As indicated in Chapter 1, the violent policing of COVID-19 public health regulations has resulted in children and adults dead in Africa, Asia, and Latin America. Police killings often involve innocent bystanders. In Brazil, children have been killed in favelas as collateral damage in police shoot-outs in their 'war on drugs' – such as 14-year-old João Pedro Mattos Pinto killed while playing with friends during a botched police raid, or an 8-year-old Ágatha Félix shot dead by police while inside a van travelling with her mother, both in poor areas of Rio de Janeiro.

And it is also important to remember that it was the deaths of young Black teenagers that led to the establishment of resistance movements to police violence and institutional racism – the Committee to Defend Black Rights in Australia after the police killing of 16-year-old John Pat in 1983, the Stephen Lawrence Campaign that led to the Macpherson Inquiry after 17-year-old Stephen's killing by a White racist gang in 1993, and the Black Lives Matter movement after the killing of 17-year-old Trayvon Martin by a neighbourhood watch captain in 2012.

The violence of neglect

Although lethal police violence (particularly fatal shootings) attracts a great deal of public attention, many deaths in police custody occur through inaction and neglect by police – a failure which represents the *violence of neglect* when authorities fail to exercise their responsibilities and duties. These deaths cannot be written off as accidental or through 'natural causes' when there is an active disregard for a detainee's well-being. When a State deprives a person of their liberty they rob that person of the ability to protect themselves. The State thus assumes a direct responsibility to safeguard the life and bodily integrity of the detainee. The Australian RCADIC found there was a significant failure by police and correctional authorities to exercise a proper duty of care and this failure directly contributed to or caused numerous Aboriginal deaths in custody. For example, in the RCADIC regional report on southeast Australia it was found that every one of the 18 deaths investigated was potentially avoidable and further that 'negligence, lack of care, and/or breach of instructions on the part of custodial authorities … played an important role in the circumstances leading to 13 of the 18 deaths investigated'.[55]

Although the circumstances of police neglect were extensively documented by the RCADIC, more recent deaths in police custody over the last 30 years continue in similar circumstances. For example, Yamatji woman Ms Dhu was in police custody for unpaid fines. She complained to police about severe pain, vomiting, and partial paralysis. She was twice taken to hospital but on both occasions sent back to the police cells. Police told nursing staff she was "faking" her illness. On the third occasion she was taken to hospital she was dying from septicaemia and pneumonia and could not be revived. There are many examples in Australia where people (and particularly First Nations people) have received rough and inappropriate treatment by police and medical staff; inadequate cell checks and supervision; and been denied access to medications and medical services by police. The type of callous disregard for well-being which was so extensively documented by the RCADIC remains a deadly problem today.

In an analysis of *The Guardian*'s database of several hundred First Nations deaths in police and prison custody since the RCADIC, it was found that:

- Police watch-houses, prisons and hospitals failed to follow all of their own procedures in 41 per cent of cases where Indigenous people died.
- The proportion of Indigenous deaths where medical care was required at some point, but not given, was 38 per cent.
- Mental health or cognitive impairment was a factor in 42 per cent of deaths in custody, and Indigenous people with a diagnosed mental health condition or cognitive impairment, such as a brain injury or foetal alcohol syndrome disorder, did not receive the care they needed in half the cases.

Police attitudes of neglect were especially prevalent for Indigenous women who were less likely to have received appropriate medical care prior to their death compared with men. Authorities were also less likely to have followed all their own procedures in cases where an Indigenous woman died in custody.[56]

In England and Wales, the vast majority of deaths arising from police intervention occur while a person is held in a custodial setting, rather than through a police pursuit or shooting. INQUEST data shows that over a 30-year period from 1990 to 2020, police fatal shootings comprised only 4.2 per cent of all deaths compared to 63 per cent in custody and 24 per cent in police pursuits.[57] The number of deaths in police custody (other than police shootings or as a result of direct physical violence) is dependent on a range of policies and practices including, to name only some, public health initiatives such as alternatives to arrest and custody, the extent of criminalisation for minor matters, the frequency of the use of police custody, access to medical assistance, as well as policies governing police pursuits, cell checks and supervision. While there is considerable international focus on police shootings, other factors are also important.

Conditions in police detention can play a part in causing death, injury, and disease. Inadequate sanitation, food, water, and overcrowding can impact on detainee's health – and particularly so during health crises such as the COVID-19 pandemic. The UN Human Rights Council identified the 'lack of basic medical attention and denial of access to medicine, make otherwise treatable conditions, such as infected wounds, asthma or diabetes, fatal'.[58] Poor conditions can also contribute to self-harm and suicide in custody. As noted previously, access to proper healthcare is critical when we know that people coming into police custody have higher rates of poor health, drug dependency, and mental illness than the general population. These problems are further compounded when police engage in physical mistreatment and torture. Indeed, some organisations such as INQUEST in the UK and the NCAT in India also measure the incidence of suicide among people after their release from police custody where the suicide may have been related to custodial experiences or the threat of ongoing state violence.

Violent responses and use of force

Police regularly use violence in 'non-fatal' forms, including police dog attacks, the use of batons, OC (capsicum or pepper) spray, hoods, tasers, the use of restraints and restraint positions,[59] and other types of crowd control. Police use of excessive force constitutes an important cause of serious injury and permanent disabilities, and the use of 'less lethal' weapons not infrequently results in death. Unfortunately, there is relatively little official data published on police use of force – like the problematic reporting on fatalities, the state does not prioritise accurate data on its use of violence against citizens. In the US the Marshall Project recently used data from the CDC to show that from 2015 to early 2021, some 400,000 people were treated in hospital emergency because of violent interactions with police or security guards. However, there is limited nationwide data in the US on the context, nature, or extent of injuries. It is also likely an underestimate of injury when it is police who decide whether to call an ambulance – and the policies and practices governing this decision vary widely among police forces.[60]

It is well established that police are significantly more likely to use violence against Black, Indigenous, and people of colour. In England and Wales during 2019–2020 Black people were nearly six times more likely to have force used on them by police than White people. Black people were eight times more likely to be 'compliant handcuffed', and over three times more likely to have a spit and bite hood/guard used on them than White people.[61] Sometimes these interventions proved fatal. In the UK, police use of restraint is identified as the cause of death in 10 per cent of cases, while it is used at some stage in 25 per cent of deaths in police custody.[62] There have been significant increases in the use of tasers – with a 500 per cent increase between 2010 and 2019. Police were nearly eight times more likely to use tasers on Black people than on White people. There has also been more frequent use of tasers against children – over 74 per cent of whom are Black or Minority Ethnic. The UN CROC have called for the prohibition of the use of tasers on children because of the impact on their physical and mental health.[63] In New York City, an examination of complaints to the CCRB regarding the NYPD's use of tasers between 2014 and 2017 showed that 59 per cent of complainants self-identified as Black – which is twice the proportion of their population in the city. Conversely, White complainants were 9 per cent of the total but are 33 per cent of the city's population.[64] In 43 per cent of all complaints, police officers gave civilians no warning before using a taser.

In Aotearoa New Zealand, racialised differences in the use of police violence are evident. Māori are six times more likely to be handcuffed, 11 times more likely to be subdued with OC spray, six times more likely to be batoned, nine times more likely to have dogs set on them, ten times more likely to be tasered, and nine times more likely to have firearms drawn compared to Pākehā (non-Māori).[65] In Australia, there has been an increasing use of tasers and OC spray as compliance tools, especially on people who are already in custody, and their inappropriate use on children, pregnant women, people with mental health issues, and First Nations people. In NSW, First Nations people comprised 29 per cent of people tasered, nearly ten times their proportion of the general population. They were also more likely to be subjected to multiple/continued taser use than other groups. A similar over-representation was evident in Queensland in the use of OC spray against First Nations people.[66] This increasing use of force by police has occurred as an alternative to the utilisation of de-escalation techniques. In some cases, this has led to or contributed to the death of the person in custody. For example, GB died in the Northern Territory after he was subjected to multiple taser applications and bursts of OC spray by police. The man had been taken into custody for a mental health assessment. The coroner found that where the deceased was not armed nor making any threats to kill or cause serious harm, 'the use of the Taser was premature and inappropriate'.[67]

Racial profiling and the use of stop and search

In January 2021, several non-government organisations in France filed a class action against the French state for racial profiling by police. It argued that police identity checks perpetuate ongoing and systemic ethnic profiling by targeting individuals of Black and Arab origin. The legal action includes affidavits from police officers which confirm the prevalence of ethnic profiling, as well individual statements from individuals who have suffered police discrimination and violence. Various research indicates that Black or Arab young men are up to 20 times more likely to be stopped by police.[68] The racism behind stop and searches is an international issue.

In England and Wales, the racially discriminatory use of stop and search powers by police has been controversial since the introduction of the *Police and Criminal Evidence Act* (PACE) 1984, more than 35 years ago. Evidence published since 1995 regularly shows that Black people are consistently between four and nine times more likely to be stopped and searched than White people. In the Inquiry into the racist killing of Stephen Lawrence, Lord Macpherson found that:

> If there was one area of complaint which was universal it was the issue of 'stop and search'. Nobody in the minority ethnic communities believes that the

complex arguments which are sometimes used to explain the figures as to stop and search are valid. In addition, their experience goes beyond the formal stop and search figures recorded under the provisions of the PACE, and is conditioned by their experiences of being stopped under traffic legislation, drugs legislation and so called 'voluntary' stops.[69]

In 2010, the Equality and Human Rights Commission concluded that racial discrimination was a 'significant reason why Black and Asian people are more likely to be stopped and searched than white people'.[70] Little has changed. Her Majesty's Inspectorate of Constabulary found that during 2019–2020, Black, Asian, and Minority Ethnic people were over four times more likely to be stopped and searched than White people; and for Black people specifically, the rate was nearly nine times greater. Over three quarters of searches resulted in 'no further action'. Drugs searches, particularly for possession, contributed substantially to racial disparity – they comprise around two thirds of all searches under the PACE and Black people are much more likely to be searched by police.[71] However, fewer drug searches of Black people result in drugs being found compared to White people. Despite this, because of the large number of searches of Black people, they are 12 times more likely than White people to be prosecuted for cannabis possession in England and Wales.[72] Police can also search a person or vehicle for offensive weapons under the Criminal Justice and Public Order Act 1994. Black people are around 18 times more likely to be searched under the legislation than their White counterparts. Only 3.7 per cent of searches result in finding offensive weapons.[73]

Some US commentators have argued there is no evidence of anti-Black disparity in police shootings because if Black people commit more crimes, then a higher rate of police killings would naturally follow. However, the counter argument has been that if racism and racial profiling impact on stop and searches and other police interventions, then the racism in police violence and killings is essentially masked.[74] Research in the US shows that disproportionate police violence against Black Americans is driven by systemic racism. Black Americans experience disproportionate levels of police contact, even for crimes that both Black and White

Americans commit at similar rates, such as certain drug offences, and for police interactions, such as investigatory traffic stops.[75] Under the stop and frisk policy, NYPD officers regularly stopped and searched hundreds of thousands of people annually. Between January 2004 and June 2012, 4.4 million people were searched, of whom 83 per cent were Black or Latinx. In 2013, a federal judge found the stop and frisk policy to be unconstitutional. The most frequent reason given by police for a stop was 'furtive movements' which could include 'changing direction', 'getting a little nervous', or 'being very fidgety'. Officers recorded furtive movements in many more stops of Black and Latinx people than White people. Police stops relative to charges and convictions are relatively low – a study of the NYPD stop and frisk programme found that well over 90 per cent of people stopped by the police were not committing any crime and did not have any contraband or weapons on them. Even after the Federal Court decision, racial disparities in police stops continue.[76] Black and Latinx women are similarly stopped by police in disproportionate numbers. They also experience racial stereotypes of women of colour as drug couriers, sexually deviant, and/or promiscuous and thus engaged in prostitution-related offences, or as bad mothers and therefore involved in offences related to child welfare.[77]

These problems are by no means confined to the NYPD. A Department of Justice investigation in 2016 of the Baltimore City Police Department found that the Department engaged in 'a pattern or practice of conduct that violates the Constitution or federal law'. Specifically, 'making unconstitutional stop, searches and arrests; using enforcement strategies that produce severe and unjustified disparities in the rates of stops, searches and arrests of African Americans; using excessive force; and retaliating against people engaging in constitutionally-protected expression'.[78] Nor have the targets of racial profiling remained static – in the post-9/11 era we can add people of 'middle eastern appearance' and suspect populations of 'illegal immigrants' to the list.[79]

On protests, 'kettling', and police militarisation

The connections between police, military and war have a history as long as the institution of police, as discussed in Chapter 2. The various convergences during the colonial period with police acting as a military force of occupation, control and dispossession showed that the police have been 'militarised' to a greater or lesser extent since their inception, depending on the colonial and domestic context. For this reason, we when talk of the militarisation of police, it is important to recognise this is neither a new nor unique phenomena. The militarisation of police is an *ongoing process* rather than a specific outcome, it is a continually recurring process that reproduces police power. As Neocleous argues, police power and what he terms 'war power' are intertwined and not surprisingly the technologies of state violence are shared.[80] However, the specificities and intensity of the 'sharing' process varies over time and are contingent on a range of local and geopolitical factors.

There have been clear links between the militarisation of policing within the US and the police training and technical assistance offered to regimes globally to suppress popular revolts and enforce political priorities. Shifts towards further militarisation occurred with Reagan and later Bush's 'war on drugs' from the early 1980s, and the post-9/11 'war on terror'. Indeed, it has been argued by Harcourt and Schrader, among others, that the model of counterinsurgency which views all citizens as a potential threat to the state has become the paradigm for contemporary policing.[81] In the decades post-9/11, various US cities have also sought police training *from* other countries – particularly from Israel, one of the most violent and repressive settler colonial states.[82] Acknowledging the negative effects of this training, officials in Durham, North Carolina introduced a policy to prevent these international collaborations because it had led domestically to 'intensifying surveillance and racial profiling as well as harsh responses to public protest'.[83] In addition, after decades of war in Iraq and Afghanistan, it has been estimated that nearly one in five police officers in the US are military veterans who bring their own training to domestic counterinsurgency.[84]

The nature and drivers of the militarised response to civil protests in the US and the role of the federal policy in arming police has been well documented and evident well before the policing of the 2020 protests.[85] Since its creation in the 1990s, the Department of Defense's Excess Property Program (or 1033 Program) has transferred military equipment to law enforcement agencies. In addition, since 9/11, further funding for military equipment to police has been provided by Departments of Homeland Security and Justice programmes for the 'war on terror'. We are all aware of the outward signs on the street – not just in the US but globally from Lagos to the favelas of Rio – the commando and army fatigues, military-grade weapons, armoured vehicles, helicopters, BearCats, and Humvees. While overt militarisation is evident in police hardware, there are also much deeper influences on police tactics and use of force.

According to Kraska, militarisation permeates through the material, cultural, organisational, and operational characteristics of law enforcement.[86] For example, police paramilitary units such as SWAT teams that were modelled on military special operations have become normalised into the everyday functions of policing, and their use has increased dramatically – for example in raiding houses for evidence of small-time drug dealing. Kraska and Williams estimate 80 per cent of SWAT deployments are proactive drug raids. Every year roughly 60,000 of these raids occur, and in 50 per cent of the cases no drugs are located nor are any arrests made. Nearly 50 per cent of the raids are conducted against Black Americans.[87] Warrants involving 'no knock' or 'quick knock' raids are common. Breona Taylor was killed by police in a 'no knock' drug raid on her apartment in March 2020 – she was not the target of the raid and the suspect was not at the house. In acknowledgment of the wrongful death, Louisville paid $12 million to Breona's family in a lawsuit. In relation to the cultural impact of militarisation, Leigh Goodmark has argued that it leads to a 'militarized masculinity' which values aggressiveness, force, and violence.[88]

Protests, containment, and violence

George Floyd's killing sparked one of the largest protest movements in US history. As has been the case in many countries, notwithstanding that the protests were in direct response to racist police violence, the protesters were met with more state violence.[89] According to HRW:

Tens of millions of protesters went to the streets in all 50 states. … The police in many places responded

... with unnecessary and excessive force and other abuses: beating up protesters, conducting mass arbitrary arrests, and deploying police and national guard forces to discourage protests ... police used less-lethal weapons to disperse protesters, including teargas, pepper spray, stun grenades, and rubber bullets – sometimes firing directly at protesters, resulting in serious injuries. [90]

The way the protest movements were policed reflected tactics of counter-insurgency containment. The tactic of 'kettling' is a premeditated operational decision designed to encircle and trap protesters through forcing them into narrow, confined spaces, and blocking any exit – and then engaging in arbitrary mass arrests often with unnecessary violence. As Neocleous has commented, the 'kettle is a microcosm of the police war of containment' deriving from the political and military containment of enemies.[91] The police tactic of kettling is used internationally – it was prevalent during the 2020 demonstrations, for example in the UK and Australia.

These policing tactical decisions are made at the top of the organisation. A study by HRW of a 'kettling' tactic against a demonstration in Mott Haven in the Bronx – where 82 per cent of the population are people of colour, mostly Black or Latinx – found that the decision to block alternative routes, trap protesters, and undertake arbitrary mass arrests was a premeditated plan. The operation was described by the NYPD Commissioner as being 'executed nearly flawlessly in the Bronx [those arrested were] outside agitators ... tearing down society [with the] intent to destroy property, to injure cops, and to cause mayhem'.[92] In other words, this was a counterinsurgency operation. These are not decisions made by individual police officers – they are policy formulated by and activated at senior ranks of the police department.[93] Perhaps the highest level of direct intervention was when then President Trump ordered the US Marshals Special Operations Group and US Customs and Border Protection's Border Patrol Tactical Unit to Portland, Oregon to protect federal property. During protests against racism and police brutality, protestors were grabbed off the street in unmarked vans, while heavily armed law enforcement in military camouflage beat people.[94] The policing of protesters and protest movements are political decisions. Furthermore, there is a clear asymmetry between the policing of progressive social movements and right-wing extremists/White supremacist movements.[95] Indeed, the 6 January 2021 attack on the US Capitol showed both this asymmetry as well as the participation of some police as White supremacists.[96]

Conclusion

An understanding of the extent and nature of violence by law enforcement agencies is an important driver to the call for defunding the police, and the call to redirect social and economic support to community-based solutions, and eventually moving to police abolition. As indicated earlier, most countries do not publish comprehensive figures on the extent of police violence. In the US, the federal government provides more informative data on the number of livestock in the country than on the number of people who die in police custody – and that is not a problem particular to the US. Despite this, we are able to piece together a frightening picture across much of the world.

Police violence is a pandemic for the poor and marginalised globally. We also know that the extent of violence varies. The US is an outlier for police killing civilians in the global north, but the US rate is much lower than many countries in the global south. The war on drugs has facilitated rampant police killings in countries like Brazil and the Philippines – leading to questions of state crimes against humanity. The examples of India, Bangladesh, and Pakistan provide insight into the routine use of torture by law enforcement to extract confessions and bribes, and impose summary punishment, in addition to extrajudicial killings and enforced disappearances.

One feature of deaths in police custody is that in many cases the deaths occur where a trivial matter provides the official reason for police intervention. In example after example, these are people engaged in small crimes of survival, or the victims of discriminatory police stop and searches, or they are innocent bystanders. Moreover, deadly violence is also only one part of the story – violence is used in multiple forms from dogs to tasers and chemical and physical restraints. And there is the violence of neglect and indifference where police fail to exercise their responsibilities and duties of care. Inadequate sanitation, food, water, the lack of access to medicine or medical attention – all these lead to unnecessarily fatal or disabling outcomes.

What this chapter repeatedly demonstrates is that the targets of law enforcement violence are inevitably poor and marginalised communities, whether by way of class, caste, race, gender, Indigeneity, ability, sexual orientation, religion and ethnicity, or other status. In many cases the targets of police repression represent the ongoing legacies of colonialism, imperialism, and slavery – these legacies intersect across divisions between the global north and south and are prevalent in, for example, Brazil, the US and Australia, where Black and Indigenous peoples are over-represented among the dead. The targets of police repression also intersect with the contemporary demands of local and global elites – the castes, the classes, the Indigenous and tribal peoples, and local communities who threaten capitalist economic development and the profits of the few from South Asia to South America to Africa – these are the victims of forced disappearances, extrajudicial killings, and criminal legal systems that legitimate state violence as a tool of authoritarian regimes. The US 'war on drugs' and 'war on terror' have impacted on domestic policing, but their international export has impacted broadly on policing and violence through the training, the sale and supply of armaments, renewed militarisation of police, and a further collapsing of police and military functions in the name of protecting security. One final point to make is that the social and political forces driving the police use of violence overlap with those driving a more punitive approach to crime and crime control. In addition to policing, these approaches place a heavy reliance on the use of imprisonment – police power and the carceral state are intertwined.

6

The protection racket

One of the core public rationales for policing is that it provides a necessary institutional response to protect citizens from crime and to maintain order. This is a powerful rhetoric that plays on people's fears and insecurities, even where they have witnessed or experienced police violence or the failure of police to provide protection or assistance. This chapter considers perhaps one of the most contested points of argument in calls to defund the police: are police necessary to ensure the safety of women against harassment, violence, and sexual assault, and do they provide these outcomes? It is argued that the evidence shows that police as an institution fail to protect women and this particularly (although not exclusively) impacts on specific groups of women from Black, First Nations, Brown, racialised, poor, and other minoritised communities.

At the time of writing this book, there were vigils in London for the killing of Sarah Everard, a White professional woman in her early thirties. A police officer was charged with her kidnapping and murder. A vigil for Ms Everard on Clapham Common in mid-March 2021 resulted in a violent police response which led to arrests and the dispersal of women who attended. There was widespread condemnation of the violence of police tactics, although a later police inspectorate report exonerated police and argued that the Metropolitan Police did not have a 'choice' but to use force.[1] The death of Sarah Everard and police violence at the subsequent vigil for the dead woman was problematic enough. However, a further dimension was the relative silence around the murders of other young women in London who were Black. Mina Smallman questioned why the deaths of her two daughters, Nicole Smallman and Bibaa Henry, killed in London nine months before Ms Everard, had received comparatively little attention and why police were slow to respond to their disappearance. In that case, two police officers were subsequently suspended and arrested after allegedly taking 'selfie' photos with the bodies of the two women. A 19-year-old male was later charged with their murder.

Emphasising the importance of the death of one woman compared to another raises the broader social value placed on different women and victims/survivors of violence particularly by reason of their race, religion, ethnicity, class, sexuality, and ability, and whether the deaths of minoritised women attract the same public outrage and police responses as White and socially privileged women.[2] At roughly the same time as the deaths of Mina Smallman's daughters, the women prisoner's advocacy group, The View, released their report *We Are Invisible* on Black and minority ethnic women's experience in the criminal legal system in the UK.[3] The report found that minority women who are victims/survivors of domestic abuse and sexual violence suffer systemic and institutional racism in the justice system. Police brutality was a recurring theme among Black women.[4] Shortly after the controversial policing of the vigil on Clapham Common, then Prime Minister Boris Johnson announced as a response to violence against women plans for increased CCTV, increased policing in 'clubs, bars and popular nightspots' and pushed for the passage of the controversial *Police, Crime, Sentencing and Courts Bill*.[5] Among other changes, the new legislation allows greater police powers to prohibit public protests, negatively impacts on Roma, Traveller and Gypsy people, expands youth imprisonment, and extends prison sentences for various offences, including up to 10 years' imprisonment for defacing statues and monuments – apparently showing a greater concern for controlling the Black Lives Matter and Extinction Rebellion movements than responding to violence against women.

How policing became the answer to violence against women

Promises of more policing and increased police and penal powers seem to be the stock answer by government to women's demands for safety and protection against harassment, violence, and rape. The World Health Organisation estimates that 30 per cent of women globally have been physically or sexually assaulted.[6] The likelihood and incidence of physical and sexual violence is increased for Black, Brown, Indigenous, women with disability, and poor women. For example, in the US one in five women of colour and one in three First Nations women experience rape, compared to one in six of all women.[7] First Nations women in Australia are 10 times more likely to be murdered than other women and twice as likely to be a victim of sexual assault. Similar levels of violence against First Nations, Metis, and Inuit women can be found in Canada, and in the US the National Congress of American Indians has described the violence against First Nations women as at epidemic proportions.[8] The UN Committee on the Elimination of Racial Discrimination (CERD) has on several occasions expressed deep concern about the incidence of rape and sexual violence against First Nations and Inuit women, the insufficient will of US federal and state authorities to take action, and in particular the need to ensure Indigenous women's right of access to justice.[9] The frequency of violence is also impacted by other factors – women with disabilities are nearly twice as likely to experience partner violence than other women, and between 4 and 10 times (depending on national data) more likely to be sexually assaulted.[10] Other violent patriarchal practices also come into play: India records nearly 20 'dowry death' murders of women a day, including bride burning.[11]

However, questions remain: how did we get to the position where more policing, criminalisation, and incarceration has become the primary answer to the problem of violence against women? And is it effective? Feminist activism in the 1970s and early 1980s was instrumental in bringing about change in the legislative frameworks and policing of violence against women, including both domestic violence and sexual assault. It was a period of 'breaking the silence' on the effects of violence on women and children and the discriminatory responses that were prevalent. In the 1970s, the focus was on providing women's shelters and rape crisis centres as well as identifying the wider systemic issues including health care, housing, childcare and the broader problems of male violence and gender inequality.[12] Although changes and developments were specific to the political dynamics of various countries, during the 1980s many governments shifted their responses to domestic and sexual violence against women. For example, in 1984 the Final Report of the US Attorney General's Task Force on Family Violence clearly argued for prioritising the role of police in domestic violence law and policy.[13] Domestic violence was defined as a crime problem that required a strong response from criminal justice agencies including police. The tenets of this position were not surprising given the extent to which historically male violence against women had been considered a 'private' and 'personal' matter and the police when they did become involved were focused on mediation.

However, it was clear at the time that a belief in the efficacy of criminalisation and mandatory or pro-arrest strategies was not shared by Black, Indigenous, and other women of colour. Aya Gruber notes that in the late 1970s Black feminists in the Combahee River Collective 'challenged mainstream feminists' commitment to "separatism" from men – a commitment that significantly underwrote feminists' comfort with invoking a violent, racist, sexist, and hierarchical penal system to discipline individual men'.[14] Angela Davis observed in the early 1980s, that few White men were prosecuted for rape, while between 1930 and 1967 almost 90 per cent of men *executed* for this offence were Black. She wrote, 'too many innocents have been offered to gas chambers and lifer's cells for Black women to join those who often seek relief from policemen and judges'. Further, police assaults on Black women, including rape, are 'heard too frequently to be dismissed as aberrations'.[15] Similarly, Beth Richie had argued that questions of race and class were lost as the anti-violence movement began to converge with the conservative law and order policies of criminalisation and mass incarceration.[16] Certainly by the late 1990s it was also clear in Australia that dominant approaches to domestic violence were not working for First Nations women: the criminalisation and removal of offenders was not addressing violent behaviour, nor respecting the wishes of women.[17]

During the 1990s, as the adoption of either mandatory or pro-arrest police strategies for responding to domestic violence became popular, developing research showed that these policies did not necessarily deter the occurrence of violence, although they did deter women from reporting violence. Research also showed that mandatory arrest policies had increased the likelihood of women being arrested more than men, and that intimate partner homicides had *increased* in US states where mandatory arrest policies were in force – most likely because of decreased reporting.[18] The impact of increased arrests for women, particularly racialised women, meant those women were subjected to even greater violence through police use of force (sometimes lethal), abusive strip searches, and custody.[19] Coinciding with this period was a rapid growth in the criminalisation and incarceration of Black, Indigenous, and First Nations women *and* the recognition that many women who were criminalised were also victims/survivors of violence and abuse.[20] The criminal justice response was to also have a negative impact on Black and other racialised men – for example recent research in Australia indicates that First Nations men who breach a domestic violence order are more than twice as likely compared to other men to be sent to prison. For First Nations women, the situation is even worse – they are more than three times as likely to be sent to prison compared to non-Indigenous women. Indeed, in Queensland nearly 70 per cent of all women sentenced to imprisonment for breaching a domestic violence order are First Nations women, although they comprise slightly more than 3 per cent of the female population.[21]

Why is policing problematic?

There are numerous reasons that show why police are not the solution to violence against women and why an increase in policing does not equate to more protection for women in general and in particular for those women from communities that are already subject to intense police surveillance. In the first instance, we know that very few women actually report violence and sexual assault to police, and this is particularly the case where the assailant in known to the victim. The International Violence Against Women Survey (IVAWS) which covered multiple countries found that less than one third of women reported experiences of physical and sexual violence to police, including in cases where they believed the violence to be serious.[22] Indeed with intimate partner violence, even where women believed their life was in danger, or they were in danger of serious bodily harm, only one third or less sought protection from police.[23] Women are more likely to seek help from family, friends, colleagues, or community services. A recent survey of migrant and refugee women's safety in Australia found that one in three women had experienced domestic and family violence. However, while half of the women disclosed the violence to someone, only a small minority (19 per cent) of those did so to police. The women were far more likely to report the violence to family and friends (84 per cent), health professionals (28 per cent), or a doctor (21 per cent). Women who had experienced domestic and family violence or other forms of criminal victimisation were less likely to trust the police or see them as fair, than other migrant or refugee women.[24]

The IVAWS noted that many women choose not to report violence because they are afraid of the 'negative attitudes' of police and others in the justice system. Research with health professionals in the US showed that 80 per cent saw contact with the legal system as 'psychologically detrimental to rape survivors'.[25] The revictimisation of women can take other forms: some women, especially Black, Indigenous, and women of colour will not report domestic and family violence to police because of a direct fear, if police are called, that their children will be removed by child welfare agencies – which has been a long-term strategy of colonial states to disrupt and separate poor and racialised families.[26]

For the minority of women who do report to police, there is no guarantee that their complaint will be taken seriously and progress through the justice system. As I prepared to write this chapter, a Sydney coroner in Australia held back tears as she delivered her findings in the case of two teenage children, aged 13 and 15 years, deliberately shot dead by their father. The mother had reported previous violence against herself and her children, but police had failed to take the reports seriously. The male perpetrator had a history of domestic violence with previous partners. The coroner found that the deaths were preventable and was highly critical of the failures of the NSW police, including the female officer who categorised the women's final complaint as 'no offence recorded'. After the deaths of her children, she subsequently committed suicide.[27]

There is a fundamental problem with the police inability to correctly identify male perpetrators. In Canada the National Inquiry into Murdered and Missing Indigenous Women and Girls (NIMMIWG) noted that Indigenous women, girls, and 2SLGBTQQIA (Two-Spirit, lesbian, gay, bisexual, transgender, queer, questioning, intersex, and asexual) people feared reaching out to police because they might be arrested and charged in situations of intimate partner violence.[28] The Australian National Research Organisation for Women's Safety (ANROWS) found that in Queensland nearly half the women killed by an intimate partner in 2017 had been previously misidentified by police as the perpetrator of violence. ANROWS found that 'racism, poor relationships with local communities, misogyny, and the patriarchal culture of the police service' negatively impacted the responses towards women, including police 'not acting on women's allegations and a lack of compassion or respect in their interactions'.[29] Meanwhile in the UK, the All Party Parliamentary Group on Women in the Penal System has found that thousands of women are 'needlessly arrested' by police, and many of these arrests are linked to incidents in the home where women had sought to defend themselves, where women were victims of crimes, or were arrested while visibly distressed, as well as when there were fears about their mental health.[30]

The evidence shows that in many jurisdictions, reports of violence against women are not taken seriously by police. The IVAWS notes that less than half of reported cases of violence against women are referred to prosecution and, in some instances, less than one quarter. Specifically, in relation to sexual assaults, police in Canada classified almost one in six reports as 'unfounded'.[31] In the US there have been reports of widespread incidents of police destroying rape kits and other physical evidence.[32] The Australian Law Reform Commission has noted that less than one in five sexual assault reports to police result in a person being charged and prosecuted.[33] When we combine the failure to prosecute with the low level of reporting to police, then the likelihood of a violent perpetrator being charged with a criminal offence is estimated by the IVAWS to be between 1 per cent and 7 per cent of the incidents of victimisation. Although varying between countries, the likelihood of conviction is an even smaller percentage of those who have been arrested, charged, and brought to trial. Racialisation and gender also come into play at the point of conviction and sentencing: for example, in the US, White women victims of rape are more likely to have successful court outcomes than other women, and in Australia, non-White accused are more likely to be convicted.[34]

Police violence against women

A further problem in relying on police for protection in matters of violence against women is that police officers frequently commit domestic and sexual violence themselves, and regularly use their authority to ensure immunity from sanctions and prosecution. In Britain, the number of police officers facing disciplinary proceedings for abusing their positions for sexual purposes has risen significantly in recent years. Of 2,000 officers accused of sexual misconduct, in nearly 60 per cent of cases no further action was taken, and in the vast majority of matters where misconduct was identified there were no criminal charges.[35]

An ABC (Australian Broadcasting Commission) investigation in Australia found police were often unwilling to take action against domestic violence perpetrators within their own departments, which contributed to a culture of invulnerability and put victims' safety at risk. An examination of incidents of domestic violence in 2017 in Victoria found that where perpetrators were also police officers, they were significantly less likely to have action taken against them and were more than four times *less likely* to be arrested, charged, or cautioned by police than when perpetrators were members of the public.[36] Similar reports in NSW identify the absence of sanctions against police, as well as the harassment of women who report domestic violence against police officers.[37] North American research also points to a higher incidence of domestic violence by police officers – some estimates suggest 15 times greater than the general population –as well as identifying the various problems that women face when police are central to accessing legal protections.[38] Leigh Goodmark has argued that intimate partner violence by police is a systemic problem exacerbated by the power, training, and socialisation of police, including the 'militarised masculinity' mentioned in Chapter 5 which valorises aggressiveness, force, and violence as legitimate ways to solve problems. Domestic violence law and policy heavily invests in police as first responders to domestic violence. Goodmark questions whether criminalisation can succeed as a policy to control domestic violence when police are meant to enforce laws they disproportionately violate.[39]

Apart from the incidence of police officers committing domestic violence, there is widespread evidence of police engaging in violence against women outside of an intimate partner relationship. The Prison Policy Institute has found that in the US women make up an increasing share of arrests (particularly for drug offences) and report much more frequent use of force than they did 20 years ago: police use of force against women quadrupled between 1999 and 2015, during the same period it doubled for men. In 2015 some 12 million women had 'non-voluntary' contact with police through various traffic stops, street stops, and with arrest warrants. Black women were three times more likely to report the use of force by police during a police-initiated stop than other women.[40] Another group of women who experience high levels of police violence and harassment are sex workers. INCITE! found that nearly 17 per cent of sex workers interviewed reported sexual harassment, abuse, and rape by police. Zero tolerance policing and the enforcement of 'quality of life' offences such as loitering, obstructing traffic, public nuisance, and disorderly conduct enable police to harass, detain, and arrest individuals they believe to be involved in sex work, and particularly street-based sex work.[41] More generally, Andrea Ritchie has noted that the war on drugs and the war on terrorism, along with ZTP, has increased the frequency and intensity of particularly Black and women of colour's interactions with police. These women experience many of the same forms of police racial profiling, brutality, and violence as men of colour, as well as gender/race specific forms of abuse.[42] Ritchie provides a harrowing account of women shot, raped, and abused by police, including when responding to domestic violence incidents. She notes the prevalence of complaints of police sexual misconduct is the second most frequently reported form of police misconduct, after the use of excessive force. 'Yet it is clearly not the second most frequently talked about', says Ritchie. She shows that many victims of police sexual violence do not come forward for fear of reprisal or not being believed or taken seriously, and that police often receive little or no punishment, when women do raise complaints.[43]

In Canada, HRW reported on abusive policing practices against First Nations women and girls, and police failures to protect First Nations women in cases of domestic violence and sexual assault. Police violence has included the use of excessive force, assaults, inappropriate use of police dogs, pepper spray, and tasers, and rape and sexual assault by police officers.[44] These incidences of abuse were compounded by the widely perceived failure of the police to protect First Nations women from violence. HRW found that, because of the injustices they have experienced, Indigenous women did not feel safe approaching the RCMP when they experienced violence: 'Police abuse undermines women and girls' safety far beyond the direct physical consequences of any physical mistreatment. The impact is felt in the reticence of Indigenous women and girls to call the police for help when they fear or have experienced violence.'[45] In 2015, the UN Committee for the Elimination of Discrimination against Women (CEDAW) found that there was a 'grave violation' of the rights of Aboriginal women in Canada through insufficient and inadequate measures to protect Aboriginal women from gender-based violence, including disappearances and murders.[46] I return to the issue of missing and murdered First Nations women and children later. In India, the National Campaign Against Torture (NCAT) and the National Human Rights Commission have detailed the killing, torture, and rape of women, including minors, by police.[47] Most of the deaths in police custody are male, however NCAT notes that a number of women have died in custody as a result of torture, 'foul play' or unknown circumstances – including a 55-year-old Dalit woman at an All Women Police Station in Tamil Nadu. Of those women who were tortured and raped by police and survived, they included, for example, the rape of a 15-year-old girl by four police officers and her subsequent sex trafficking.[48]

Beyond the fear of police violence, there are multiple reasons for women not reporting violence to police. In Australia, inadequate police responses to First Nations women who experience violence have the result that women are reluctant to seek assistance from police.[49] Similarly, research in Belize in Central America found the lack of reporting by women was a result of previous negative outcomes with police.[50] In India, the data from the National Crime Records Bureau shows a steady increase in crimes against women – up by nearly 8 per cent between 2018 and 2019.[51] The country has been the site of shocking police responses to women who have been killed, sexually assaulted or abused in the community. To take just one example, in September 2020 where a 19-year-old Dalit woman died after being gang raped and tortured, the Uttar Pradesh police immediately and forcibly cremated the body against the wishes of her family whom the police detained in their home. The police denied the young woman had been raped, despite her dying declaration. The NCAT has observed the problem of the 'hasty cremation' of bodies by police to hide evidence and prevent post-mortem. Writing in the *Economic and Political Weekly*, Nathan and Thorat noted, regarding the failure of police to protect Dalit women and girls: 'We hold the police and the state responsible for their inaction to register complaints and not arresting the accused. … Every case reveals that the state machinery has turned a blind eye [and] through its apathetic response, violated rights of victims to access justice and has nullified human dignity.'[52]

Similar comments have been reiterated frequently enough. The CEDAW concluded in relation to India that there was 'continuing impunity' for the increasing violent crimes against women and girls, particularly rape and abduction; that this violence especially impacted on marginalised castes and communities, including Dalit and Adivasi women, and that key state officials continually downplayed the 'grave criminal nature of sexual violence against women and girls'.[53] In the case from Uttar Pradesh, subsequent protests concerning the young woman's rape and death were described by the state government as part of an 'international conspiracy' and subsequently the government had a number of journalists, activists, and protestors arrested and charged with terrorism, sedition, and conspiracy offences.[54]

In neighbouring Pakistan, there were nationwide protests in September 2020 demanding police reform after the Chief of Lahore Police stated that a woman who had been raped by two men in front of her children on a highway in Punjab was to blame because she should not have been traveling 'without her husband's permission' on a motorway late at night.[55] A similar attitude that women were to blame for being raped was reflected by Prime Minister Imran Khan in June 2021. The Global Gender Gap Report for 2021 ranks Pakistan at 153 from 156 countries for gender inequality. Various reports indicate in Pakistan there are almost 12 rape cases reported daily, with only 0.3 per cent of accused being convicted, as well as around 1,000 'honour' killings annually. The CEDAW has drawn attention to the high prevalence of violence against women, the social acceptance of domestic violence, the under-reporting of violence, and the impunity for perpetrators in Pakistan.[56] According to the Human Rights Commission of Pakistan, the issues that face women are starkly shown by the prevalence of domestic and sexual violence and are exacerbated by other patriarchal factors including 'so-called "honour" killings, acid attacks, extended family dynamics, social restrictions on movement and jobs, inequality and abject poverty, forced and arranged marriages'. Only one in two women report feeling safe in their own home.[57]

Missing and murdered First Nations, Black, and marginalised women and children

There is a road in northern British Columbia, Canada called the Highway of Tears. This stretch of the Yellowhead Highway runs for around 700 kilometres and was named after the estimated 40 unsolved cases of missing and murdered First Nations women associated with that location.[58] The story of the failure to investigate the disappearances and murders of Aboriginal, Black, and other marginalised women and children goes to the heart of the failure of police to protect racialised and vulnerable women and children – to take their disappearances and deaths seriously. It is a story that can be found in various forms in multiple countries. In India it is a story of hundreds of thousands of adults who are recorded missing each year, nearly two thirds of whom are women, and the tens of thousands of children similarly recorded as missing annually.[59] Most come from Dalit, Adivasi, or other marginalised communities. The numbers for both adults and children have been increasing. Children make up about two thirds of those who are abducted and end up trafficked for forced labour, sex work, or domestic slavery. Activists put the number of missing children much higher than the official figures – up to half a million each year. The reason for the discrepancy is that police do not record notifications, or parents are too poor or scared to attend police stations and do not have the resources to follow-up with police.[60] Police corruption also comes into play where police are either directly part of trafficking networks, or brothel owners and traffickers bribe local police to maintain their silence and inaction.[61] One might argue that if the Indian police were provided with more resources, they would achieve better outcomes. But what do we find when we look at highly resourced police services in the global north? In England and Wales, Black people are four times more likely to be reported missing relative to their population size. There is particular concern about the number of missing Black children and the failure to recognise the seriousness of these cases.[62] In the US more than half a million people go missing annually and more than half of those are children under the age of 18 years. Black American children make up well over one third of this group, although they are only 14 per cent of American children. It has been noted that Black families can be hesitant to call police to report their children missing because of distrust. When Black families do report their children missing, they can be misclassified as runaways or criminals. As a result, police do not provide 'amber alerts' unlike when White children are classified as missing.[63] There is also the issue of tens of thousands of missing Black women annually and missing First Nations women and children in the US.[64]

In Australia, there are many examples of missing or murdered First Nations women and children which have involved inadequate police investigations characterised by various failures and shortcomings. These include police failure to follow up on crucial leads, the delay in collection of evidence due to racial assumptions made by investigating police officers because of the victim's Aboriginality, political inaction in the decision to prosecute by attorneys-general and public prosecutors, and other systemic oversights and shortcomings. These issues have been further exacerbated by a lack of interest within the mainstream media over the deaths of Indigenous people. The Bowraville case highlights these problems. In the space of 5 months between

September 1990 and January 1991, three Aboriginal children went missing from a small NSW community with a population of a little over 1,000 people. It has a history as an Aboriginal mission and the area where many First Nations people in the town live today is still known as the 'the mission'. It was from the mission that three Aboriginal children – Colleen Walker-Craig aged 16 years, Evelyn Greenup aged 4 years, and Clinton Speedy-Duroux aged 16 years – went missing. The initial police investigations in the Bowraville cases were riddled with incompetence and inaction often arising from racist assumptions about First Nations people. When Colleen Walker disappeared, the missing person report from the family was not taken seriously, there were no searches or other formal action undertaken. There were later delays in calling in specialist homicide detectives, failures to follow up on crucial leads including witness statements, and delays in the collection of evidence. One could only compare the difference in police responses, the level of resources which would have been deployed, and the public interest generated by the mainstream media, if three White children who all lived on the same street in a small rural community had disappeared within a matter of months. Colleen Walker-Craig's body was never found, although some of her clothing was located in a nearby river. The remains of Clinton Speedy-Duroux and Evelyn Greenup were located within a few kilometres of Bowraville. The families have continued to demand justice. In August 2016, 25 years after the disappearances, then NSW Police Commissioner Scipione delivered a formal apology to the Bowraville families for inadequacies in the initial police investigation. He stated: 'I want to publicly acknowledge that the NSW Police Force could have done more for your families when these crimes first occurred and how this added to your pain, as a grieving community.'[65]

The Bowraville story bears similarities to events in other regional and remote centres across Australia. It is not an isolated case. In 1987 in the remote NSW township of Bourke, two teenage Aboriginal girls – Mona Smith aged 16 years and Cindy Smith aged 15 years – died in terrible circumstances after accepting a ride in a vehicle driven by a White middle-aged man who was drunk and subsequently crashed the car. The driver sexually molested one of the girls as she was dying or shortly after she had died. The police investigation was minimal. The driver was never arrested nor fingerprinted, little evidence was collected and some that was collected went missing. The driver was acquitted of culpable driving and the charge of interfering with a corpse was withdrawn. The family have continually sought an explanation from police – in March 2020 Police Commissioner Fuller announced that the police investigation had been 'adequate'.[66] Some 35 years after the girls' deaths, and a constant struggle by the families, on 14 July 2022, the NSW State Coroner confirmed that the inquest into the deaths of Mona Lisa and Cindy Rose Smith would be resumed.[67] The examples of Bowraville and Bourke have been repeated across the nation, with no or substandard investigations by police into the deaths of First Nations women and children.[68] In August 2022, it was announced that the Australian senate would conduct an inquiry into missing and murdered First Nations women and children.[69]

In Canada there were years of political agitation by First Nations women and supporting organisations over the incidence of missing and murdered Aboriginal women and children. In 2004, Amnesty International had identified a number of cases of disappearances of Aboriginal women and the failure of police to conduct serious investigations.[70] In 2013, HRW again drew attention to the problem of police apathy towards investigating violence against Aboriginal women and girls.[71] A report by the RCMP in 2014 found that there were 164 Aboriginal women considered missing at that time, and there were 225 unsolved cases of either missing or murdered Aboriginal women.[72] UN human rights committees also weighed into the debate, noting the disproportionate homicides and disappearances of Aboriginal women, and in 2015 called on the Canadian government to establish a national public inquiry into missing and murdered Aboriginal women and girls.[73] The Canadian Liberal Government established the NIMMIWG in 2016. The Inquiry reported in 2019. More than 2,380 people participated and 468 family members and survivors of violence shared their experiences. The Inquiry revealed a persistent and deliberate pattern of human rights abuses and systemic racism within the police. The report outlined routine police indifference to First Nations people, the failure to investigate, to take statements from witnesses, and to treat matters of missing and murdered First

Nations women and children either urgently or seriously. To justify their inaction, police utilised racist and sexist stereotypes of Indigenous women as prostitutes, as drunks, as criminals, as negligent parents, and so forth.[74] The police consistently devalued the lives of Indigenous women.

> The women were deemed as disposable. And it was very, very tragic; their lives were tragic. You know, they were human beings; they were sisters, mothers, daughters, loved ones, wives; partners, aunties, grandmas. They were human beings worthy of dignity and respect, and that wasn't accorded to them in life.[75]

The Inquiry found that the police failed to ensure justice and protection, and failed to provide adequate, bias-free policing services. The treatment of First Nations women, girls and 2SLGBTQQIA people was discriminatory and contributed to systemic harm.[76] Further, the Inquiry found that the violence against Indigenous peoples in Canada was genocidal. The connection between the deaths and endemic violence was and is founded in the colonial violence, racism, and oppression which is embedded in everyday life and institutional structures (including the police). This violence amounted to genocide.[77]

Conclusion

There have been long-standing criticisms dating back to the 1980s of a public policy approach to violence against women which relies on stronger policing, criminalisation, and penal sanctions. These criticisms have received greater traction in recent decades along with the growing intellectual and political movements against mass incarceration which have coincided with the interest in abolitionism, and the comparatively newer BLM and Defund the Police movements. Alongside this there has been a wider acknowledgment of the centrality of intersectional analysis in understanding the profoundly negative effects of criminal law reforms on Black, Indigenous, and women of colour.

It has been noted that 'to see policing and punishment simply as feminist solutions is an act of bad faith when the injustices of mass incarceration—the confinement of 2.3 million people, predominantly Black and Hispanic men [in the US]; the brutal conditions of detention; the lasting legal discrimination faced after release, to name but a few—are widely known'.[78] Decolonial feminists have also been critical of a criminal legal approach: reliance on criminalisation furthers the colonial and patriarchal continuities of punishment within countries of the global south and north.[79] Broadly speaking this has given rise to a critique of carceral feminism – that is a critical opposition to the reliance on policing, criminal prosecution, and imprisonment as a core solution to violence against women. Feminist abolitionists have argued instead for the development of non-state, community-controlled responses that protect women, hold offenders accountable, and address the underlying causes of violence.

It is argued that criminal legal interventions are 'extremely poor at dealing with the underlying causes of criminal behaviour and make a negligible contribution to addressing the underlying consequences of crime in the community'.[80] The failures of these interventions are manifold. For example, they fail at the symbolic and political level because the justice institutions, including police, lack legitimacy within many communities; the interventions fail by leaving women socially and economically worse off; they have led to increased levels of criminalisation of women; and they fail by escalating the violence against women and children if imprisoned men return more traumatised after their imprisonment experiences. It has been suggested that rather than seeing domestic violence as a criminal legal problem, it can be more usefully understood and responded to as a public health, economic, community, and human rights issue – a point discussed more fully in later chapters.[81]

The call to defund the police is an important part of this critique of carceral feminism because police both directly and indirectly soak up so much of the resources that might be available to provide socially beneficial responses in health, housing, education, and employment. For example, in the US, nearly nine times the amount of grant funding from the federal *Violence Against Women Act* goes to the criminal legal system compared to housing, despite repeated studies that show housing is 'the single greatest need identified by people subjected to abuse'.[82] Indirectly, a carceral approach soaks up society's resources because the criminalisation and imprisonment of women further generates a raft of additional costs from operating a bloated system of criminalisation and incarceration. These costs include all the social, health, and economic costs associated with, for example, child welfare, lost educational and employment opportunities, and so on.

The distinction between carceral feminism and feminist abolitionism is an important underpinning to the debates between those who seek greater reliance on policing and the processes of criminalisation, and those who are committed to circumscribing and ultimately removing criminalisation from state responses to domestic and sexual violence against women. This is putting the issue in a somewhat simple polarity and there are different positions argued along this spectrum.[83] However, there is a fault line which ultimately separates abolitionism from reformism and that is whether the proposed changes expand or contract the criminal legal system. We can see this line currently in debates within Canada and Australia over whether to criminalise coercive control or controlling behaviour within intimate partner relationships along the lines that have already occurred in the UK, Ireland, and proposed elsewhere.[84] The strongest opposition to the proposed changes in Australia has come from First Nations women who see the legislation as further empowering police to criminalise Indigenous women rather than protect them – a legitimate fear given the data on criminalisation already canvassed in this chapter.[85] It is also apparent in arguments over the utility of women-led or all-women police stations used in some parts of India and a number of Latin American countries. They have been advocated recently as a solution to violence against women in Australia. First Nations women are especially critical of the proposal to expand policing when there is already such strong evidence that First Nations women are extensively criminalised, reluctant to contact police, and desire community-controlled interventions within a framework of Indigenous self-determination.[86] There is also considerable debate over whether women-led police stations have been effective in curbing violence against women or in improving police response to women in those countries where they have been established.[87]

In short, rather than protecting women from violence, there are significant failures by police in taking violence against women seriously — through the failure to record reports, to act on information, to investigate serious crimes, and through the use of demeaning stereotypes of racialised women. In addition, police are a major source of violence, especially for Black, First Nations, women of colour, and other marginalised women. Perhaps then we can leave the last words to Andrea Ritchie, author of *Invisible No More*, 'What's clear is that police are not preventing violence — they're perpetrating violence, and they are being lifted up as the answer in the aftermath of the violence. Through that, they are able to perpetrate even more violence'.[88]

7

Disabling policing, protecting community health

Many videos went viral after the military coup in Myanmar in February 2021, however, one that was particularly disturbing were the images of a group of police publicly beating a young man who had a physical and cognitive disability.[1] There is an absence of systematic evidence internationally on the extent of police violence, including lethal violence, against people with disabilities and mental ill-health – this absence is part of the state's strategic ignorance which disavows knowledge of the targeted victims of state violence noted in Chapter 5. However, we know from individual cases and research data that the problem is extensive. Some of the most well-known police killings in the US which spurred the BLM movement involved Black Americans with disabilities, including Eric Garner, Tamir Rice, Tanesha Anderson, Freddie Gray, and Sandra Bland.[2] In Canada in the 3 months between April and June 2020 in the lead-up to mass protests over police killings, six people died during mental health-related contact with police: Ejaz Ahmed Choudry, Rodney Levi, Chantal Moore, Regis Korchinski-Paquet, Caleb Tubila Njoko, and D'Andre Campbell. All were Black, Indigenous, or people of colour. Four were shot dead by police. The other two fell from balconies after police intervened. The circumstances of these deaths provided a powerful impetus to Canadian calls to defund the police and to provide non-punitive support for people in need. Similarly, in Australia, police fatal shootings and violence against people with disability have been detailed in evidence to recent state and federal royal commissions into mental illness and disability. It has also been a source of First Nations activism in relation to deaths in custody. According to *The Guardian*'s database Deaths Inside, during 2018–2019, nine First Nations people with disability died in police custody.[3]

There is extensive police intervention into the lives of people with mental ill-health and cognitive impairments, and policing is a key part of the disablist and ableist processes of state control. I use the term *dis/abling* to encompass these dual processes of (i) the directly disabling effects and outcomes of police violence and trauma which cause disability, and (ii) police intervention, criminalisation of, and violence against people with disability because of ableist assumptions of what constitutes normative behaviour. There has been a profound penetration of policing and the carceral system into the repressive management of people with disability – both creating and reinforcing the social stigma and disposability of such a significant group of people. The evidence underlines the intersections of race, class, gender, and other social divisions with the state's dis/abling violence. The policing of disability is not a new phenomenon, but it has intensified with the neoliberal contraction of social support and the growth of the carceral state. Further, police decisions affecting people with disabilities compound through the carceral system, often justifying more extreme legal measures. As will be evident in this chapter, it is impossible to conceptualise policing without understanding its dis/abling effects. Centring disability is fundamental to the defund the police project and abolitionism more generally.

Before launching more fully into this discussion, it is necessary to draw attention to the problematic nature of how disability is responded to globally.

Worldwide one billion individuals have a disability. Many people with disabilities live in conflict settings or in developing countries. … In many countries, they are subjected to violence and discrimination. People with disabilities are also often deprived of their right to live independently, as many are locked up in institutions, shackled, or cycled through the criminal justice system. [Many] abuses are a result of entrenched stigma and a lack of community-based services.[4]

Criminalisation and imprisonment are not the only mechanisms of control, as other forms of surveillance, confinement, restriction, and regulation exist both within and outside state-based institutions. Some 80 per cent of people with disabilities globally live in low to middle income countries where private institutions, religious-based centres, and families can play a major role in enforcing captivity.[5] However, policing and prisons are also a vital part of control and confinement, and the use of state violence is ubiquitous. As we will come to see, prisons in countries like Australia, Canada, and the US hold more people with mental illness than psychiatric hospitals – the point being that police and prisons are central to the state's processes of dis/ablement. In other countries, police often play a role in feeding people with disabilities into places of confinement which are distinguishable from the prison, but are still systems of carceral control, both state and private.

At this point, a clarification of terminology is necessary. Although not always recognised in the law, literature, or official data, there is a distinction to be made between mental ill-health and cognitive impairment. Mental ill-health is a *temporary or continuing* health problem that affects functioning such as anxiety disorders, psychoses and personality disorders. A cognitive impairment or cognitive disability is an *ongoing impairment* such as an acquired brain injury, dementia, fetal alcohol spectrum disorder, and autism spectrum disorders.[6] In addition, cognitive impairments and mental illness can and often do co-exist – such as acquired brain injury and anxiety disorders. Sometimes in the literature, mental ill-health and cognitive impairment are simply referred to as 'disabilities' without distinction, and it is not always clear who is included or not. For the purposes of the discussion, I use the term 'disability' to cover both groups – except where it is appropriate to refer separately to mental ill-health or cognitive disability.[7] A political and sociological model of disability emphasises that people are *dis/abled* by attitudinal, social, political, economic, and environmental barriers that prevent participation and actively disable individuals. In other words, it is not the condition itself but the social responses and *dis/abling processes* to the condition that are deeply problematic.

Policing and criminalisation are important processes in actively dis/abling people, and indeed, in more extreme cases, killing people with mental ill-health or cognitive impairment. Further, the disabling effects of policing intersect across racial, gendered, and other social divisions which intensify oppression and the risk of state-sanctioned maiming and death. It is the active process of dis/abling (or what Puar calls debilitation[8]) which is highlighted in the role of the police and the carceral state in producing a criminalised and disabled population. Disability activists internationally have provided a compelling voice to the arguments for defunding the police and the need to transfer resources into non-stigmatising and non-punitive processes for support.

Policing dis/ability: not a new, but a resurgent problem

As noted in Chapter 2, historically, police performed a central role in controlling people with disabilities. During the 19th century and later, police were engaged in the long history of institutionalising the mentally ill and cognitively and physically disabled, alongside those who were vagrant, poor, or seen as a threat to public order and stability.[9] Indeed in contemporary India, laws relating to beggary are still used to confine people with disabilities in various institutions.[10] The period of hyper-incarceration since the 1980s, at least in parts of the global north, has reinvigorated the police role in dis/abling significant sections of the population. It has been tempting to argue that policework itself has changed *from* law enforcement *to* maintaining social control and managing disadvantaged people – that police have become the 'carers' of last resort, and a 'lead agency' in responding to people with disability.[11] However, the historical record challenges the simplicity and passivity of this argument – a core function of policing has always focused on actively controlling populations who in some way *contest* capitalist exploitation and the legitimacy of rule, and indeed the police were key well before the 1980s in the control and institutionalisation of people with disabilities.

Having said that, the neoliberal retraction of social supports – the increasing homelessness, stagnant wages, cuts to public services, and the decades-long failure to invest in community mental health resources across many countries – has increased demand for repressive state agencies to take a more proactive role in containing the generative social and economic problems of capitalism. This demand for repression has been matched by policing strategies, including ZTP, which are proactive in criminalising the types of public order 'lifestyle' offences likely to involve poor, unsupported people with disabilities (such as homelessness-related activities or behaviours). The ravages of neoliberalism and the current criminalisation of disability has occurred at a time of profound and entrenched poverty. People living with disability are significantly more likely to be unemployed, to be poor, on low incomes, to have inadequate access to health services, and to be homeless.[12] In addition, disability is more likely to be manifested in poor and racialised communities precisely because the material conditions of poverty (such as lack of access to medical care, affordable healthy food, environmental factors and so on), combined with marginalisation and structural racism create the conditions for disability.[13] Not all people with disability experience poverty and disadvantage, but it is clear globally that disability is disproportionately evident in poor, marginalised, and racialised communities – both within over-developed capitalist societies as well as the global south. These are precisely the communities where proactive public order policing is *actively* engaged in criminalising poor people in the public sphere, many of whom live with one or more disabilities. Thus, the criminalisation of disability follows the same path as criminalisation more generally, which picks up people who are poor, unemployed, homeless, and from minoritised and disenfranchised populations.

People with disability have increased risks of criminalisation and are treated differently from those without disability. People with disabilities are more likely to be arrested, questioned, and detained for minor infringements of public order. Both the Royal Commission into mental health services in Victoria and the federal Australian Disability Royal Commission found that people with disability were particularly criminalised for minor offences relating to homelessness, begging, vagrancy, drug/ alcohol use, public transport fare evasion, offensive behaviour, and unpaid fines.[14] Similar findings have been made in the US.[15] The statement given by Justen Thomas provides an example of these compounding problems.

> My name is Justen Thomas. I gave evidence at the Disability Royal Commission. I am a 43-year-old

Aboriginal man with an intellectual disability and epilepsy. I was homeless as a young person and I started to get fines for sleeping on trains. I was never able to pay my fines and it escalated to a big issue where I was getting locked up for fines. When I got arrested I didn't understand the police or the court system and I ended up in prison many times. The cycle ended when I finally got the help and support I needed.[16]

A community health survey in Canada found that nearly 35 per cent of people with a mental health problem or substance dependency reported contact with the police in the previous 12 months. There is also a high prevalence of homelessness. For example, studies have shown that people with mental ill-health make-up three quarters of people accessing homeless services.[17]

Police across many countries typically have extensive powers to intervene and apprehend a person who is thought to be suffering from mental ill-health. For example, in England and Wales the police can remove a person from a public place to a 'place of safety' if there is a risk of harm to self or others. A police station is designated as a place of safety. The Independent Police Complaints Commission (IPCC) review of 333 deaths in police custody, referred to in Chapter 5, found that although police stations should be used as a last resort, this was not the case in practice, and not surprisingly that using police custody as a place of safety in reality can 'exacerbate the individual's condition'. More than one in six of the 333 people who died in police custody were detained under s136 of the *Mental Health Act* or were identified as having mental health needs when apprehended. Most were in custody for offences related to public order, public drunkenness, or property damage.[18] In Victoria, Australia, the legislation allows for police officers to apprehend a person if they 'appear mentally ill and may be of serious and imminent harm to themselves or others'. Evidence to the Victorian Royal Commission detailed how confronting and upsetting being apprehended by police can be for people with a disability and the distress caused by police involvement in mental health responses.[19]

Police spend significant time on policing disability. Approximately 10 per cent of all police interactions in the US involve people with mental health conditions.[20] Similarly, in Sydney, Australia, on average 10 per cent of police time is spent policing people with mental health conditions. The role of policing mental health disorders and cognitive impairment has grown with, for example, a ten-fold increase in the number of 'mental health events' recorded by NSW police between 2000–2009, and this was on top of a 500 per cent increase during the previous decade. Similarly, in Canada, police in Ontario and British Columbia have reported significant annual increases in attending 'mental health occurrences' over recent years.[21] However, these increases in police focus should not be seen as simply a *passive* response for two reasons. First, police are defined and enabled as the appropriate responders in contrast to other forms of community-based and/or state-assisted interventions; second, proactive police strategies which focus on public order offences are likely to criminalise people with disabilities. As noted in Chapter 3, calls to police regarding homeless people are usually not about criminal behaviour. However, police intervention generates arrests for minor public order offences, particularly for people with disabilities.

In addition, there is widespread evidence of police actively resisting an acknowledgment of a person's disability and as a result police then fail to fulfil any procedural requirements that might be required when a person being detained has a disability. Studies of police attitudes towards people with disability reveal the use of derogatory language, negative or paternalistic stereotypes, and assumptions about 'normality' that frame police discretionary decisions to intervene and criminalise.[22] Further, it is clear that people with disability are more vulnerable to police violence and misconduct and have distinctive challenges in making complaints about police. A police complaints legal clinic in Melbourne revealed that almost half the formal complaints which they lodged against police involved people with a disability.[23]

Police decisions affecting people with disabilities compound through the carceral system. People with disability are more often refused bail and are more likely to receive a custodial sentence due to a lack of community-based options. They are thus exposed to extended and repeat incarceration, building up a long criminal record for minor offences. The nature of their impairment may cause trouble with memory, attention, impulse control, and communication. Their behaviour may be misinterpreted as non-compliance, rudeness, defiance, or indifference. The ability to conform with the legal requirements of, for example, bail, probation, and parole may be impaired – thus furthering ongoing police interventions and imprisonment. People become caught within the net of criminal justice with cycles of arrest, court, and imprisonment from which they are unable to extricate themselves. Being caught in cycles of criminalisation is itself harmful to recovery and to maintaining social support.[24] Indeed, for some – particularly racialised peoples – it leads to gross miscarriages of justice. To take just one recent example, in May 2021, two Black men who had cognitive impairments and were also brothers were awarded compensation for wrongful convictions after 31 years spent in prison.[25]

It has been estimated in the US that 64 per cent of jail inmates, 56 per cent of state prisoners and 45 per cent of federal prisoners have mental ill-health.[26] Reportedly, some 44 states and Washington DC have 'at least one jail that houses more people with mental illnesses than the largest state psychiatric hospital', while less than 13 per cent of incarcerated people report receiving any treatment for mental illness during their sentence.[27] In Australia, 40 per cent of prisoners reported a previous diagnosis of a mental health condition, while physical and cognitive impairments are also significantly more prevalent than in the general population.[28] Several reasons are put forward for the mass incarceration of people with disabilities, including selective enforcement, repeated arrests for low level offences, and inadequate provision of community treatment.[29] The result is a constant flow of people with disabilities in and out of the prison system on short sentences. HRW found that in many countries the conditions for prisoners with disabilities are extraordinarily harsh and degrading. For example, in South Sudan, individuals were imprisoned for being said to show evidence of mental ill-health or cognitive impairment. Very few were accused of a criminal offence, and they could not appeal their imprisonment. Many had no release date. 'Some of these prisoners are chained day and night while naked and soiled in excrement, unable to access proper health care'.[30] In Uganda, those incarcerated in rural prisons are required to work the land for the profit of prison governors or contracted to private landholders. 'The elderly, individuals with disabilities, and pregnant women, are frequently caned, or are even stoned, handcuffed to a tree, or burned, when they refuse to perform hard labor'.[31]

While a key argument presented here is that the incarceration of people with disabilities is dependent on police intervention in the first instance, it is also important to recognise that the resulting confinement can take place outside the prison. Police play a role in sending people to private and state-based institutions and faith-based centres where they are kept in abusive situations. Police can also put pressure on families to shackle and imprison family members. One mother in Bali, Indonesia shared with HRW why she had chained her son with mental ill-health for over 10 years:

> We took Ngurah to more than 40 traditional healers where they poked him with a stick and put herbs in his eyes but it didn't work. We didn't know what to do. When Ngurah kept getting lost, the local police and community blamed and put pressure on us. We felt ashamed so we decided to chain him.[32]

In India it has been noted that there are various institutions where people with disabilities are incarcerated, including 'mental hospitals' and residential facilities. The majority of States have 'Beggars' Homes' which are used to detain people. Disability advocacy organisations have affirmed that:

> Many 'beggars' homes' have been converted into 'old age homes' or 'disabled homes', where people who are homeless, elderly or destitute and people with disabilities are 'lumped' together without any reasonable accommodation, services or care. The Beggary Act does not provide for minimum standards, safeguards or monitoring. ... The role of the police in 'round up' operations which ensure people are taken forcibly to these institutions has been observed.[33]

In India, as elsewhere, there are many accounts of police violence against people with disabilities. The institutions are over-crowded, dirty, and lack sanitation; those detained are subjected to abuse, prolonged detention, involuntary treatment, and violence.[34]

Police fatal shootings and other violence

The *Washington Post* database on police fatal shootings shows that between 2015 and September 2021, some 23 per cent of those killed had a mental illness.[35] More broadly it has been estimated that between one third and one half of people killed by police in the US have mental ill-health, cognitive impairment, or other disability.[36] Other studies in Australia, Canada, and the UK on fatal police shootings indicate similar findings.[37] Some of the independent data collections put the figures even higher: the Deadly Force database in Canada estimated that during 2000–2020 some 68 per cent of people killed in police encounters had mental health or substance abuse problems, or both.[38] Although it is difficult to locate police use of force data involving people with disabilities, there are investigations which suggests a significant problem. For instance, the US Department of Justice, Civil Rights Division investigations of the Baltimore, Ferguson, and Seattle Police Departments all found extensive and unnecessary force against people with disabilities, and the New York City CCRB examination of taser-related complaints against the NYPD between 2014–17 found that a significant number of cases involved complainants 'who appeared to have been in the midst of a mental health crisis' at the time they were tasered.[39] Research in Victoria, Australia, found that police were more than twice as likely to use OS spray against people with mental illness.[40]

Disability intersects with other social categories of race, class, gender, and sexuality to magnify marginalisation and to increase the risk of police violence.[41] Black, Indigenous, and other racialised communities are over-represented among police killings of people who are in a mental health crisis or have cognitive disabilities in the US, the UK, Australia, and Canada. In England and Wales, the Runnymede Trust noted that Black and minority ethnic people are twice as likely to feature in mental health-related deaths in police custody than others, and particularly those deaths involving restraint by police officers.[42] In Canada, Black and Indigenous people with mental ill-health are over-represented among those fatally shot by police.[43] In Australia, *The Guardian*'s database Deaths Inside, indicates disproportionate numbers of First Nations people with disability dying in police custody.[44]

A fundamental feature of the lives of criminalised people with disability is that they have also been subjected to frequent and recurring forms of non-state violence, including inter-personal violence and violence in non-prison institutional settings. The rates of violent victimisation are higher than in the general population.[45] These issues come to the fore particularly when considering women with disabilities and their contact with police. Women with disability are almost twice as likely to experience partner violence than other women, and between four and ten times more likely to be sexually assaulted. Around half of women with cognitive disability are sexually assaulted before the age of 18.[46] An investigation of 850 police records of rape allegations in Australia found that cases involving victims with a disability were least likely to lead to criminal charges against an offender and were twice as likely to be rejected as false. A similar examination of rape and sexual assault police files in New Zealand found that of the complaints made by women with cognitive disability or mental ill-health, only 13 per cent were regarded by police as genuine.[47] In India, HRW has reported police inaction and the refusal to register complaints when women and girls with disabilities attempt to report sexual violence, including gang rape.[48] Thus, women with disability experience both violence in the community *and* police violence. The statement of Dorothy Armstrong to the Australian Disability Royal Commission captures this intersection.

> I have an acquired brain injury. ... I first noticed that there was something different about my thinking patterns when I was 16 or 17. I also have mental health issues. I have experienced a lot of physical violence and homelessness during my life. ... My first direct experience with the police was because of someone else's crime. I was 17 years old. ... I called a police station because my handbag had been stolen. I was raped by a police officer who worked on the case. ... After this experience and many more incidents I have

learned to be terrified of police. ... Getting help was challenging. I struggled to get my story right or in the right order. Often police did not believe I was a victim of domestic violence or they did not follow up on my complaint. ... Once I was attacked by three men and went to Geelong Police Station. My clothes were ripped and I was screaming and bloody. A police officer came out and yelled at me to "fuck off".[49]

Low reporting rates to police are compounded by the gendered attitudes held by police – some research suggests two consistently held myths about women with disability: that they are promiscuous and that their stories are not credible. These intersect with other social stigmas including that women with disabilities have less worth than other women, and the gendered stigmas attached to being a female victim of sexual violence.[50] This is further intensified by racist myths that pervade police responses to Black, Indigenous, and women of colour. Assumptions about 'normality' and 'abnormality' infuse police decisions regarding their intervention, the use of violence, and criminalisation. Andrea Ritchie has written eloquently on the tragic consequences of the controlling narratives that frame police interventions into the lives of Black women with disability – for example, their supposed inhuman or superhuman strength – and the role of scientific racism in the conceptualisations of disability and disorder.[51] All these narratives come into play in justifying the police killing of Black, Indigenous, and women of colour – as they did recently in Australia where a police officer shot and killed 29-year-old Yamatji woman 'JC' who suffered from mental ill-health and had been previously imprisoned. During a mental health episode she was surrounded by eight police officers. As she stood there motionless, one police officer killed her with a fatal shot. He was acquitted of murder. The court heard that 'JC' had 'to be taken down' like she was some wild deranged animal.[52]

Unresolved trauma is ubiquitous in the lives of people with disabilities who have survived both criminalisation and victimisation. Experiences of trauma are compounded particularly by gender, race, Indigeneity, and sexuality. Survival techniques and resistance to victimisation may be labelled as offending behaviour and can lead to further criminalisation.[53] Geoffrey Thomas is a 59-year-old Aboriginal man who self describes as having a cognitive brain impairment, psychosocial disability, chronic depression, and other disorders. He provided a written statement to the Australian Disability Royal Commission where he talks about being arrested at age 15 and 'bashed by the police'. Decades of policing, imprisonment, and institutional violence followed.

> I feel like too often police are immediately aggressive toward me and assume the worst about me. ... Authorities in general need to improve the way they deal with people who are experiencing psychosis or serious mental health issues. There is no way that a person in that situation is going to cope with authoritarianism. ... If you start threatening someone who is already feeling mentally and psychologically threatened, they will lose the plot every time.[54]

The medicalisation of disability as abnormality is also used to justify police violence. Disability becomes an underlying medical condition that explains police murder and represents killing as excusable or inevitable. For example, the autopsy report for George Floyd, signalled 'underlying conditions' including hypertension and a previous COVID-19 diagnosis – which enabled an inaccurate narrative that Floyd's disability contributed to his death as opposed to the officer's knee on his neck. Or that a deaf victim who failed to hear a police command to stop was thus 'legitimately' shot and killed.[55] We see this also with the advent of the so-called 'excited delirium syndrome' which is used by police to defend the use of (fatal) force as well as to explain sudden deaths of people in custody. Although it has been raised by authorities to 'explain' many deaths in custody in the US, the UK, and Australia, it has not been medically recognised internationally outside of a small group of doctors in the US. In the UK the Angiolini review of deaths in police custody criticised its use, and in July 2021 the American Medical Association issued a policy advising that it should be avoided in attributing cause of death.[56]

The great misnomer: police welfare checks

One of the greatest misnomers in the history of policing is the idea that police officers can conduct *welfare* checks on vulnerable people, including those suffering from mental ill-health and cognitive impairments. In many countries, police 'welfare checks' or 'wellness checks' on people with disabilities are common. For example, in the UK it has been noted that it is not unusual for a medical practitioner, social services, or other agency to request police to check on someone when they cannot be contacted or have not attended an appointment.[57] Similar use of police is made in the US, Australia, and Canada. It is also common for family and friends to request police to check on someone, or for the person with the disability or mental illness to call police. Canadian data suggests that more than half of all requests to police were made by family, friends, or were self-initiated, rather than by an agency.[58] It is difficult to determine how many of these police checks end in violence, arrest, and in some cases death. However, these outcomes are frequent enough to have become one of the major drivers in the calls to stop police involvement in responses to people with disabilities. As the US-based Consortium for Citizens with Disabilities (representing over 20 key advocacy bodies) has stated, 'stories of people with disabilities killed by police during wellness or welfare checks abound'.[59] Among many examples, the Consortium refers to the death of Osaze Osagie in March 2019, a 29-year-old Black man with autism and schizophrenia, who was shot and killed by police after his father called local police to make a mental health wellness check on him.

In Canada, the deaths of Choudry, Levi, Moore, Korchinski-Paquet, Njoko and Campbell between April and June 2020, *all* arose in the context of wellness checks by police. In response, the Canadian Mental Health Association issued a Statement on Police and Wellness Checks pointing out perhaps what should be obvious, 'mental illness is not a crime'.[60] The Association observed that the deaths were 'the most recent in what has been a terrible history of fatalities involving people in mental health crisis situations. Systemic racism, including anti–Black and anti-Indigenous racism, has gravely increased the risks associated with experiencing a mental health crisis'. In Australia, there are many examples of police killings of people with disabilities after family members have requested help – such as the death of Yamatji woman 'JC' referred to previously.[61] Even where police intervention does not lead to death there are multiple accounts of police violence, arrest, and criminalisation arising from what should be a supportive check on someone's well-being, particularly when a large group of police arrive to 'check' on a single person.[62]

When contrasted with the idea of a *welfare* check on a person with a disability, the violence of policing becomes manifestly obvious. The contradiction between violence and welfare is so overladen that it cannot be ignored and not surprisingly many government and independent agencies have expressed concern over the police role in the 'management' of disability in the community. They have variously aimed to limit or remove police involvement and transfer responsibility to other areas of community and/or government responsibility.[63] Certainly, not all of the organisations calling for change would see themselves as abolitionist in their focus – however, they do clearly argue for removing police from crisis and welfare responses to mental ill-health and disability and for increased funding into the community sector.[64] There is potential for broad-based solidarity in building non-carceral community-based approaches based on principles of care rather than force, and for a significant retraction in the police/carceral state.[65]

Conclusion

In bringing this chapter to a close I want to draw some of the links between policing disability and the idea that policing itself is inconsistent with protecting and enhancing community safety and public health. The relationship between policing and community health can be conceptualised at various intersections. One is the manner in which police violence is itself a public health issue, like other forms of violence such as family and intimate partner violence, or gun violence. In other words, it is a significant cause of death, disability, and ill-health. Second, policing is linked to public health to the extent that policing and criminalisation are brought into play for social issues which could otherwise and more appropriately be responded to as community health concerns, such as mental ill-health and drug and alcohol addiction.[66] Third, policing and criminalisation are key regulatory responses to social and economic conditions which we know to be determinants of ill-health – for example, homelessness and poverty – and indeed further exacerbate these problems through cycles of criminalisation and imprisonment. Finally, policing as an activity *joins* the violence of (dis)ablism with racism, sexism, and other forms of discrimination and exclusion which negatively affect a person's health. By this I simply mean that state violence against people with disability is coupled with racial, sexual, and other forms of violence.[67]

Understanding the connections between disability and policing brings to the fore these public health concerns. A profoundly neglected area has been the extent to which police violence and brutality causes or directly contributes to physical and cognitive disability and mental ill-health. There is a growing public health literature discussing the role of police violence as an individual and community health issue, particularly for Black, Indigenous, and people of colour. In the context of disability and mental health, Alang and colleagues show that death, injuries, psychological stress, racist public reactions, economic stress and systemic community disempowerment can arise from police brutality and racism.[68] More specifically, it is clear that police violence often results in disabilities – this can include for example the number of people who have become blind as a result of being shot with rubber bullets or other projectiles, or have acquired brain injuries or become paralysed as a result of police violence. It can also include those whose mental ill-health was caused by or deteriorated as a result of the trauma of police abuse, including those who have committed suicide as a result.[69]

Many public health practitioners and organisations have increasingly moved towards an abolitionist position. As Deivanayagam and colleagues note: 'We define abolitionist public health as work directed towards the dissolution of the PIC [prison industrial complex], recognition of its discriminatory roots, and the implementation of interventions that tackle the social, economic and political determinants of health at the root of societal problems, thus making policing obsolete.'[70] The American Public

Health Association (APHA) has released two policy statements in recent years relevant to this discussion. In 2018 the APHA released its *Addressing Law Enforcement Violence as a Public Health Issue* policy which notes that law enforcement violence is a critical public health problem that impacts on marginalised communities. The policy argues strongly for a defund the police and divestment/investment proposition when it calls for the 'reallocation of funds from policing to the social determinants of health'.[71] According to the APHA: 'This type of approach includes increasing access to housing, expanding educational and employment opportunities, increasing access to mental health and substance use treatment, and restoring a sense of safety by addressing interpersonal and institutional factors contributing to perceptions of safety and experiences of discrimination.'[72] At its 2021 Annual Conference, the APHA adopted a more general policy on carceral abolitionism, calling for decarceration, divestment from carceral systems, and investment in the social determinants of health, decriminalisation, and a commitment to non-carceral measures for accountability, safety, and well-being.[73] The final sections of this book pick up on these ideas. Following a discussion of the contemporary failure of police reform mechanisms in Chapter 8, there is more specific consideration in Chapter 9 of limiting, retracting, and eventually replacing police power with a logic and programme of community solidarity and care.

8

The failure of reform

Over the last 50 years, there have been numerous high-profile judicial inquiries, presidential commissions, royal commissions, and national reports into one policing crisis after another across a spectrum of countries. While these reports have varied in terms of scope and specific content, there are many commonalities in the broad focus of recommendations, particularly in the need to change police through a suite of internal police reform mechanisms and improved measures for accountability. The key police reform priorities which are often identified (and endlessly repeated from one inquiry to the next) include enhancing community policing, introducing diversity quotas and recruitment initiatives, technical solutions such as body cameras, a greater reliance on evidence-based policing (EBP), and various measures to improve citizen complaints systems and accountability mechanisms. Added to this catalogue is recommended investment in an the almost never-ending list of training courses: in de-escalation techniques, in cross-cultural awareness, anti-racism and unconscious bias, in the use of force and physical restraints, to identify signs and symptoms of mental illness, in community policing and community-based crime reduction programmes, in responding to domestic violence and sexual assault, and so on.

This chapter turns to the failure of reform and the problem of police reformism. The discussion focuses on the limitations of programmes of reform in affecting meaningful change. Given the number of inquiries and recommendations and the failure of empirical evidence, research, or practice to show significant improvements, it appears to be a case of not learning from continual failure and instead doing more of the same over again.[1] However, in a deeper sense, and from a perspective of the impact on police as an institution, reformism reinvigorates and reinforces the centrality of the institution of policing rather than challenging it. Indeed, police are able to command even greater resources through reforms, and police power is enhanced rather than contested. What we do not see on the reform lists is a recommendation for the retraction of policing. In contrast, the Defund the Police demand has been for divestment of resources from police and investment in community structures. It is a perspective which works towards diminishing police power by questioning the necessity of police – thus unlike reformism, the institutional role of police is no longer seen as unassailable.

The forlorn hope of police inquiries and the liberal reform agenda

The early 1990s saw the publication of prominent, state-funded investigations in response to crises in policing occurring in various countries. In the United States, the Independent Commission on the Los Angeles Police Department (the Christopher Commission) on the beating of Rodney King was published in April 1991. In Australia, the RCADIC was published in the same year. In Northern Ireland, the Report of the Independent Commission on Policing for Northern Ireland was published in 1998, meanwhile the South African Truth and Reconciliation Commission (which dealt with human rights abuses relating to policing in apartheid South Africa among other issues) was established in 1995 and presented its report to government in two parts in 1998 and 2003.

In Britain, the Scarman Inquiry into the Brixton riots had reported in 1981. The Inquiry held that the cause of the riots was unemployment, poverty, and social deprivation. Scarman believed that both community policing and saturation-style militarised policing could co-exist and that solutions to policing could be found in changing police attitudes and prejudices. His recommendations also relied on social and economic reforms (which were ignored) and on an expanded programme of police training on community and race issues and the establishment of community consultative committees. As Sivanandan commented, Scarman failed to recognise the structures of institutionalised racism within British society and his recommendations 'did nothing more than put new gloss over old policies'.[2] Indeed, Stuart Hall noted,

> Scarman put his trust in [police training] as a way of trying to get to grips with the racialization of routine police work. ... Racism Awareness Training ... was so patchily introduced, the trainers so inadequately prepared, the programme so lacking in senior managerial authority or integration into wider policing practices, to be grossly inadequate on the ground to the liberal purpose intended.[3]

Nearly 20 years after Scarman, Macpherson issued his report on the racist killing of Stephen Lawrence and identified the problem of institutional racism. However, the government response did not prioritise the investigation of complaints and accountability, and as Hall commented at this time, "a few Racism Awareness Training films are no doubt at this very moment being prepared ... with the laughably ineffectual results about which we already have overwhelming evidence".[4] Another 20 years after the McPherson report, policing and institutional racism continued to be heavily criticised in the 2017 report by the British member of parliament David Lammy.[5]

In Australia, controversy over the reform of police and criminal legal institutions continues 30 years after the 1991 RCADIC. In 2018, the federal government requested multinational consultancy firm Deloitte to review the implementation of the 339 recommendations from the RCADIC. In what was largely seen as a self-serving exercise for government: Deloitte determined whether recommendations had been implemented based on the assessments and responses of state, territory, and federal governments. Not surprisingly it was found that nearly 80 per cent of recommendations were either fully implemented or mostly implemented – an estimation roundly challenged by academics, media, and human rights organisations. Meanwhile, the over-representation of First Nations people in prison is at record highs, and deaths in police and prison custody continue in situations of violence and neglect similar to those originally identified by the RCADIC.[6]

Of the multiple inquiries that could be referred to in the United States, the focus here is on three reports, each roughly 25 years after the other: the Kerner Commission in 1967, the Christopher Commission in 1991, and the President's Task Force on 21st Century Policing in 2015. The National Advisory Commission on Civil Disorders (the Kerner Commission) was appointed by President Johnson to inquire into riots across 23 American cities during the mid 1960s. The Kerner Commission recommendations included improved community policing and strategies to enhance community support and legitimacy, recruitment of Black Americans into the police, reviews of training, and improvements to police complaints mechanisms.[7] The recommendations also included wider use of non-lethal weapons and chemical agents as methods of riot control. In addition, Kerner made recommendations to address racial and economic inequality, which were largely ignored. However, some of the Kerner Commission's recommendations relating to police and what Johnson was increasingly referring to as a 'war on crime' were acted upon. According to Schrader, the increased allocation of federal funding to police, with bipartisan support, laid the 'foundations of the carceral state: aggressive policing, mass incarceration, and the engulfing of the state's welfare capacities by penal demands', all in the name of police reform.[8]

The Independent Commission on the Los Angeles Police Department (the Christopher Commission) was established following the beating of Rodney King in 1991. The Christopher Commission found there was a significant number of LAPD officers who repeatedly used excessive force against the public and that the problem of excessive force was aggravated by racism and bias. Recommendations from the Commission followed a well-trodden path designed to address improvements in training (including cultural awareness), diversity recruitment, complaints and disciplinary procedures, and various management issues. Failure to adequately implement the recommendations, particularly those related to accountability, were noted during the 1990s.[9]

After the police fatal shooting of Michael Brown in Ferguson, Missouri, President Obama established the President's Task Force on 21st Century Policing. The Task Force was given 90 days to 'identify best policing practices and offer recommendations on how those practices can promote effective crime reduction while building public trust'.[10] It reported in 2015. The President's Task Force identified six 'pillars' around which it organised the report and recommendations: building trust and legitimacy, policy and oversight, technology and social media, community policing and crime reduction, training and education, and officer wellness and safety. As several commentators have noted, the reforms were familiar territory: better training, police–community relations, diversification, and various other procedural tweaks.[11] The priority of trust and legitimacy belied a conservative approach that focused on strategies to ensure that citizens trusted the police and obeyed the law, and was not directed at fundamentally changing policing. As noted at the time, the solutions proposed by the Taskforce 'will strengthen police, expand their budgets and insulate them from public criticism. ... [T]he reforms are designed to increase the legitimacy of the police. But they will also make the police's powers more extensive'.[12]

The focus on trust and legitimacy in the 2015 Taskforce Report was perhaps not surprising. In late 2014, the US Department of Justice had launched the National Initiative for Building Community Trust and Justice in six locations with the aim of improving relationships and increasing trust between communities and the police and justice agencies. One of those sites was Minneapolis. As Robin D.G. Kelley observed, these reforms have not made communities safer, despite the fact that, prior to the police killing of George Floyd, 'the city's police department was a poster child of reform. Minneapolis's diverse force was well-trained in mental health crisis intervention, implicit bias, de-escalation, and praised for being exceptionally compassionate'.[13]

In a nutshell, the liberal reform agenda sets out to strengthen policing, not to primarily challenge it. It does not question the nature and role of police power in upholding and protecting the structural inequalities and systemic abuses embedded within society. The liberal reform agenda has absolutely no sense of history, either of the institution of police nor of its own continually failing agendas. The inadequacies of the liberal reform agenda are what makes it so appealing to the institutions it seeks to reform, because it inevitably strengthens them through *more* human, financial and technological resources to support the ongoing institutional systems of power. US President Joe Biden captured this liberal agenda in his 2022 State of the Union Address, 'We should all agree: The answer is not to defund the police. It's to fund the police. Fund them. Fund them. Fund them with resources and training'.[14] If more public money is continually thrown at police for reform, we should question the nature of the reform agenda.

Diversity

The proposal to increase diversity within police ranks has a long history. One form of it dates back to the late 19th and early 20th centuries in relation to employing more women in police forces to better respond to needs of women citizens.[15] The rationale is the same today: if we could employ more women, LGBTQIA+, Black, Indigenous, ethnic, religious or cultural minoritised groups within the police, then the organisation will change the way it works to be more reflective of the needs of citizens, and as a result, increase its overall legitimacy and trust among the wider population. Further, the reforms can have a common-sense appeal to them: take a recent example from India published in the *Hindustan Times*, which describes the importance of diversity for Indian police: 'Not being inclusive and not having adequate representation from diverse communities adversely affects police response and performance especially in its dealing with marginalised sections of society. Access to justice for such disadvantaged communities becomes more difficult.'[16]

There are several major problems with this approach. First, for a variety of reasons, most police forces seem incapable of diversifying their recruitment. Moreover, there is an expedience to this approach – such as putting up a few posters or running some recruitment advertising campaigns – that does not require substantive change to the organisation. Second, it ignores the historical function of policing which has adversely targeted and terrorised the very groups it now seeks to include. Third, the assumption that diversification changes the policing of diverse groups within the community, or indeed changes policing more generally, seems dramatically misplaced. There is an essentialism to the basic idea that identity based on gender or ethnicity or race will trump institutional culture and practices, rather than become absorbed into the fabric of police work regarding, for example, stop and searches, the use of force, profiling and the targeting/overpolicing of particular types of offences, social groups, neighbourhoods, or other locations.

There are many examples that could be used to illustrate the problems with achieving diversification. In India there are reserved positions within police forces for scheduled castes (Dalit), scheduled tribes (Adivasi), and 'other backward classes'. In addition, the Ministry of Home Affairs require State governments to increase the representation of women to at least 33 per cent of the police force. Only a small minority of the 28 States and eight Union Territories have filled their reserve quotas, and the proportion of women in police forces nationally is 12 per cent.[17] At the present rate of change it will take decades for many States, and in some cases more than 100 years, to meet the target for women officers.[18] The marginalised groups that are recruited into the police remain concentrated in the lower echelons of the force, and reflect the broad social, political, and economic hierarchies of power in Indian society. A particular colonial relic has been preserved whereby constables are required to work as orderlies (essentially personal servants) for senior officers, thus reinforcing their subservience.[19] These problems of recruitment, racism, and entrenched discrimination within the police are hardly particular to India. In Australia, First Nations people are under-represented by about one third in the composition of the nation's police.[20] In addition, there is a long history of complaints of racist treatment towards Aboriginal officers within the police service.[21] It is not surprising that employment targets are not met. Furthermore, if police power reproduces caste, class, gender, and racial divisions within the institution, as in both the Indian and Australian examples, why would we expect police practices towards the public to be fair and inclusive?

What happens though when police forces do diversify? In the US, the composition of police forces is roughly equal to the national population figures, particularly for Black and White officers. Alex Vitale has reviewed the evidence on whether the racial background of an officer affects the use of force. He concludes that 'most studies show no effect ... a few indicate that black officers are more likely to use force or make arrests, especially of black civilians'.[22] At a departmental level, 'More diverse police forces fare no better in measures of community satisfaction, especially among nonwhite residents. ... Both New York and Philadelphia have highly diverse forces ... both have come under intense scrutiny for excessive use of force and discriminatory practices such as "stop and frisk"'.[23] As discussed in previous chapters, individual policing involves discretion, but it is also driven by operational priorities set by local, divisional, and departmental directives which are themselves guided by the broader political context of crime control policies. Tough on crime and law and order agendas inevitably target poor, working-class and racialised communities. The nature of police power does not change because an officer is a woman or Black.

Training

After half a century or more of recommendations for improved police training, we might have expected that various public inquiries would have grown tired of recommending more of the same. However, like appeals to diversity, the expectations that training will improve policing and resolve problems of racism, violence, and discrimination remains deeply embedded in the liberal agenda for reform. It's an easy recommendation to make – one that involves little thought, can be applied to almost anything, and gives the appearance of addressing the issue in a practical, achievable and measurable way. Most importantly it does not upset anyone unnecessarily (particularly senior police and police unions) and is good for business – police receive more resources, consultants and trainers make money, and police can claim greater professionalism. However, the evidence of effective change is far from compelling.

Stuart Hall's scathing comments on British attempts at 'Racism Awareness Training' during the 1980s and 1990s were cited previously. Yet, advocates continue to promote anti-racism, diversity, and implicit bias training. In relation to the US, the research indicates this training has no long-term impact on problems 'like racial disparities in traffic stops or marijuana arrests; both implicit and explicit bias remain'.[24] While anti-bias training may impact for short periods of time, it does not last. Many police officers, including those involved in police killings, have received various de-escalation, anti-bias and cultural awareness training. For example, the NYPD implemented anti-bias and de-escalation training, and over half of the patrol force has been 'certified in a crisis intervention training involving de-escalation techniques'.[25] In 2018, NYPD officers had implicit bias training as part of a $4.5 million contract with Fair and Impartial Policing.[26] A later evaluation found that while police had a greater awareness of bias and discrimination, there was no reduction in disparities in enforcement.[27] Part of the problem is that strategies like ZTP will inevitably focus on low level offending by poor people, which will also more likely be Indigenous, Black, or communities of colour. As Alex Vitale remarks, that's not because of the biases or misunderstandings of police officers, it 'is how the system is designed to operate'.[28]

Much of the other training in police academies and in the field militate against de-escalation training. Indeed, in the case of the killer of George Floyd, officer Derek Chauvin was an operational field trainer at the time.[29] Particular use of force techniques like chokeholds may be banned by police departments, but still used in practice, as was the case in the police killing of Eric Garner. Further, it is not only use of force but who it is used against – as demonstrated throughout this book, lethal and non-lethal violence is directed against racialised and marginalised groups. Human Rights Watch suggests that legal changes such as those introduced in New York state after the death of Eric Garner which prohibit the use of chokeholds, 'while welcome, will likely have little effect on policing because they rely too much on an officer's easily abused discretion and, without more fundamental changes, can be replaced by other easily abused uses of force'.[30]

Indeed, part of the problem with police training is the over-emphasis on deadly force. Various commentators have detailed the use of independent training companies in the US that train both police and military personnel and emphasise 'military-style approaches and the "warrior mentality"'.[31] In addition, there is the number of serving police who were former military personnel. This issue came to the fore in Australia during 2022 when a former soldier and then a Northern Territory police officer Zachary Rolfe was charged with murder after shooting dead a 19-year-old Aboriginal youth Kumanjayi Walker from Yuendumu while the youth was being held down by another police officer. He was acquitted by a jury with no Aboriginal members. Rolfe had a history of multiple assaults on Aboriginal people during arrest, of allegedly falsifying reports in three of the incidents, and negative comments about his honesty by a judge.[32] Ex-military recruits are sought after by police services in many countries, and may be offered waivers on certain requirements, given other preferential recruitment, and provided with additional benefits. It is difficult to locate the number of ex-military serving in police forces, although research from the US shows that 19 per cent of police officers are veterans and that it is the third most common occupation for veterans after truck driving and management.[33] A national survey of police officers in the US also found that 28 per cent reported current or prior military service.[34] US research indicates that former military personnel are significantly more likely than other police to have fired their weapons while on duty, are over-represented among police who have had use-of-force complaints filed against them, and are over-represented in fatal police shootings.[35]

One area of substantial discussion on police training relates to people with a disability. As noted in Chapter 7, this has become particularly relevant in recent years because of the significant number of people with disabilities killed by police, especially during what are meant to be welfare checks.[36] Reforms to policing have focused on changes to police training, operational procedures, and guidelines, and have proved to be completely inadequate because they misunderstand the nature of policing – particularly when non-compliance escalates the police response.[37] The Police Accountability Project observes that in Victoria, Australia, the police Operational Safety and Tactics Training and more specifically the Tactical Options Model reinforce the problem, 'When a person who police are interacting with becomes distressed, upset, argumentative, swears or otherwise displays uncooperative behaviours, police "scale-up" their response accordingly. This escalated response then prompts further distress, fear or anxiety, to which police respond to accordingly'.[38] Added to the problem has been an increasingly armed and aggressive police response to people with disabilities despite decades of reform attempts.[39] There appears to be no evidence that police disability awareness training has improved the knowledge and skills of police officers: a systematic review of the published literature on training provided to police officers found limited evidence for the effectiveness of police disability sensitivity programmes.[40] The prevalence of people with disabilities in police shootings and as victims of other police violence does not appear to have reduced in frequency despite various training programmes.[41] Changes to training also does not appear to have impacted on police responses to people with disability who have been victims of sexual violence, particularly women.[42]

A further area where there has been constant demand for improved police training, with seemingly poor results, has been in response to domestic violence. As noted in Chapter 6, criminal justice responses have been ineffective and negatively impact on First Nations, Black, and other minoritised women and men. Although the need to improve police training is a constant refrain, research indicates that police culture impacts on decision-making around domestic violence through, for example, the 'pervasive, stereotypical assumptions about victim behaviour' and whether there is 'visible or physical violence'.[43] A US National Institute of Justice Report found that general domestic violence training for police does not necessarily change attitudes toward domestic violence or, more important, change police behaviour.[44] As Goodmark has observed,

> Hundreds of millions of federal dollars have already been committed to the training of police officers on domestic violence, with equivocal results for people subjected to abuse. ... Resources should be used on services for people subjected to abuse instead of continuing to pour money into police coffers for training that does not seem to fundamentally change the quality of the law enforcement response to domestic violence.[45]

The focus on training diverts attention away from larger questions around the ineffectiveness of policing and criminalisation approaches to domestic violence because it disregards 'the structural issues that drive abuse, and that rob women of autonomy and ignore women's needs'.[46] These questions go to the heart of the problem of police reform through training. It takes no account of the role of police as an institution in maintaining inequality: economic, racial, ableist, and gendered. It ignores the deeper cultural values that underpin policing – embedded ideas of the legitimate victim, the stereotypical offender and what 'real' crime looks like. And there is the tangible problem of what the Australian RCADIC referred to as a failure of the duty of care, or what Vitale calls a 'problem of values' which we see writ large over and over in deaths in police custody – it is the sheer indifference by police to a person's well-being and whether they live or die.

Technologies and techniques

Technical fixes for police abuse are also popular – the idea that the deployment of 'less than lethal', 'non-lethal', and other technologies will improve policing. It was advocated by the Kerner Commission in the US back in the mid 1960s with the use of tear gas, and has been furthered ever since: tasers, CS spray, and now body cameras are the most recent development. The two basic points in relation to technical fixes like tasers are that firstly, they are in fact lethal and maiming when used incorrectly or abused by police officers, and second, they have supplemented lethal weapons, not replaced them.[47] Chapter 5 has already discussed the misuse of tasers and CS spray by police and the targets of misuse – in particular Black, First Nations, and people with disabilities.

Over recent years, police body-worn cameras have been promoted as a way to ensure the accountability of police. A systematic review of the evidence on body cameras found that they did not have clear or consistent effects on most officer or citizen behaviour,[48] with some studies in the US showing higher rates of civilian deaths where cameras are deployed.[49] Perhaps there is a belief that the footage justifies the action. As a number of commentators have noted, the images are not neutral – they are open to the interpretation of experts through a frame-by-frame analysis which can reconstitute events in particular ways. Further, the cameras individualise interactions and sever them from the socio-political context in which they occur: a police stop may look innocent but it fails to capture the racist targeting of particular individuals – 'the recorded image is never neutral in a racist society'.[50] A major issue is also the lack of police compliance. The *Washington Post* database on police fatal shootings showed that there were body camera recordings of only 14 per cent of 6,578 deaths between 2015 and September 2021.[51] Despite the widespread distribution of body cameras to the NYPD from 2017 onwards, the CCRB complaint investigations confirm that police routinely fail to follow the NYPD policy which requires officers to activate their cameras in various instances. Further, police use various signals to indicate to other officers whether their cameras are activated or not.[52]

The struggle for police legitimacy is not only about the use of technical fixes provided by hardware like body cams and tasers. It is also about policing *techniques* in the broader sense, which involve legitimation through the application of methods and procedures, especially those that can claim authority as being in some way neutral and scientific. ZTP was based on a simplistic and deeply conservative theory which fitted well with police managerialism of the 1990s; it provided a rationale for the allocation of police resources towards less serious public order offences and for the accountability of line managers – not to the public or the policed but to senior managers and politicians who could claim tactical victories in the war on crime, on drugs, on terror, etc. ZTP lives on with variations on 'hot spot' policing and a focus on minor crime in poor communities. However, the modalities of police power and language have changed with the rise of EBP, problem-oriented policing, and predictive policing. According to the blurb of a recent book, 'Evidence-based policing is based on the straightforward, but powerful, idea that crime prevention and crime control policy should be based on what works best in promoting public safety, as determined by the best available scientific evidence'.[53] Problem-oriented policing has some overlap with EBP, and focuses on effectiveness in resolving crime problems. EBP poses the question of what works in policing. A critical approach to EBP is to ask: What works best for whom, and for whom does policing work? While there are multiple critiques of EBP on the basis of its narrow conceptualisations of evidence, it is the wider lack of reflexivity that is questioned by the calls to defund the police. The appeals to evidence and science displace the need to question police power as a requisite condition for maintaining embedded systems of inequality and oppression. Ironically enough, some have called for a greater investment in EBP as a response to the Defund the Police movement with the view that if we know what works and, just as importantly, what doesn't work (like police body cams and anti-bias training), we can create more efficient and accountable police.[54] However, as Betts notes, EBP has reached a hegemonic position in policing which silences and excludes other ideas about policing from consideration, and reinforces state definitions of crime and criminality.[55] Further, EBP assumes that police policy is determined on the basis of rational assessment; and that science itself is neutral. The mathematical 'science' of predictive policing particularly highlights the latter problem.

Predictive policing has emerged with the development of new algorithmic techniques for the predictions of crime which aims to stop crime before it occurs. It relies on data from a range of sources, including, for example, facial recognition technologies, police body cams, video surveillance systems, automatic vehicle number plate recognition and social media data.[56] Various corporations sell software to police departments including Microsoft, Amazon, ShotSpotter, Mark43, and Axon (who are also the major manufacturer of tasers and police body cameras). However, algorithms and AI involve assumptions which have adverse social consequences, particularly for racialised groups – a problem which is evident in various scenarios from the London Metropolitan Police's Gangs Matrix database to the policing of Black teenagers in Melbourne.[57] Ugwudike demonstrates that the 'structural and creational dimensions of prediction technologies … can give rise to racialising effects such as the over-prediction of risks ascribed to racialised people'.[58] The evidence rebuts the liberal ideology of race neutrality and the claim that scientific standardisation eliminates racial bias. In 2020, more than 1,400 US mathematicians signed a petition criticising PredPol, a corporation that produces software for predictive policing, because of racial biases in the software. PredPol software was used by the LAPD.[59] The *Stop LAPD Spying Coalition* showed that:

> The same month LAPD stopped using PredPol, it announced a surveillance framework entitled 'Data-Informed Community-Focused Policing' that claims police will now use mass data to 'measure results, improve efficiency, and provide overall accountability'. Soon after, PredPol reincorporated as Geolitica and undertook a nearly identical rebranding, changing its slogan from 'The Predictive Policing Company™' to 'Data-Driven Community Policing'.[60]

ShotSpotter is another company that has come under scrutiny for its gunshot detection technology, especially after it was linked to the police killing of a 13-year-old boy in Chicago in early 2021. The technology uses acoustic listening devices to identify gunshot locations and relies on algorithms and AI. ShotSpotter is in use in 124 cities and counties mostly in the US, but also in Puerto Rico, the Bahamas, and South Africa.[61] Research based on a study of 68 large US cities found that the results suggest that 'implementing ShotSpotter technology has no significant impact on firearm-related homicides or arrest outcomes'. The authors argue that policy solutions relating to the carrying of firearms may represent 'a more cost-effective measure to reduce urban firearm violence'.[62]

Community policing

An item on many reform lists is community policing, not necessarily as a mechanism for democratising policing, but certainly as a process for building police legitimacy. In the 1980s, it was connected to 'problem solving policing', whereby the police were to build relationships and work with communities to solve local crime problems. However, it was always difficult to see how community policing would sit with the problem of overpoliced racialised, marginalised, and Indigenous communities – especially when these communities see themselves as the object of constant police surveillance, continual stop and searches by police, saturation policing, and intervention by aggressive police paramilitary units.[63] This was a problem that Stuart Hall identified with the Scarman Inquiry back in 1980s, and is just as relevant today: community policing is overridden by racialised and oppressive police practices, and various 'community consultative committees' have very little power to change police practice.[64] Community policing is perhaps the most over-used legitimating idea behind the liberal agenda for police reform. It dates back to the Peelian concept of the London police and has never disappeared from our policing vocabulary since. Yet as demonstrated in this book, it has always been part of a mythology of policing. Community policing was largely irrelevant to colonial policing; and today it is difficult to imagine anything more removed from the community than phalanxes of riot police shooting tear gas, rubber bullets, and at times live rounds into fleeing crowds.

If we fast forward more than three decades from Scarman to President Obama's 2015 Task Force on 21st Century Policing, we find community policing is again a key recommendation. In the same year, the NYPD launched a community policing plan 'One City: Safe and Fair Everywhere' to develop positive police and community relationships. An independent review of the programme found that it had stalled. In commenting on the NYPD plan, HRW observed that:

> activists have found that community policing serves to legitimize and expand the role of police in everyday lives, and contributes to a greater police presence and surveillance without solving the underlying social problems that contribute to crime. Where Human Rights Watch has examined 'community policing' reforms, we have made similar critiques and observed that they tend to emphasize the public perception of police without changing harmful behaviors.[65]

As has been noted often enough, police community consultative committees tend to be hand-picked and do not represent the targets of police interventions. Yet even if they were comprised, for example, of the poor, the homeless, and people with disabilities, it is legitimate to question whether they would have any serious impact on policing strategies. Community policing exists to police the community, not to control the police.[66]

Police accountability

Criminal prosecutions of police officers involved in lethal violence are rare, and convictions even rarer. For example, not one police officer in England and Wales has been found guilty of murder or manslaughter following a death in custody or after police contact since INQUEST started recording deaths in 1990, despite nearly 1,800 deaths either in police custody, through police pursuits or from police shootings.[67] These are global problems. In South Africa, the civilian oversight body, the Independent Police Investigative Directorate (IPID) has been accused of poor investigations and closing cases prematurely to boost its performance indicators, despite a 9 per cent increase in complaints against police.[68] In Kenya, killings by police are unaddressed. The Independent Policing Oversight Authority (IPOA) has been unable to investigate and prosecute over 2,000 incidents of police killings currently on its files. It has managed six successful prosecutions since its establishment in 2011.[69] Similarly, in Ghana, there is a lack of police oversight which continues 'the influence of the colonial militaristic orientation to policing, with its quintessential lack of accountability and respect for the fundamental rights of citizens'.[70] In Malaysia, HRW has outlined deaths in police custody, violence, and abuse of human rights, and the lack of transparency and any meaningful system of accountability.[71]

Accountability and oversight mechanisms are notoriously limited through lack of independence, effectiveness, and legitimacy. In contrast to this reality, the UN High Commissioner for Human Rights has found that because of the heightened duty of care placed on the State for individuals who are deprived of their liberty, there is 'a presumption of State responsibility for deaths in custody which can only be rebutted through a prompt, impartial, thorough and transparent investigation carried out by an independent body'.[72] There is no shortage of regional and international human rights standards and academic literature outlining the effective processes that *should* apply to police accountability mechanisms.

The standards are typically not realised, although some countries fall short of them more than others. We might consider the Independent Police Complaints Council (IPCC) in Hong Kong where the Chief Executive chooses the Chair. After violent police responses to pro-democracy demonstrations in 2019–2020, some 8,000 complaints were filed against police, only 242 were referred to the IPCC and of these only two officers were reprimanded for 'harsh language'.[73] In India, despite a Supreme Court directive in 2006 on police reforms, only one state is fully compliant and two states partially compliant with the Court's directive relating to the establishment of police complaint authorities.[74] Moreover, it is difficult to meaningfully talk about accountability mechanisms in jurisdictions where the use of torture is routine, extrajudicial killings are frequent, and corruption by police, other justice officials, and politicians is commonplace.

There are many hopeful statements on the need for civilian oversight – such as the US President's Task Force on 21st Century Policing who opined that 'there are important arguments for having civilian oversight even though we lack strong research evidence that it works'. The 'arguments' by the Taskforce reiterate the importance of police legitimacy – of paramount concern to those whose primary aim is the preservation of existing policing institutions.[75] Even where multiple mechanisms for oversight exist, these may all fail to deliver accountability. For example, after the violent abuse by the NYPD of protesters in 2020, HRW considered the current available avenues of accountability including internal oversight, independent external oversight bodies (there are three bodies for the NYPD), judicial oversight, and other avenues such as civil lawsuits. It documented their limitations and failings and concluded that

> Despite the harm caused to the protesters, and violations of international human rights law, constitutional civil rights protections, and the NYPD's guidelines, police officers and their supervisors are unlikely to face any disciplinary or legal consequences. This is due to a deeply entrenched system that prevents meaningful scrutiny and allows officers and police departments to commit abuses with impunity. Existing structures

in the United States to hold police officers to account for misconduct and abuses are largely ineffective.[76]

Similarly, in Canada, the NIMMIWG report found that police services are able to 'infringe and violate the human rights of Indigenous women ... without remedy and recourse'. The Inquiry found that existing oversight and accountability mechanisms were inadequate and failed to 'elicit the confidence of Indigenous peoples'.[77]

There are a range of technical questions about the nature of oversight bodies in terms of understanding their effectiveness – are they truly independent (not just institutionally but also culturally and politically), are they resourced properly, can they initiate their own inquiries and investigations (with civilian investigators), are hearings public, and so on.[78] These are important questions, however, there are also issues with criminal prosecutions and civil claims that limit accountability, including the various legal processes in many countries that protect police from successful prosecution or being dismissed from their employment, for example, Law Enforcement Officers Bills of Rights, qualified immunity or immunity when acting in good faith, and the requirement for prosecutions to be approved by government.[79]

Even the best systems of oversight and accountability are often limited by the relative *political* power of police institutions and police associations, and thus the success rate for police complaints remains low. Ultimately the questions of oversight and accountability relate to the nature of policing itself and police power. Increases in policing and police powers, exceptional laws for the various 'wars' on drugs, terror and crime, the apparent easy collapsing of police and military roles, the rise of 'presumptive enemies' who may not have committed offences, and the political champions of always 'more police' have all militated against effective police scrutiny.[80]

Conclusion

This chapter points to the failure of police reform and raises some fundamental questions for advocates of defunding the police and for abolitionists more generally. We know that most police reforms represent stories of constant failure. Yet despite this they are endlessly repeated. Meanwhile, policing is expanding into new terrains on the back of corporations using Big Data for systems of surveillance and control, while also strengthening connections in old terrains including the police/military/colonial nexus. The routine use of violence, the profound racial and other disparities in policing, and the failures of police accountability and oversight challenge policing's foundational legitimating ideologies of consent, fairness, and the rule of law and which underpin liberal agendas of reform. The limits of incremental reforms in bringing about real change are painfully obvious.

The question that arises, then, is how do we respond to police reform? Many commentators have argued that movements for police accountability and reform – like Defund the Police – must look not to 'reform' police, but to reduce their scope and power. At the same time, they should also be working towards transformative justice practices and demanding the provision of jobs, housing, education, and healthcare.[81] Abolitionists speak of an abolition horizon – the future point of police and carceral abolition. Ruth Wilson Gilmore states that abolition is about 'building the future from the present'.[82] This work of building involves strategic decisions about reform – about understanding which reforms take us closer to the horizon of abolition.[83] There is a fault line which ultimately separates abolitionist views of Defund the Police from reformist positions and that is whether the proposed changes expand or contract policing (and the criminal legal system more generally). It is about being able to distinguish between 'reformist' and 'non-reformist' demands for change. Reformism expands and strengthens the existing policing and penal system, rather than challenging it. Indeed, criminal legal institutions are able to command ever greater resources through reformism, and police and penal power is enhanced, not contested. The types of reforms advocated for by various governmental inquiries discussed in this chapter are clearly reformist: greater resources for training, technological fixes, non-lethal alternatives, and various new and old techniques (EBP, community policing, predictive policing, etc).

In contrast to reformism, changes which diminish the role of police include, for example, redirecting calls for service away from police, developing community safety programmes that do not rely on police and penal power, disarming police, and legal and policy changes that decriminalise behaviours or otherwise reduce policing and shrink police and carceral budgets. The importance of any one of these changes is that they are not simply seen as an end in themselves (although the end is a social benefit), but they are contextualised within an overall strategy to replace policing. What we replace policing with is the subject of Chapter 9. For now, though, it is important to recognise that not everything suggested here is clear-cut.

At the mid-point on the Defunding the Police spectrum between abolitionism and reformism, there are multiple ambiguous grey areas. For example, is the democratic control of existing police institutions and an effective system of police accountability achievable? Will prosecuting police officers for murder and other acts of violence ensure justice? There are not always straightforward, definitive answers to these questions. As Mariame Kaba recognises,

> People think you're either interested in reform or you're an abolitionist – that you have to choose to be in one camp or the other. I don't think that way. For some people, reform is the main focus and end goal and for some people, abolition is the horizon. But I don't know anybody who is an abolitionist who doesn't support *some* reforms.[84]

The question of police accountability is probably the most difficult of all, particularly when there is both a widespread demand that civilian oversight boards respond to complaints against police and that police be prosecuted for criminal offences, while at same time recognising the 'justice system' is incapable of actually delivering justice – in fact the *most* it delivers is the furtherance of its own carceral ends through imprisonment. Alternative approaches to achieving justice are required and there is a need to engage in dialogue and reflection that works to build solidarity across various endeavours. We know that collective action and protest outside of the criminal legal system can force governments to respond – however piecemeal that may be. However, collective action can do much more than this in building other ways of responding to the concerns of communities that do not require policing at all.

9

What is to be done?

Before we directly address the question, it is important to restate some of the basic propositions from the Defund the Police movement, and abolitionism more generally. The first is that it is about presence, not absence. It is focused on building the type of society that does not require heavily armed police and mass imprisonment. For Ruth Wilson Gilmore, for example, it is both a long-term goal and a practical policy programme that requires investment in social goods that enable a productive life. 'It's obvious that the system won't disappear overnight … no abolitionist thinks that will be the case'. Reforms are needed, but they need to be reforms that actually change the order.[1] As Patrisse Cullors acknowledges, 'we need to have a *movement around divestment* – to divest from police and prisons and surveillance and to use that money to reinvest in the communities that are most directly impacted by poverty and the violence of poverty'.[2]

The second proposition which is foundational to answering the question of what is to be done is developing a movement built around alliances. The Defund the Police movement has brought together a range of groups across differing perspectives and with various agendas. While there may be a common view on the need to take resources away from police and to expand and develop community responses to social needs, there is less uniformity on the question of abolitionism – that is whether the police and prisons should be abolished. Gilmore has consistently stressed the need for creating and building alliances – the need to build a popular front to make connections and pursue transitional goals: 'Solidarity is something that's made and remade and remade. It never just is', thus it is good practice for 'people engaged in the spectrum of social justice struggles to figure out unexpected sites where their agendas align'.[3] Building alliances also needs to avoid what Davis and Martinez referred to as the 'oppression Olympics'.[4] Building coalitions for challenging, defunding, and moving to abolish the police requires thinking about the connections between groups of people who bear the brunt of state violence, criminalisation, and imprisonment, and the common interests and connections that exist, rather than emphasising hierarchies of oppression. Dean Spade speaks of the need to develop 'a multi-issue and solidarity-based approach because … lives are cross-cut by many different experiences of vulnerability'.[5]

This leads to the third proposition, which is the need for ways of doing things that do not involve police. Mariame Kaba and Andrea Ritchie's disarmingly simple question, 'why are we asking the police to stop being the police over and over again?' belies the greater complexity about alternatives or options.[6] The minimalist view of Defund the Police is that government should reallocate resources away from police to other sectors – supported by arguments such as those at the Brookings Institute that increases in funding for police do not significantly relate to a decrease in crime, but support, for instance, for education and employment does. Or a similar argument in the UK that 'sensible' public policy decision-making requires assessment of the most effective ways of expending public resources.[7] A more significant demand is for a radical democratisation of the state which challenges policing as a practice that occurs beyond the police and the criminal legal system and involves social welfare, child protection, education and health systems in the web of policing Indigenous, racialised, working-class, and other marginalised peoples. Here the political programme is more ambitious and seeks to 'transform the state by building democratic institutions that distribute social, economic, and political power more equitably'.[8] Finally, to what extent do we need to think beyond the state? Mutual aid approaches pursue transformative change by addressing community needs through collective action outside of the state.[9] Further, for decolonial theorists like Mignolo, there is no hope of reforming state processes because the state is a fundamental dimension of the colonial matrix of power. Thus decoloniality, 'is not a task that States could enact'.[10]

The final proposition is the recognition that the state is a colonial state in which the police and the military are core components. Therefore, the struggle to defund the police must be a struggle for decolonisation. The popular challenge to police violence and unaccountability has extended in various forms across most parts of the world, and there is a strong connection between the political and intellectual programmes of abolitionism and decolonialism. This book has argued that the foundations of the contemporary institutions of policing are found in the interplay between the centre and periphery of the colonial experience. However, neither the praxis of decolonialism, nor the programme of Defund the Police, can be universally prescribed – it will be differentiated along a range of axes, determined by historical and contemporary contingencies. Despite the global uprising in 2020 against police and state violence, the profile of BLM and Defund the Police and indeed contemporary abolitionism more generally, has tended to be dominated by the countries of the global north, especially the US. As Angela Davis and colleagues have argued, 'US-centric discourses and organising can saturate contemporary abolitionist political movements, reinforcing and deepening US imperialism and potentially eliding local histories of violence and resistance'.[11] The local histories of police oppression and resistance have been a theme throughout this book.

In summary then, the discussion on practical options to police power is built on the premise of activism in creating solidarity for change across a spectrum of broadly like-minded groups. It sees this struggle as global and decolonial, defined in its specificity by the multiple intersecting groups who bear the burden of police violence and oppression: women, Indigenous peoples, Black and other racialised groups, people with disabilities, and people living in poor, working-class, and overpoliced communities. It calls for imaginative and radical change to remove policing as we understand it through an arrangement of alternative strategies and institutions – not all of which can be laid out in advance.[12]

Practical options/structural change

There is no shortage of practical options[13] for reducing police numbers, police interventions, police budgets, and police power. Many community-based organisations, philanthropic and other research centres, and individuals have provided extensive evidence of viable options for reducing the police presence within society. These are the intermediate steps we can take to reduce policing and restructure our relationships, in Mariame Kaba's words, 'on the way to abolition'.[14] And there are lists of reformist changes that should not be supported because they further entrench police power – including the specific examples of reformism identified in Chapter 8.

It needs to be emphasised that the precise focus of any programme for change is dependent on local historical, political, legal, and administrative contexts which will vary considerably from state to state and country to country – not every item listed here is an issue in every jurisdiction, but many are. Box 9.1 is an amalgamation of multiple sources from activist organisations and scholars working to develop options and programmes for change – it does not claim to be either comprehensive or prescriptive.[15]

Box 9.1: Moving towards a decolonial and abolitionist horizon for policing: some examples

Citizen and community action

- Increase public awareness of the social, health, political, and financial costs of policing.
- Increase public awareness of the failure of police to 'solve crime' and ensure community safety.
- Build open-access databases that identify violent and 'problem' police; cost their drain on the community.
- Build open-access databases that identify key corporate sector interests that support, invest, and profit from policing and the carceral state. Lobby shareholders and promote divestment from these corporations.
- Organise for decreasing police budgets and propose citizen budgets.

- Introduce 'Copwatch' and similar programmes to observe, document, and prevent police violence and harassment.
- Support and promote the use of reparations for victims of police violence.

Replace police through building community-based interventions

- Replace police with civilian centres (such as proposed Offices of Neighbourhood Safety or similar), to coordinate and service community-based alternatives.
- Channel police calls for service away from police to alternative community options.
- Build community-based interventions that address harms and/or provide safety and support without police: for example, non-criminalising responses to gun violence, domestic violence, neighbourhood disputes, homelessness, mental health crises, disability, young people, and drug and alcohol addiction.
- Remove police from schools and provide support services for students and staff.
- Remove police from public transport systems and replace with more transport staff.
- Remove police from motor vehicle and traffic enforcement, and use unarmed civilian traffic management officers (for example, as a local government function).
- Support local justice reinvestment where it is a community developed process for support and change.
- Develop the use of restorative and transformative justice principles and frameworks for addressing harms.

Police administration

- Support suspending the pay of police while under investigation, dismissing police involved in the use of excessive force, and removing their benefits.
- Work to abolish police unions and police bills of rights.
- Separate forensic labs and coronial systems from law enforcement.
- Work to promote elected independent civilian police accountability boards *only* if they have power to challenge the structural power of police,

for example, with a focus on systemic harms caused by police, and the power to re-allocate budget and other resources away from policing and toward other community initiatives.

Disarm and demilitarise the police

- Advocate for disarming police.
- Block new military and surveillance equipment acquisition.
- Withdraw police participation in police/military training and other joint programmes.
- Abolish Border and Immigration police.

Decriminalise particular offences and other legislative changes

- Decriminalise drug offences.
- Decriminalise offences criminalising sex workers.
- Decriminalise offences criminalising people in LGBTQIA+ communities.
- Decriminalise offences that criminalise homeless people and people with disabilities.
- Decriminalise so-called 'quality of life' offences such as begging, panhandling, etc.
- Abolish cash bail and jail time for non-payment of fines.
- Redirect funding from police and prisons to community services.
- Introduce greater police transparency through mandatory reporting on stop and searches, deaths and injuries during arrest and custody, the use of firearms, and non-lethal weapon use.

Indigenous self-determination, sovereignty, and decolonial strategies

- Challenge the sovereignty of the state and the right to police.
- Introduce Indigenous-defined options for developing and maintaining community safety (such as community patrols, supervising community sanctions).
- Introduce anti-violence and healing strategies that respect Indigenous law and culture, and are cognisant of the impact of colonial trauma.
- Replace state systems of child removal with networks of kinship and community care.

Social services and health

- Remove policing functions in child protection and family services.
- Remove policing and criminalising functions in mental health and disability services and settings.
- Remove policing and criminalising functions in social security.
- Remove criminalising policies and practices in public housing.
- Remove policing through forced medicalisation and treatment.

It is not possible in the context of this book to discuss every strategy identified in Box 9.1 and there is considerable literature which already does.[16] Here I provide a focus on a number of general issues and strategies that are particularly important, given the nature of police violence and repression.

Citizen and community action is essential in building support and solidarity for diminishing and removing police presence, and for providing community education around what police do, how much they cost, and what they don't do (solve crime). There are various community education 'toolkits' available in multiple countries, and there is no need to repeat their content here.[17] One area of community activism where there has been less attention is the development of open-source databases, for example, with the development of 'problem police' databases in the US. These include open-source police brutality databases to fill the gap in the lack of public information on a range of issues relating to death and violence caused by officers. As noted in Chapter 5, there are various databases on police killings, but this is only a fraction of the story. For example, the Accountable Now site is collecting data on police use of force from a variety of sources.[18] Databases have been established on police officers accused of misconduct, such as the Citizens Police Data Project in Chicago which identifies individual officers and provides aggregate statistics, including on officers with ten or more complaints against them who generate 64 per cent of all complaints.[19] In New York the Cop Accountability Project has the CAPstat database based on civil rights lawsuits against NYPD. It can be searched by name, badge number, and location.[20] In addition, *The Washington Post* has developed an interactive website on the financial costs of police misconduct to the community.[21] The newspaper collected data on nearly 40,000 payments at 25 of the nation's largest police departments over the last decade and identified more than $3.2 billion spent to settle claims against officers. The database is searchable by city, officers, type of lawsuit, and settlement. A further financial development is bond analysts' calling for the incorporation of the cost of lawsuit settlements for police misconduct, as well as municipal budgets with 'over-reliance' on fines, and indicators in inequality when rating the value of municipal bonds.[22] There is also the opportunity to build divestment campaigns around the corporations that profit from policing, similar to those that name the corporate sector players that profit from prisons and immigration detention.[23]

Disability activists demand an end to policing

Many disabled people all over the world find themselves in situations of precarity: poverty, marginalisation, and confinement. Policing and carcerality are integral to controlling disability globally, but the extent to which they do that and how they achieve these ends differ depending on context.[24] Activist responses vary but are aimed at decarceral options. However, much of the literature on defunding the police and abolitionism in the disability space emanates from the global north. The specificity of this origin does not make it 'wrong', but we also cannot expect that it can be emulated without understanding specific contexts.

One of the most frequently cited community-run and responsive models for mental health crisis support that does not involve police is the Crisis Assistance Helping out on the Streets (CAHOOTS) programme in Eugene and Springfield, Oregon and has been adapted in other parts of the US.[25] It is based on harm reduction and trauma-informed care, and operates as a consensus-based collective. The programme operates 24/7 and dispatches unarmed civilian teams of crisis intervention workers and medics or nurses to respond to emergency and non-emergency calls involving people experiencing behavioural health crises – calls which would normally be directed to police. More than 60 per cent of the clients are homeless, and 30 per cent live with severe and persistent mental illness.[26] CAHOOTS provides a range of functions, including: unarmed de-escalation, crisis counselling, suicide prevention, conflict mediation, grief and loss support, welfare checks, substance abuse support, housing crisis, harm reduction, information and referral, first aid and non-emergency medical care. It also offers connections and transportation to various medical and social services to help support clients' longer-term needs.[27]

The services are non-coercive, and prioritise informed decision-making by the person in crisis. The use of trained civilians who have lived experience of behavioural health conditions as crisis workers highlights the importance of peer responders as an effective and accessible crisis intervention strategy.[28] The most common types of calls diverted from police to CAHOOTS are welfare checks (35 per cent), transportation to services (35 per cent), and for public assistance (66 per cent); some calls may require more than one response type. Of the estimated 24,000 calls responded to by CAHOOTS in 2019, only 150 required police backup – approximately 0.6 per cent.[29] It is estimated that COHOOTS's call out costs are around one third to one quarter the cost of police.[30]

While the CAHOOTS model is US based, there are core principles which underpin the approach that have broader applicability. A fundamental starting point is to avoid the mistake of responding to disability by furthering the criminal legal system through more police training, more specialist courts, more state-controlled diversion programmes, and so forth. There are examples of co-response models to mental health crises in various countries outside the US. However, most still involve police. CAHOOTS shows that only a tiny percentage of requests actually require a police response. The principle at play here is the need to remove police and the criminal legal system from the assistance being offered. The combination of a medic to address medical needs, and a trained peer support worker with lived experience to be able to offer understanding and support and de-escalate a crisis situation are paramount. It is precisely the opposite of police responses which often rely on compulsion and loss of dignity and can easily escalate into force and violence.

Removing police from response teams is an important development, but it does not in itself expand the availability of community-based mental health and other services such as accommodation and support. Services are fundamental. How they are developed, who they are delivered by, and to whom they are accountable are also vital issues. If an approach like CAHOOTS does not have options for further referral and assistance, then the same dilemma of eventual criminal legal intervention and/or forced medicalisation remains. Simply removing police from initial intervention reduces the likelihood of violent encounters but ultimately does not work as a decarceral approach unless there is an increase in available community-based services.

Community responders

Rechannelling calls for police service can take multiple forms, from providing alternative community-based responses to calls about noise complaints, homeless people, people with disability including for welfare checks, as well as property offences and motor vehicle accidents where reports are made essentially for insurance reasons. The principle behind community responders offers opportunities for developing responses to a broader range of issues. Community responders should be 'credible messengers' who have 'strong ties to the community, oftentimes with a personal history of overcoming violence or justice system involvement, who are able to connect to community residents based on their shared background and experiences'.[31]

There are two areas of common calls for service to emergency police numbers where community responders could intervene. First, they could attend calls related to homelessness, behavioural health crises, and substance (mis)use. These calls might currently be classified by emergency dispatchers as wellness checks, disturbances, drug overdoses, intoxicated persons, or mental health crises. These responders would then typically include a peer responder and a paramedic.[32] The second group of calls for service relate to so-called 'quality-of-life' matters and low-level community conflicts that do not require a mental health team. These might include calls that are classified as suspicious persons, disorderly conduct, noise complaints, juvenile disturbances, or trespassing.[33] There has been considerable discussion on how the community responder model works, and practical options of community responder schemes which are already in place.[34] Violence interrupters have been promoted as trained 'credible messengers' who use their social standing to mediate conflict before it escalates.[35] The decriminalisation of public order or 'quality of life' offences and street level drug offences would assist in both removing a police presence and with developing community responder models. It has been proposed that civilian offices of neighbourhood or public safety at city or regional levels could fulfil significant tasks in organising non-police civilian services, such as violence interrupters, transformative mentoring and transitional employment and training for justice-involved residents and in coordinating responses to calls for service.[36]

What is to be done about violence against women?

Aya Gruber, the author of *The Feminist War on Crime*, has commented that:

> The evidence is clear: dialling back aggressive policing, even without other changes, promises to benefit women, especially those living in low-income communities of color. Investing in programs proved to reduce violence and increase victims' well-being, instead of policing, is even better. The question 'What about domestic violence?' is better understood not as a critique of defunding the police but as an argument *for* it.[37]

Like many other areas of more progressive social policy, substantial work has been completed on options for responding to domestic violence which do not involve the police and criminalisation as a stock response.[38] Leigh Goodmark invites us to consider a different path from the criminal legal system that instead incorporates economic, public health, community, and human rights policies. Economic abuse is a form of domestic violence experienced by the majority of women in violent relationships, and economic instability prevents women from leaving abusive relationships. Individual and structural programmes that increase economic security for women are an important alternative to criminalisation policies.[39] Likewise, public health responses to domestic violence can involve prevention and interventions at various points from pre- to post-harm or abuse and at individual and structural or population levels.[40] In 2017, the US CDC published a report on approaches that are effective in reducing domestic violence. The report highlighted social, economic, and environmental programmes which are shown to be effective in reducing violence including prenatal care, housing, employment, free preschool, and access to green urban spaces.[41] Domestic violence and sexual assault also prevents women from realising their human rights as full and equal citizens and the violence also reinforces systemic and intersectional forms of discrimination against minoritised women. As shown throughout this book, the failure of policing and the criminal legal system to protect women from violence is a global problem.

In 2001 a joint statement by INCITE! and Critical Resistance called on social justice movements to develop strategies and analysis that address *both* state and interpersonal violence, particularly violence against women. The statement identified the need to initiate community-based responses to violence that do not rely on the criminal legal system *and* have mechanisms that ensure safety and accountability for survivors of sexual and domestic violence.[42] The statement noted that transformative practices emerging from local communities should be documented and disseminated to promote collective responses to violence. Today, many community-based organisations are working outside of the state and the criminal legal system to stop violence against women, including Sisters Inside in Australia, and Sisters Uncut in the UK. Both organisations are abolitionist and support direct action against state violence and racism as well as domestic violence and sexual assault. Sisters Inside supports sovereignty and self-determination for First Nations peoples in Australia.[43] Sisters Uncut has initiated direct action opposing state violence perpetrated against migrants in detention and through forced deportations. It has also supported First Nations' struggles for sovereignty and protest movements in Canada.[44]

In the US, organisations such as Sista II Sista, the Coalition Against Rape and Abuse (CARA), the Audre Lorde Project's 'Safe Outside the System', Survived and Punished, and INCITE! are working within transformative justice frameworks to respond to domestic and sexual violence in ways 'that address social as well as individual accountability and transformation, and that do not reinforce or funnel more resources towards the main perpetrators of sexual, gender, racial, colonial, and class violence—the police and the carceral state'.[45] Although not necessarily abolitionist in their outlook, other sexual assault and domestic violence organisations are promoting options that shift the focus away from policing and criminalisation. In June 2020, some 46 sexual assault and domestic violence state coalitions signed the 'Moment of Truth' statement which called for reframing the idea of public safety, removing police from schools, decriminalising survival, providing safe housing for everyone, and investing in care, rather than police.[46]

Many Indigenous women have argued that stopping violence against women must simultaneously involve opposition to the violence of the colonial state – that a decolonial position and advocacy for Indigenous sovereignty and self-determination are essential. Sarah Deer of the Muscogee (Creek) nation argues for a synthesis of safety and sovereignty whereby tribal communities can respond to and address crime in a culturally appropriate way.[47] Not all First Nations positions will be completely abolitionist, but at a minimum many demand the removal of policing as a first response, and do not see incarceration as a solution. In Australia there has been strong First Nations support for 'on-country' or place-based approaches to domestic and family violence. Work with communities across northern Australia found that programmes were needed which were underpinned by social and emotional well-being, and which focused on a range of issues facing Indigenous people, including 'unresolved grief and loss, trauma and abuse, domestic violence, removal from family, substance misuse, family breakdown, cultural dislocation, racism and discrimination, and social disadvantage'.[48]

As Figure 9.1 shows, Aboriginal Law and Country are at the centre of responses, immediately followed by Indigenous practices that support and strengthen Law and Country. As one moves further away from the centre of the circle, non-Indigenous responses become more visible with, finally, non-Indigenous justice institutions like the police, courts, corrections, youth justice, and child protection agencies essentially outside the circle. Female and male Elders and respected persons need to be at the

Figure 9.1: Placing law and country in the centre

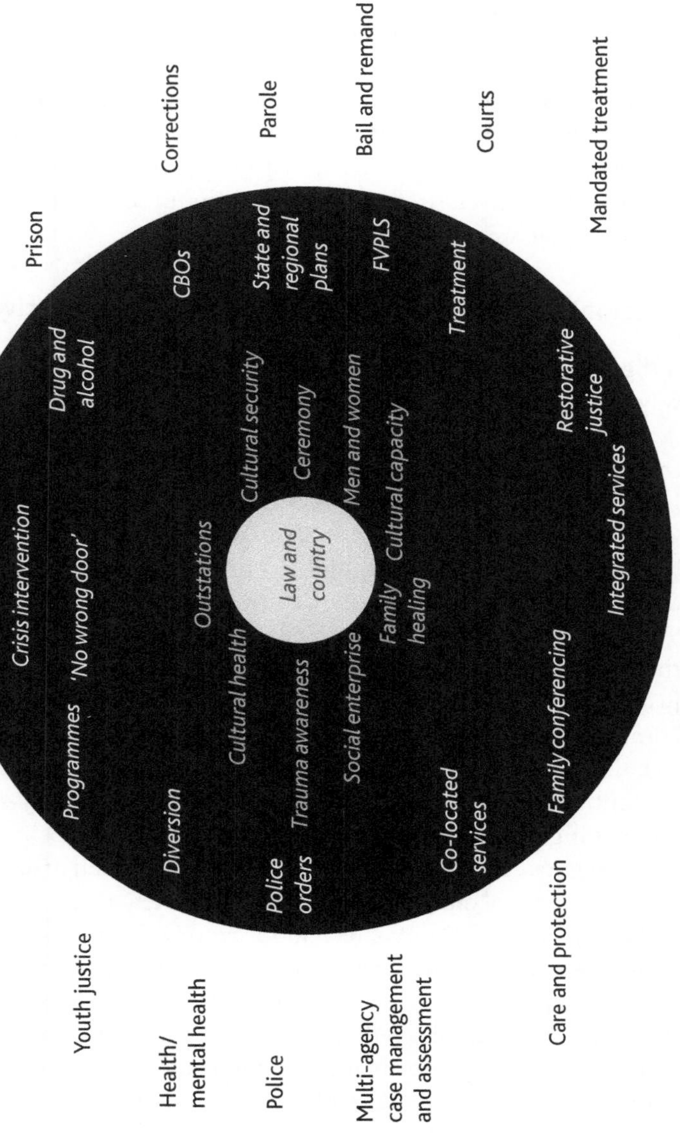

Law and country

Cultural security
Ceremony
Men and women
Family
Cultural capacity
healing

Outstations
Cultural health
Trauma awareness
Social enterprise

Programmes
'No wrong door'
Crisis intervention

Drug and alcohol
CBOs
State and regional plans
FVPLS
Treatment

Diversion
Police orders
Co-located services
Family conferencing
Integrated services
Restorative justice

Prison
Corrections
Parole
Bail and remand
Courts
Mandated treatment

Youth justice
Health/ mental health
Police
Multi-agency case management and assessment
Care and protection

Source: Blagg et al, 2018: 60. Reproduced with permission – CC BY 4.0.

181

centre of intervention wherever possible, and there needs to be greater recognition of the important role Aboriginal-controlled interventions play in preventing family and domestic violence. Mainstream systems should defer to Indigenous organisations and any role for non-Indigenous institutions must be peripheral to Aboriginal justice: 'Achieving meaningful reductions in family violence hinges on a decolonising process that shifts power from settler to Aboriginal structures', that utilises Aboriginal law and culture, and involves 'strengths-based and community-led solution solutions that are culturally safe'.[49]

Decolonial and Indigenous community defence initiatives

Indigenous activism has been fundamental to challenging the way state police operate, and it has also been at the forefront of developing various autonomous or semi-autonomous modes of Indigenous community safety. There is a perception among many Indigenous people that western criminal justice interventions are 'extremely poor at dealing with the underlying causes of criminal behaviour and make a negligible contribution to addressing the underlying consequences of crime in the community'.[50] The failures of these interventions are manifold. They fail at the symbolic level because there is little or no ownership of justice institutions, including police; they fail by escalating community disorder when imprisoned men and women return to communities even more traumatised than before; and they fail by continuing to separate Indigenous families – which is seen as an ongoing strategy of colonialism.

Indigenous communities have a right to security, and practices of maintaining social order are required to legitimately support, ensure, and maintain community safety and harmony. While Indigenous people deserve the same level of community safety as other people, 'what remains an issue is the way this security is provided: how it is structured and administered; how it is embedded culturally; how, and to whom, it is made open and accountable'.[51] Developing and extending Indigenous modes of community safety have become an important part of Indigenous governance and capacity-building often at a localised level. They have developed in response to ineffective and colonising state police who are seen as violent, oppressive, and lacking both political and cultural legitimacy. In some settler colonial states, such as Canada and Australia, the challenge by Indigenous people has extended to contesting the sovereignty of the colonial state over Indigenous people – thus denying the foundational legitimacy of the state criminal legal system.[52] In other states such as South Africa and Zimbabwe, it has been noted that Indigenous bottom-up approaches have developed to provide security when policing services are either unavailable, ineffective, corrupt and/or violent and more broadly when 'state policing falls short of providing security for citizens as it remains deeply rooted in colonial practices'.[53]

There are a wide variety of justice approaches that are organic to Indigenous communities and include, among others, reintegration/diversionary projects, holistic healing programmes, various anti-violence strategies, Indigenous sentencing courts, community justice groups, justice reinvestment projects, community patrols, and safe houses. These justice strategies seek to enable more effective responses to sanctioning, community reintegration, rehabilitation, social and emotional well-being, and trauma healing.[54] They draw their legitimacy from Indigenous culture and the collective right to self-determination (as found in the UN Declaration on the Rights of Indigenous Peoples) For example, contemporary First Nations community safety patrols question the way state policing is built on bureaucratic authority and the threat or use of violence. The patrols represent a different vision of community engagement and authority to state-based police: the external authority of the state is replaced by local cultural authority; and bureaucratised state-centred methods of crime control are replaced by an organic approach to community need which focuses on assistance, prevention, mediation, and persuasion rather than reactive force.[55]

The work of community patrols requires us to rethink the concept of policing as it is understood within dominant criminological and legal discourses.[56] The colonial logic of policing founded in the constant potentiality of state violence and imprisonment is replaced with a different logic of care, of thoughtfulness and sensitivity to community and individual needs – community patrols are a form of counter policing.[57] They are consistent with decolonial and abolitionist calls to replace current policing practices with community control, interventions that promote harm reduction, individual and community well-being, and social justice. Another innovative development in Australia has been a radical reinterpretation of justice reinvestment (JR) by Aboriginal communities as a way of building and exercising local authority over justice issues and which aligns with the collective right of self-determination. Indigenous approaches 'transform an understanding of the [JR] process beyond simply a technocratic means of crime control and decarceration, to one that is centrally concerned with Indigenous controlled governance'.[58] In this approach the community defines the core problems for maintaining social order and the best way to respond to those issues.[59]

Changing drug policies

The war on drugs has taken a shocking toll on human lives globally, from the police killings in places like Brazil and the Philippines, to the vast numbers of people imprisoned for drug offences or drug-related crimes internationally and often serving extraordinarily long (mandatory) sentences. Internationally, more than 30 countries have the death penalty for drug offences, with China, Vietnam, Saudi Arabia, and Iran among the most frequent executioners. In addition, there is the distortion of local economies and the profound corrupting influence on political and governmental institutions (including the police, military, and judiciary). As many have argued, the war on drugs has only ever been tangentially related to stopping illicit drug use. Rather, it has been about extending and ensuring imperialism, it has been about supporting corrupt and violent regimes, and it has been concerned with exercising control over Black, Indigenous, racialised, and poor communities. As Carvalho has commented in relation to Latin America, 'If the intent is to reward corrupt actors while propping up arms manufacturers, the prison industry and entrenched law enforcement bureaucracies, then the war on drugs has been successful'.[60] The Global Commission on Drug Policy found two prominent outcomes of the war on drugs were: 'The growth of a huge criminal black market, financed by the risk-escalated profits of supplying international demand for illicit drugs; [and] extensive policy displacement, the result of using scarce resources to fund a vast law enforcement effort intended to address this criminal market.'[61] Policing has, either as matter of policy or convenience, inevitably targeted those on the bottom-rung – consumers, small-scale farmers, low-level dealers, and carriers – who are the easiest targets without the power, influence, and money to ensure their freedom.[62] These insights are not new. In the US context, Michael Tonry argued in 1995 that drug legislation was racist because it heavily criminalised some drugs (ice) over others (cocaine) and had a foreseeable impact of massive disparities in arrests, convictions, and imprisonment for Black Americans.[63] The war on drugs also has a gendered impact – in many countries in Asia and Latin America, convictions for drug offences are the main cause of imprisonment for women, mostly for low level offences such as transporting drugs. In 2018 the UN estimated that 35 per cent of women in prison worldwide were incarcerated for drug offences, compared to 19 per cent of men. There is also the collateral punishment of their children.[64] In addition, when police have instigated localised 'crackdowns' on drug markets, research in Australia, the UK, and the US has found that levels of violence (including homicide) increase.[65]

Progressive reform to policing and drug laws is not difficult to conceive. The central aim should be to make policing irrelevant to drug policies. Decriminalising drug use, possession, and low-level sales is a first step in getting police out of the drug enforcement industry. Decriminalisation also impacts on the illicit drug market. Removing the large profits that can be made from the sale of illegal drugs can dramatically change both the market and the dynamics of political and law enforcement corruption. In the context of Defunding the Police, it has been estimated that globally over US$100 billion is spent annually on drug law enforcement. In contrast in 2019, US$131 million was spent on harm reduction in low- and middle-income countries.[66] Beyond decriminalisation, what is needed is a public health approach of harm reduction in the community for drug users which is led by peers with lived experience and that rejects forced treatment, drug detention centres, and imprisonment.[67] There are multiple programmes and approaches to providing support: needle and syringe programmes for safe injecting, pill testing, help lines, therapeutic treatment centres,

Hepatitis C testing and treatment, providing support for people with complex trauma, and school education to name only some. Although not perfect, Portugal has long been held as an example of a decriminalised approach to drug policy.[68] In those countries where people are detained by police when affected by alcohol there is also a need for a public health approach that removes intoxicated people from police control.[69] Second, there needs to be alternative opportunities for those in poverty and dependency who form the never-ending supply of low-level workers for the drug trade, as well as alternative livelihoods for the small farmers, sharecroppers, and day labourers dependent for their survival on supplying the narcotics trade. Simultaneously, it is also necessary to recognise the long history to the traditional cultural, medicinal, and ceremonial uses of coca, opium, and cannabis which is 'still widespread in many places around the world today among Indigenous peoples, minorities and religious groups'.[70]

The problem is not one of finding solutions, it is rather the absence of political commitment by governments domestically and internationally who find adherence to punitive law and order policies more attractive irrespective of their staggering human and financial cost.

Disarm and demilitarise

Discussion of drug policies leads directly to the question of militarisation and policing. In previous chapters, the international role of the US in financing and training of police and military has been noted, including police training conducted by the military, and military forces themselves being trained in internal security matters, with the functions of both being blurred.[71] However, there has also been extensive discussion in earlier chapters of the historical and contemporary intersections between colonial policing as militarised and the failure to reform the colonial structure of policing. Although there may be variations at different times – for example in South Africa, the attempted demilitarisation of the police after the end of Apartheid in 1994 and the more recent remilitarisation since 2009 with increased state repression and rising police violence and deaths in custody – the basic problem of police power within colonial contexts remains. In the

South African example, the police have changed from ensuring the privilege and control of the White minority to a new war on the poor presented as a 'war on crime'.[72] We need to be careful, as Neocleous suggests, to not perpetrate the myth that police power is separate to military/war power or that it can be fair, legitimate, transparent, and just.[73]

Having said that, how can we approach the question of what is to be done? What political demands and policy options are there to decrease police power? Reducing the lethality of police is part of the larger struggle of constraining and ultimately removing the institutional structures of policing. The issue of the militarised profile of the police was clearly brought to the fore during the global protest movements in 2020. For those protesters facing heavily armed police equipped with military hardware, the argument that police have always had a domestic militarised role can seem unhelpful. Certainly, police can kill without weapons, *vide* George Floyd. However, the ready availability of lethal weapons is also clearly related to killing and maiming by police. Towards the end of 2021, medical journal *The Lancet* published an editorial on fatal police violence as a public health issue in which it identified strategies to reduce police violence. Of relevance here is that these strategies 'must include demilitarisation of police forces, but with the broader call to demilitarise society by, for example, restricting access to firearms'.[74] As was noted in Chapter 5, we know that in countries where police are not routinely armed such as the UK, Norway, and New Zealand, there are comparatively fewer fatal shootings by police. In contrast, among countries in the global north, the US, Canada, and Australia have much higher rates of fatal shootings. For example, Australia regularly has three to four times more fatal shootings compared to England and Wales, although it has less than half the general population.[75]

Indeed, the disarming of police has taken on a particular resonance with the rise of the BLM movement. For example, in 2019 after the police shooting of Kumanjayi Walker, senior Aboriginal Elders in the Yuendumu community (NT, Australia) called for the disarming of police.

> Karrinjarla muwajarri meaning we want a ceasefire. No more guns in our communities. It must never happen

again. The police must put down their weapons. We have been saying this since the beginning. We cannot walk around in fear in our own homes anymore. ...We do not want any police officers to live and work in our communities with guns and other lethal weapons.[76]

Community Elders also called for an end to ex-military police officers and asserted that senior elders and Aboriginal community police 'must be decision-makers in policing matters': 'We are the First Nations peoples but we are still being disrespected and ignored. We are all so full of anger and grief. It is a racist system ... we are powerful decision-makers. We, as the Warlpiri Nation ... demand an end to guns in our communities.'[77] Disarming the police is a radical demand, but is completely consistent with the localised control over policing which colonised people have been insisting on for decades. It is also consistent with outcomes sought in public health literature. The introduction of harm-reduction policies and strategies must challenge the 'models of hostile, racialised interactions between civilians and armed agents of the state'.[78] Disarming police is an important part of the overall strategy that requires replacing state violence with investment in the types of programmes and services determined by affected communities.

Conclusion

The answers are clear: we need to dramatically reduce the role of police in addressing a range of social, political, and economic problems, including through decreasing the size of police forces. We need to invest in communities to promote public safety through reallocating money to services that address the issues that impact on community safety, such as homelessness and poverty, and those that improve access to good quality health care, mental health support, education, and economic opportunity.

However, divesting from police and investing in community is more than simply a matter of moving money. Divesting has ethical, political, and social dimensions – it signifies that we no longer imbue and endow police with legitimacy, authority, and power; that we want an end to institutional violence and racism; that we see community-based approaches as both more effective and more legitimate in responding to social issues; that we no longer see the cult of criminalisation and violence as the best way to help people who are homeless, who have been harmed or who are in some other way in need of assistance. It is also about reversing the years of neo-liberal retraction of government social services while the state happily increased the budgets to service police repression and the infliction of harm on those left abandoned and seen as disposable.

As has been underlined in this book, these changes will not happen overnight. They require building alliances across various groups and they require political strategies for change. While the issues of police repression and violence are largely global, the alliances and the strategies they pursue will be determined by specific contexts. Although colonialism has influenced the nature of policing and its targets across much of the world, the struggles against state violence are also influenced by local conditions. As shown in Chapter 4, in the past, the opposition to police violence and racism gave rise to new forms of community-based organisations and resistance, and this will no doubt continue to be the case as the contemporary BLM and Defund the Police movements already attest.

For many, the longer-term vision is the demise of police power and a horizon which is both abolitionist and decolonised. This book focuses primarily on the institution of police, the reasons for divesting from police, and the alternatives available to achieve that result. However, it also recognises that this is only part of the bigger picture. The logic of policing underpins, is embedded in, or intersects with, multiple state agencies. Thus, we need to challenge the expansion of police and carceral power into our daily lives through a web of social institutions well beyond the police. A fundamental part of any political programme will be the ability to distinguish reforms or options for change which take us closer to an abolitionist future rather than simply reinventing and re-empowering existing institutional frameworks. Further, as has been argued throughout this book, the institution of police is deeply rooted in the exploitation and control that were foundational to colonialism and imperialism, and still today it reveals itself as the most intense and transparent examples of state violence and terror. The 're-imaginings' that are required to move beyond state systems of control must be based on broad solidarity. While liberal reformers might continue with various programmes to reform the police, the abolitionist challenge of removing state policing and carceral systems and re-imagining community safety has been accepted by many diverse groups. They include those working in areas such as public health, radical social workers, critical disability workers, LGBTQIA+ advocates, people from Black, Indigenous and other minoritised communities, activists in the labour movement, and the people in the street demanding an end to police violence.

Notes

Chapter 1

[1] Throughout this book, police and policing are used interchangeably with law enforcement officials and law enforcement. Following the UN Code of Conduct for Law Enforcement Officials, the definition includes officials who are exercising police powers, especially arrest or detention. This can include border control, specialist squads, and other security forces, including the military, where they are exercising police powers in a domestic setting. It can include other seemingly anomalous groups such as Forestry and other Land Management officials who engage in policing roles, and in countries such as India have been widely implicated in torture and murder.

[2] Vitale, 2017; Maher, 2021.

[3] See www.changethenypd.org/nycbudgetjustice; www.peoplesbudgetla.com/peoplesbudget/

[4] Millie, 2014; Fleetwood and Lea, 2020.

[5] M4BL, 2020: 4. The Movement for Black Lives is a coalition of more than 50 organisations, and includes the Black Lives Matter Network established by Patrisse Cullors, Alicia Garza, and Opal Tometi in 2013. There are multiple organisations within the broader social movement.

[6] Cited in Kushner, 2019.

[7] Kaba, 2021.

[8] See www.aljazeera.com/news/2020/5/31/mapping-us-police-killings-of-black-americans

[9] Cited in Heatherton, 2016: 36.

[10] Independent Police Investigative Directorate, 2021: 38.

[11] Amnesty International, 2020. On the judicial inquiry see www.edition.cnn.com/2021/11/15/africa/lekki-tollgate-judicial-panel-report-intl/index.html

[12] Human Rights Watch (2020a) noted that at least six people died from police violence in first 10 days of the curfew in Kenya, and the Nigerian National Human Rights Commission (2020) found there were 18 extra-judicial killings by law enforcement agencies in the first 2 weeks of the lockdown in Nigeria.

[13] Human Rights Watch, 2021: 390.

[14] Human Rights Watch, 2020a. 'Nigerian forces fire on protesters', *New York Times*, 20 October 2020; 'George Floyd's killing prompts Africans to call for police reform at home', *New York Times*, 8 July, 2020.

[15] Aborisade and Gbahabo, 2021; Onuoha et al, 2021.
[16] See www.amnesty.org/en/latest/news/2021/08/indonesia-papuan-protest ers-shot-beaten-and-racially-abused-by-security-forces-new-research/; www.aseantoday.com/2020/06/southeast-asia-on-the-black-lives-matter-protests-how-they-covered-it/; www.bbc.com/news/world-asia-50236 481; www.scmp.com/week-asia/politics/article/3087204/george-floyd-kill ing-stirs-asian-feelings-regions-own-racial; www.thejakartapost.com/news/ 2020/06/04/papuanlivesmatter-george-floyds-death-hits-close-to-home-in-indonesia.html
[17] Mahtani, 2020.
[18] Human Rights Watch, 2016a: 1–2; National Human Rights Commission, 2018: 44; National Campaign Against Torture, 2020: 6.
[19] Kalhan et al, 2020. Historian Ramachandran Guha described the impact on migrant workers as the 'greatest manmade tragedy' in India since the Partition, *The Hindu*, 24 May, 2020, and this was prior to the devastation caused by the pandemic after April 2021.
[20] Ravi, 2020.
[21] Human Rights Watch, 2021: 319. In West Bengal, police allegedly beat a 32-year-old man to death after he stepped out of his home to buy milk. Human Rights Watch, 2021: 318.
[22] https://www.americamagazine.org/politics-society/2020/06/22/black-lives-matter-movement-latin-america-protests] Human Rights Watch, 2021: 452–5.
[23] See www.bbc.com/news/world-latin-america-53484698; www.nytimes. com/2020/06/29/opinion/latin-america-racism-police.html
[24] BBC (2021); Dickinson, 2021.
[25] See https://newsinteractives.cbc.ca/longform-custom/deadly-force
[26] See www.theglobeandmail.com/canada/article-more-than-one-third-of-peo ple-shot-to-death-over-a-decade-by-rcmp/
[27] See www.theconversation.com/black-lives-matter-outrage-must-drive-pol ice-reform-in-aotearoa-new-sealand-too-139965
[28] See www.theconversation.com/despite-432-indigenous-deaths-in-cust ody-since-1991-no-one-has-ever-been-convicted-racist-silence-and-com plicity-are-to-blame-139873
[29] Bobin, forthcoming. See also www.france24.com/en/20200613-protest ers-gather-in-paris-for-fresh-march-against-racism-and-police-brutality.
[30] Elliott-Cooper, 2021: 4–5. www.theguardian.com/us-news/2020/jun/ 06/now-is-the-time-londons-black-lives-matter-rally-looks-like-a-turn ing-point.
[31] See Thompson (2021a) on the protests in Germany, France, and Switzerland, and racialised policing more generally; also www.time.com/5851165/germ any-anti-racism-protests/
[32] Petre, 2021: n.p.
[33] Strong, 2018: 267.
[34] Egwu, 2020.

[35] www.feminisminindia.com/2020/06/17/unnamed-george-floyds-india-episodic-police-brutality-2019-20/

[36] Miki, 2021: 304.

[37] Dahir, A.L., Maclean, R. and Chutel, L. (2020); see also McMichael (2016).]

[38] Cunneen and Tauri, 2017.

[39] Amnesty International www.amnesty.org/en/countries/middle-east-and-north-africa/israel-and-occupied-palestinian-territories/report-israel-and-occupied-palestinian-territories/

[40] Sekhri, 2020.

[41] Hope (2021); Anders (2021).

[42] Anti-Security Collective, 2021.

[43] Jacobs et al, 2021.

[44] See Ben-Moshe's response to these issues in the context of disability, deinstitutionalisation, and prison abolition, (2020: 111–12).

[45] Jannetta, 2020.

[46] Barker et al (2021).

[47] Heatherton, 2016: 35.

[48] Davis, 2003: 106.

[49] Mignolo, 2017: 15.

[50] Cunneen et al, 2013.

[51] Simon, 2007: 6.

[52] Harcourt, 2018: 6; Schrader, 2019a.

[53] Davis, 2003: 108.

[54] Desai, 2020: 3–4; Kaba, 2021: 14–17.

[55] Kaba, 2021: 15.

Chapter 2

[1] Following the Peelian principle that 'the police are the public and the public are the police'.

[2] See www.nationalarchives.gov.uk/education/resources/georgian-britain-age-modernity/new-police/; see also https://www.nationalarchives.gov.uk/education/resources/georgian-britain-age-modernity/new-police/

[3] Harring, 1983; also Vitale, 2017: 36–9.

[4] Porter, 2020.

[5] Sälter, 2014: 1251

[6] Named as a specific phenomenon in an 1816 London report as part of the increasing crime problem in the 'Metropolis' and evidence for the need of new police. See Cunneen et al, 2015: 3–5.

[7] For example, see Brogden, 1981 and Jones, 1982.

[8] Cunneen et al, 2015: 2–23.

[9] Garton, 1987: 74–79. Similarly, in Ireland the police played a central role in the management and institutionalisation of the mentally ill and disabled; see McNamara, 2021.

[10] Brogden, 1982.

[11] Reiner, 2010: 67–110.

[12] See, for example, Geary, 1985.

[13] Jones, 1982.

[14] Sinclair, 2008: 173–87. Sinclair and Williams (2007) also note that there was 'cross-fertilisation' between colonial and 'British' models of policing. The policing of social protest and industrial disputes in Britain has taken on the more militarised profile of what might be regarded as the 'colonial' model.

[15] Anderson and Killingray, 1991.

[16] The Colonial Police Services was established in 1936 to standardise imperial police forces (Sinclair, 2006).

[17] Blanchard, 2014: 1839–40.

[18] Tankebe, 2008: 74.

[19] Killingray, 1991: 119.

[20] Fanon, 1967: 29.

[21] Anderson and Killingray, 1992; Blanchard, 2014; Bloembergen and Klinkers, 2014: 1201–2.

[22] Blanchard, 2014: 1842–3. He quotes Albert Memmi, writing in the mid 1950s, that 'a machine-gun burst into a crowd of colonized causes him [the coloniser] merely to shrug his shoulders'; see also Bobin, forthcoming.

[23] Blanchard, 2014: 1843.

[24] Blanchard, 2014: 1843; and Bobin, forthcoming.

[25] Anderson and Killingray, 1991; Sinclair, 2006: 26.

[26] Bobin, forthcoming.

[27] Tankebe, 2008: 71; Blanchard, 2014: 1840.

[28] Volmer, cited in Go, 2020: 1207.

[29] Hönke and Müller, 2016: 8.

[30] Sinclair, 2008: 176.

[31] Sinclair, 2008; Bobin, forthcoming.

[32] Arnold, 1992: 58; Stockwell, 1992: 122.

[33] Blanchard, 2014: 1845.

[34] Sinclair, 2006.

[35] Vitale, 2017: 40–2; also Go, 2020.

[36] Roberts, 2005; Dunbar-Ortiz, 2014; Owen, 2016.

[37] Cited in Cunneen and Tauri, 2017: 50, and see generally, pp 49–57; see also Moses, 2000.

[38] The Colonial Frontier Massacres Project has reconstructed a detailed timeline and map of the massacre of Indigenous people between 1788 and 1930 in Australia. Police, native police, soldiers and magistrates, were involved in at least 50 per cent of all massacres. See https://c21ch.newcastle.edu.au/coloni almassacres/

[39] Evans, 2021: 8–9.

[40] Vitale, 2017: 43–4.

[41] There is broad-ranging literature of this, but see, for example, Stannard, 1992; Royal Commission on Aboriginal Peoples [RCAP], 1996; Dunbar-Ortiz, 2014; Cunneen and Tauri, 2017.

[42] RCAP, 1996: 185.

[43] RCAP, 1996: 288–9.

[44] Cunneen, 2001: 66–75.

[45] Cunneen and Tauri, 2017: 52–5.
[46] Indeed, in Australia, reservations or missions were sometimes referred to as 'prison farms', and the people living there as 'inmates'; Cunneen, 2001: 54.
[47] Cunneen and Tauri, 2017: 55–6.
[48] Chartrand, 2019.
[49] Vitale, 2017: 45–7.
[50] Correia and Wall, 2018: 154–5.
[51] Davis, 1998: 99.
[52] Alexander, 2010: 28.
[53] Ritchie, 2017: 29–31; Vitale, 2017: 47.
[54] Ifill, 2007: 75.
[55] Oklahoma Commission to Study the Tulsa Race Riot of 1921, 2001: 167.
[56] Sinclair, 2006: 7; Harcourt, 2018: 19–35.
[57] Hönke and Müller, 2016; Go, 2020.
[58] Vitale, 2017: 42.
[59] Schrader, 2019a: 7. For French overseas police technical assistance programmes in the 1960s, see Bobin, forthcoming.
[60] Schrader, 2019: 170–1.
[61] Schrader, 2019a: 155–7.
[62] Schrader, 2020.
[63] Green and Mora, 2021.
[64] Whitlock, 2019; https://www.washingtonpost.com/graphics/2019/investi gations/afghanistan-papers/afghanistan-war-army-police/
[65] Hönke and Müller, 2016: 1.
[66] Cain, 1993: 323.
[67] Tatour and Tatour, forthcoming.
[68] Blanchard, 2014: 1838.
[69] Dunbar-Ortiz, 2014.
[70] Tankebe, 2008: 75.
[71] Kolsky, 2010: 63.
[72] Smith, 2005; Baldry and Cunneen, 2014; Deer, 2015; The National Inquiry into Missing and Murdered Indigenous Women and Girls [NIMMIWG], 2019a: 17.
[73] Ritchie, 2017: 21; also Baldry and Cunneen, 2014; Deer, 2015.
[74] To paraphrase Kaba and Ritchie, see Kaba, 2021: 63–7.
[75] Blanchard, 2014: 1844–5.
[76] Cunneen, 2009; Fassin, 2013; Schrader, 2021.

Chapter 3

[1] Chicago: www.chicago.gov/city/en/depts/cpd/auto_generated/cpd_miss ion.html; Maharashtra: https://citizen.mahapolice.gov.in/Citizen/MH/ CitizenCharter.aspx; London: www.met.police.uk/police-forces/metropoli tan-police/areas/about-us/about-the-met/vision-and-values/
[2] Schrader, 2021: 3.
[3] Coyle, 2022.
[4] Asher and Horwitz, 2020.

5   Brown et al, 2021. Police responded to 35,924 calls which were sorted into 241 categories then collapsed into 5 major types.
6   Ray, 2020: 1.
7   'Investigating police responses to homelessness', Global Investigative Journalism Network, www.gijn.org/2022/01/31/q-a-investigating-police-responses-to-homelessness/
8   See Chapter 4.
9   www.bls.gov/charts/census-of-fatal-occupational-injuries/civilian-occupations-with-high-fatal-work-injury-rates.htm
10 https://www.safeworkaustralia.gov.au/sites/default/files/2020-11/Work-related%20traumatic%20injury%20fatalities%20Australia%202019.pdf
11 Allard and Prenzler, 2009.
12 Hine, 2020; www.theconversation.com/road-crashes-assaults-and-being-spat-on-the-dangers-facing-australian-police-in-the-line-of-duty-137594
13 The Police Roll of Honour Trust. Although fluctuating somewhat, similar numbers for previous 5 years are as follows: 2019: 5; 2018: 3; 2017: 9; 2016: 2; 2015: 4; www.policememorial.org.uk/
14 Federal Bureau of Investigation, 2021; see also National Law Enforcement Officers Memorial Fund, 2020.
15 A total of 1,126 deaths in 2020 with 96 per cent killed in police shootings. See Police Violence Report, 2020 www.policeviolencereport.org/. In the absence of official data on police killings, Mapping Police Violence collected data from media reports, obituaries, public records, and databases like Fatal Encounters and the *Washington Post*.
16 Prison Police Initiative, 5 June, 2020; www.prisonpolicy.org/blog/2020/06/05/policekillings/. An earlier study found that the rate of civilian deaths by police shootings was 31 times higher in the US (Knutson and Noree, 2010).
17 See https://news.northeastern.edu/2020/04/16/000-people-in-the-us-are-killed-every-year-in-police-shootings-how-many-are-preventable/
18 Gramlich, 2017.
19 Gramlich, 2020.
20 See www.bbc.com/news/uk-49986849
21 Holmes and Fitzgerald, 2017.
22 See https://www.baltimoresun.com/maryland/baltimore-city/bs-md-ci-crime-policy-20191230-zk2v2auuhbgq3f7zsh3t7rt6cm-story.html
23 The use of firearms in a homicide generally results in lower clearances rates (Liem et al, 2019: 98). Murder rates vary significantly in different regions, from around 10 per million population in Europe, East Asia, and Oceania (Australia and New Zealand), to 50 per million in the US, and to 259 and 242 per million, respectively, in Central and South America (Office of National Statistics, 2021).
24 Liem et al, 2019: 82.
25 Bricknell and Doherty, 2021; Office of National Statistics (UK), 2021.
26 The use of other weapons and methods in murder cases is more likely to leave physical evidence (Liem et al, 2019). It is also important to note that most research on this subject is from developed countries, and 'less is known about

which factors … are associated with homicide clearance rates in developing countries' (UN Office on Drugs and Crime (UNODC), 2019: 68).

[27] Gramlich, 2017.

[28] van Dijk et al, 2007.

[29] van Dijk et al, 2007: 109–11.

[30] Naudé et al, 2006.

[31] Gramlich, 2017.

[32] Miles-Johnson, 2013.

[33] West and Gandhi, 2006.

[34] AHRC, 2014; Victorian Equal Opportunity and Human Rights Commission, 2014; Rowe and Dowse, 2021.

[35] BBC, 2014.

[36] References in original omitted. McManus et al, 2019.

[37] Pew Research Centre, 'Majority of public favors giving civilians the power to sue police officers for misconduct', 9 July, 2020. www.pewresearch.org/politics/2020/07/09/majority-of-public-favors-giving-civilians-the-power-to-sue-police-officers-for-misconduct/. The CATO research also found that Black respondents believed that police were too quick to use lethal force (73 per cent compared to 35 per cent of White respondents) and that police tactics were generally too harsh (56 per cent compared to 26 per cent of White respondents); McManus et al, 2019.

[38] La Vigne, 2017: 1.

[39] La Vigne, 2017: 2.

[40] Hayes, 2018: 32.

[41] Hayes, 2018: 37–8.

[42] Hayes, 2018: 38.

[43] Runnymede Trust, 2021: 17.

[44] Tankebe, 2008: 76.

[45] Tankebe, 2008: 77.

[46] For example, in the UK, the Macpherson Report and in Australia the Royal Commission into Aboriginal Deaths in Custody (Johnston, 1991; Macpherson, 1999).

[47] Findlay, 2004: 72–7.

[48] Goldson et al, 2021: 100–28.

[49] Cunneen et al, 2015: 225–7; 232–3.

[50] Goldson et al, 2021: 106–8.

[51] Bridges, 2015.

[52] Goldson et al, 2021: 108–9, 114–16.

[53] See www.france24.com/en/europe/20220627-turkish-police-release-all-activists-detained-during-istanbul-pride-march?utm_source=substack&utm_medium=email

[54] James et al, 2016: 14.

[55] Tomsen, 2002; Tomsen and Kirchengast, 2019.

[56] NSW Legislative Council Standing Committee on Social Issues, 2021.

[57] Her Majesty's Inspectorate of Constabulary and Fire & Rescue Services, 2018: 93.

58 Ronan, 2020.
59 Goldson et al, 2021: 4–7.
60 Rowe and Dowse, 2021: 211–12.
61 Justine Damond Ruszczyk (Minneapolis, 2017); Henry Louis Gates Jr. (Cambridge, Massachusetts, 2009).

Chapter 4

1   Seale, 1967: 7; emphasis in the original.
2   See https://www.collectiveliberation.org/wp-content/uploads/2015/01/ BPP_Ten_Point_Program.pdf
3   Cited by Attwood and Markus, 1999: 252–3, and see Goodall, 1996: 335–6; Attwood, 2003: 318–49; Lothian, 2005.
4   Interview with Bruce McGuinness in Foley et al, 2014: 136.
5   Harcourt, 2018: 136–8.
6   Newton, 1973. Also see Kelly, 2020, and see www.pbs.org/hueypnewton/ actions/actions_survival.html
7   Bassett, 2019: 352.
8   Bassett, 2019.
9   See https://www.collectiveliberation.org/wp-content/uploads/2015/01/ BPP_Ten_Point_Program.pdf
10 The quote was taken from the American Indian Movement website: www. static1.squarespace.com/static/5564875fe4b0a715f94b3b42/t/558850b7e 4b010cd4058b0d6/1434996919389/AIMPastPresentFuture.pdf. The website has been taken down. A discussion of the origin of AIM can be found at https://www.mnopedia.org/group/american-indian-movement-aim and of the AIM patrols at https://www.mnopedia.org/group/aim-patrol-minn eapolis.
11 See www.legalrightscenter.org/our-history.html
12 See www.legalrightscenter.org/our-history.html
13 Foley, 2001: 11–12.
14 Cited in Howell, 2014: 72.
15 Foley, 2001: 13.
16 On mutual aid, see Spade, 2020.
17 Hall et al, 1978.
18 Gilroy, 1987 [1982].
19 Sivanandan was the Director of the Institute of Race Relations and the founding editor of the journal *Race and Class*. Sivanandan, 1990: 135.
20 Gordon, 1985: 162–3.
21 Gordon, 1985: 162–3.
22 Chaudhary, 2019.
23 Gilroy, 1987 [1982]: 109.
24 Gilroy, 1987 [1982]: 108–14.
25 Hall, 1980: 257–8.
26 Hall, 1980: 266–8.
27 Cowell et al, 1982.
28 Sim et al, 1987.

29 Tribune (1986).

30 Geary, 1985: 146–67.

31 Quoted in Gordon, 1985: 161.

32 Sivanandan, 1990: 131–7.

33 Gilroy, 1987: 125–6.

34 Sim et al, 1987: 32–9.

35 Sim et al, 1987: 32.

36 Quoted in Sim et al, 1987: 34.

37 See Elliot-Cooper, 2021: 53–60 for a discussion of the murder, the investigation, and the aftermath.

38 Macpherson, 1999: para 46.1.

39 Macpherson, 1999: para 45.7.

40 See www.theguardian.com/uk/2013/jun/23/stephen-lawrence-undercover-police-smears

41 Elliot-Cooper, 2021: 57.

42 For a discussion of this debate at the time and particularly in relation to various positions on the Left within criminology, see Sim et al, 1987: 39–59.

43 Elliot-Cooper, 2021: 57–8.

44 Elliot-Cooper, 2021: 57–8.

45 Burger, 1988: 96. Helen Corbett is referred to by her previous name 'Boyle' in the publication.

46 Johnston, 1991.

47 Cunneen, 2001: 97–102; 121–3.

48 Human Rights and Equal Opportunity Commission (HREOC), 1991: 387.

49 Office of the Aboriginal and Torres Strait Islander Social Justice Commissioner, 1996.

50 Cunneen and McDonald, 1997.

51 House of Representatives Standing Committee on Aboriginal and Torres Strait Islander Affairs, 1994; Cunneen and McDonald, 1997.

52 Amnesty International, 1993.

53 Amnesty International, 1997: 8.

54 Cunneen, 2007: 26–28.

55 Maynard, 2017: 14–15.

56 Ransby, 2018: 3.

57 Kelley, 2020. Critical Resistance: www.criticalresistance.org/about/history/; INCITE! www.incite-national.org/history/; SistaIISista: Burrowes, 2018.

58 Angela Davis noted that 25 of the 28 members of the organising committee for the 1998 meeting were either women or non-binary; Davis et al (2021).

59 INCITE!, 2001.

60 See www.incite-national.org/stop-law-enforcement-violence/

61 Burrowes, 2018: 389.

62 Burrowes, 2018: 378.

63 Wilson and Kelling, 1982.

64 Kelling went on to argue that policing required consent, cooperation, and collaboration with the community. He distanced himself from zero tolerance policing, indicating that it was not a credible policing philosophy.

65   Cunneen, 2003: 144–57.
66   And, in more extreme cases, the use of torture, as in the case of Abner
     Louima in a Brooklyn police station in 1997.
67   Cunneen, 2003: 149–50.
68   Stenson, 2000.
69   Crenshaw, 2020: 15.

Chapter 5

1   Human Rights Council, 2019.
2   A death in police custody is variously defined to include deaths arising from
     police pursuits, road traffic incidents, fatal shootings, fatalities caused during
     police restraint, deaths arising from torture and beatings, medical conditions,
     suicides, or other causes while in custody.
3   Rodríguez, forthcoming.
4   www.washingtonpost.com/graphics/investigations/police-shootings-datab
     ase/?itid=lk_interstitial_manual_10. The year 2021 is tracking for over
     1,000 deaths, with 927 recorded as at 22 September, 2021. Other public
     non-government databases include *Fatal Encounters* (www.fatalencount
     ers.org/), *Mapping Police Violence* (www.mappingpoliceviolence.org/) and
     The Counted (www.theguardian.com/us-news/series/counted-us-police-
     killings)
5   The study estimated that over a 40-year period there were 17,100 more
     deaths due to police violence than the 13,700 reported deaths (GBD 2019
     Police Violence US Subnational Collaborators, 2021). An earlier 2018 study
     using CDC data reported that, based on 27 States, more than 92 per cent
     of deaths in law enforcement 'legal interventions' were from shootings, and
     the rate of Black male deaths was approximately twice that of White males
     (Jack et al, 2018).
6   See the *New Scientist* for details, https://www.newscientist.com/article/
     2246987-us-police-kill-up-to-6-times-more-black-people-than-white-
     people/
7   See https://www.inquest.org.uk/bame-deaths-in-police-custody .
8   Angiolini, 2017: 92.
9   'European' is the Authority's classification. Independent Police Conduct
     Authority, 2012: 3, 29.
10   Doherty and Sullivan, 2021.
11   See www.theguardian.com/australia-news/series/deaths-inside
12   See https://newsinteractives.cbc.ca/fatalpoliceencounters/
13   See www.cbc.ca/news/canada/manitoba/iteam/deadly-force-cbc-analysis-
     1.4603696
14   United States, Canada, Australia, Netherlands, New Zealand, Germany,
     England & Wales, Japan, Iceland, Norway. See www.prisonpolicy.org/blog/
     2020/06/05/policekillings/
15   Farmer and Evans, 2020: 54.
16   The Centro de Investigación y Docencia Económicas found that in Venezuela
     the absolute number of people killed by the State is even higher than in

Brazil, despite having a population – in absolute terms – almost seven times less. Civilian death rate through police fatal violence exceeds 15 per 100,000 inhabitants, a record higher than the *general* homicide rate in the vast majority of countries of the world (2019: 167).

[17] https://www.bbc.com/news/world-asia-50236481.

[18] ICC, 2021. See also Gallagher et al, 2020.

[19] See www.npr.org/2021/05/07/994588467/u-n-calls-for-investigation-as-police-in-brazil-kill-at-least-24-in-rio-drug-raid

[20] For a police massacre in May 2022 that killed 21 people in a Rio favela, and another in July 2022 that killed at least 18 people, see www.theguardian.com/world/2022/may/24/brazil-police-raid-rio-favela-death-toll, and see www.theguardian.com/world/gallery/2022/jul/22/deadly-police-raid-rio-de-janeiro-brazil-in-pictures?CMP=share_btn_link

[21] Centro de Estudios Legales y Sociales, 2018: 47.

[22] Human Rights Watch, 2020b: 83–4; 2021: 105–8.

[23] Metaal and Youngers, 2011: 5–7.

[24] Metaal and Youngers, 2011: 5–7; de Carvalho Silva and Langeani, 2019; Carvalho, 2020.

[25] Carvalho, 2020.

[26] This is not to suggest that police use of torture is only a problem in these South Asian countries, or indeed the global south. We see it in the global north as well – for example the Chicago detective and commander Jon Burge and his 'midnight crew'. Between the early 1970s and 1990s he was accused of torturing hundreds of people (mostly Black) to extract forced confessions. In 2015 the city approved a $5.5 million reparations package for the victims. See the Chicago Police Torture Archive and Chicago Torture Justice Memorials (www.chicagopolicetorturearchive.com/about and www.chicagotorture.org/).

[27] National Human Rights Commission, 2018: 44; NCAT, 2020: 6; Human Rights Watch, 2021: 318. The NCAT number does not include people killed by the police outside of a police station (for example, while being apprehended or assaulted).

[28] Human Rights Watch, 2016a: 1–2.

[29] National Human Rights Commission, 2018: 44; NCAT, 2020: 6.

[30] NCAT, 2021: 131.

[31] NCAT, 2021: 133–6.

[32] NCAT, 2020: 8.

[33] NCAT, 2020: 112–21.

[34] 'India's police stations are human rights threat, says chief justice', *The Guardian*, 10 August 2021. https://www.theguardian.com/world/2021/aug/10/india-police-stations-human-rights-threat-chief-justice. In 1961, Justice Mulla of the Allahabad High Court in a judgment said, "I say with all sense of responsibility, there is not a single lawless group in the whole of the country whose record of crime comes anywhere near that of the organized gang of criminals known as the Indian Police Force" (*State vs Mohammad Naim*, Criminal Misc. Case No. 87 of 1961).

35 Common Cause and CSDS, 2019: 131.
36 Committee against Torture, 2019: para 14.
37 See https://www.bbc.com/news/world-south-asia-12057400
38 Committee against Torture, 2019: para 17; Uddin, 2020; Human Rights Watch, 2021: 78.
39 Uddin, 2020.
40 Sultana and Dey, 2020.
41 Human Rights Watch, 2016b, 2021; National Commission on Human Rights (NCHR), 2019.
42 Human Rights Watch, 2016b: 2.
43 NCHR, 2019: 23–5.
44 Human Rights Watch, 2021: 518.
45 Country Reports on Human Rights Practices, 2020.
46 Human Rights Watch, 2016b: 1.
47 Cited in Human Rights Watch, 2016b: 21.
48 Waseem, forthcoming.
49 Santos, 2021: 8.
50 Latour and Latour, forhcoming.
51 Saskatoon police arrested First Nations young people, drove them out of the city and abandoned them during winter months. A number of victims died from hyperthermia – 17-year-old Neil Stonechild was one of the deaths. A subsequent judicial inquiry found that initial police investigations were 'superficial and totally inadequate'. See Wright, 2004: 212.
52 Independent Police Complaints Commission [IPCC], 2010: 14. The IPCC was replaced in 2018 with the Independent Office for Police Complaints. See also the Lindon and Roe (2017: 30) study for the decade ending June 2015.
53 Johnston, 1991.
54 Thompson, 2021.
55 Wootten, 1991: 63.
56 Allam et al, 2020.
57 Source: INQUEST case work and monitoring. www.inquest.org.uk/Pages/Category/statistics-and-monitoring. INQUEST defines police custodial deaths as deaths that take place while the individual is in contact with police, whether or not they have been arrested, or that happen shortly after that contact. The death may not necessarily have occurred inside a police station. Self-inflicted deaths following contact with police or deaths as a result of domestic violence where the police have been involved are not included.
58 Human Rights Council, 2019: para 33.
59 Restraint is often broadly defined to include the use of manual holds, handcuffs, specialist devices ('restraints' such as hoods, leg restraints), and 'less-lethal' weapons, including tasers, CS and OS sprays, and rubber bullets, etc.
60 Weichselbaum et al, 2021. Police and security forces can actively prevent medical attention, as in the Lekki Toll Gate massacre referred to in Chapter 1.
61 Her Majesty's Inspectorate of Constabulary, 2021: 4–5. See also Noor, 2018.

[62] Lindon and Roe, 2017: 33–4. The IPCC (2010) study of 333 deaths in police custody found that people from Black and minority ethnic groups were significantly more likely than White people to die while being restrained by police.

[63] Runnymede Trust, 2021: 20.

[64] Civilian Complaint Review Board, 2019: 11, 20.

[65] Thom and Quince, 2020.

[66] Crime and Misconduct Commission, 2005: x, 29; NSW Ombudsman, 2012: 99. In Western Australia, the Corruption and Crime Commission investigated the use of tasers and OC spray after First Nations man Kevin Spratt was tasered seven times in a little over a minute by two police officers. The Commission found that the tasering was an 'undue and excessive use of force which was unreasonable and unjustified'. Two senior police officers were later found guilty of assault and sentenced to suspended jail terms and fines. Corruption and Crime Commission, 2012: 1.

[67] Cavanagh, 2010: 42.

[68] See www.justiceinitiative.org/newsroom/justice-initiative-joins-groups-in-giving-notice-of-class-action-lawsuit-against-french-government-for-ethnic-profiling-by-police

[69] Macpherson, 1999: para 45.8.

[70] Equality and Human Rights Commission, 2010: 6, 13. The Commission also notes that the introduction of counter terrorism legislation has increased police powers to stop and search and their frequency has steadily increased during the 2000s.

[71] Eastwood et al, 2013.

[72] Her Majesty's Inspectorate of Constabulary, 2021: 5–6. Runnymede, 2021: 17.

[73] Runnymede, 2021: 18.

[74] See for example the discussion in the *New Scientist*, www.newscientist.com/article/2246987-us-police-kill-up-to-6-times-more-black-people-than-white-people/

[75] See, for example, the Sentencing Project (2018) and the Urban Institute (Nembhard and Robin, 2021).

[76] Human Rights Watch, 2020c: 89; Ray, 2020.

[77] Ritchie and Jones-Brown, 2017: 22–3.

[78] US Department of Justice, 2016: 3.

[79] Harris, 2020.

[80] Neocleous, 2021a: 11.

[81] Harcourt, 2018; Schrader, 2019.

[82] Tatour and Tatour, forthcoming.

[83] Schrader, 2019: 18.

[84] Schrader, 2019: 18–19.

[85] ACLU, 2014; Vitale, 2017; Harcourt, 2018; Kraska and Williams, 2019; Schrader, 2019; Go, 2020.

[86] Kraska, 2007.

[87] Kraska and Williams, 2019: 145, 148, 150. See also ACLU, 2014.

88 Goodmark, 2015. See Chapter 6.
89 During the George Floyd protests, *The Guardian* documented 950 instances of police violence against civilians and journalists. https://www.theguardian.com/us-news/2020/oct/29/us-police-brutality-protest.
90 Human Rights Watch, 2020c: 12–13.
91 Neocleous, 2021b: 183.
92 Human Rights Watch, 2020c: 49.
93 See also the training documents obtained by The Intercept https://theinterc ept.com/2021/05/05/nypd-george-floyd-protests-training/
94 Levinson et al (2020).
95 Cunningham, 2022. Also Vitale, 2017: 197–220.
96 Johnson, 2021.

Chapter 6

1 www.theguardian.com/uk-news/2021/mar/30/police-handling-of-sarah-everard-vigil-appropriate-says-watchdog
2 Richie (2012: 126) discusses the similar phenomenon in the US – referred to as the Missing White Woman Syndrome – in terms of both media and police disregard for violence against Black women compared to White women.
3 See www.theviewmag.org.uk/
4 www.independent.co.uk/news/uk/home-news/black-and-minority-eth nic-women-criminal-justice-system-bme-a9581956.html
5 See www.bbc.com/news/uk-56410943
6 World Health Organisation, 2021.
7 Terwiel, 2020: 422.
8 Cunneen and Tauri, 2017: 8, 80, 93; National Inquiry into Missing and Murdered Indigenous Women and Girls [NIMMIWG] (Canada), 2019b.
9 Cited in Cunneen and Tauri, 2017: 79–80.
10 Sobsey, 2000; Australian Bureau of Statistics, 2021. Other women more likely to experience sexual assault include those who are homeless, identify as lesbian, gay, bisexual, trans, and gender diverse, or have intersex variations (AIHW, 2020).
11 National Crime Records Bureau, 2020: 196.
12 For the US analysis see Richie, 2012: 65–98.
13 For the US Taskforce see Gruber, 2020a: 101–3. Internationally, the United Nations' Committee on the Elimination of Discrimination Against Women (CEDAW) introduced requirements for States to provide information on the incidence of violence against women and measures adopted to respond to it (1989) and to expand the definition of discrimination to include gender-based violence (1992). In Australia, the federal government's role began with developing the National Agenda for Women in 1986. The Canadian federal government began consultations for a Family Violence Initiative in 1988.
14 Gruber, forthcoming.
15 Davis, 1982: 172–3.

[16] Richie, 2012: 19. See also Davis, et al (2022: 102–8) for discussion of the role of Black, Indigenous and women of colour opposing the growing movement towards carceral feminism during the 1980s and 1990s.

[17] Aboriginal and Torres Strait Islander Women's Taskforce on Violence, 1999.

[18] Iyengar, 2007; Gruber, 2020a: 67–83; Gruber, 2020b.

[19] Ritchie, 2006: 141–2.

[20] Cunneen and Rowe, 2015: 10–13.

[21] Douglas and Fitzgerald, 2018: 42, 46.

[22] Survey countries included Australia, Costa Rica, Czech Republic, Denmark, Greece, Hong Kong, Italy, Mozambique, Philippines, Poland and Switzerland. Johnson et al, 2008: 137–8.

[23] Johnson et al, 2008: 142.

[24] Segrave et al, 2021: 8–12, 43.

[25] Johnson et al, 2008: 136.

[26] In the US, see Ritchie, 2006: 140; in Australia see Cunneen and Rowe, 2015: 20; in Canada see NIMMIWG, 2019a: 38.

[27] Coroners Court of New South Wales (2021).

[28] NIMMIWG, 2019a: 38.

[29] Nancarrow et al, 2020: 79.

[30] Oppenheim, 2021.

[31] Johnson et al, 2008: 145–6.

[32] See www.washingtonpost.com/dc-md-va/2022/08/02/rape-kit-evidence-destruction-police/?wpisrc=nl_mustreads

[33] Australian Law Reform Commission, 2010: 26.17.

[34] Johnson et al, 2008: 148.

[35] See www.nytimes.com/2021/10/31/world/europe/uk-police-sexual-misconduct.html

[36] See www.abc.net.au/news/2020-10-19/police-in-australia-are-failing-to-take-action-against-domestic/12757914?nw=0

[37] See www.abc.net.au/news/2022-04-15/josie-officer-convicted-domestic-violence-nsw-police-force/100981846

[38] Goodmark, 2015: 1183–1246; Roslin, 2016: 319–29.

[39] Goodmark, 2015.

[40] Prison Police Initiative, 2019.

[41] INCITE!, n.d, a.

[42] Ritchie, 2006: 139; 2017.

[43] Ritchie, 2017: 109–10.

[44] Human Rights Watch, 2013: 50–65.

[45] Human Rights Watch, 2013: 66.

[46] CEDAW, 2015: 47.

[47] National Human Rights Commission, 2018: 54, 198. Numbers of registered cases include both rapes and deaths in police custody which are not disaggregated. National Campaign Against Torture, 2020.

[48] National Campaign Against Torture, 2020: 108–117. See also the rape of a 13-year-old Dalit girl by a police officer when she went to the police station

to report a gang rape in April 2022, www.abc.net.au/news/2022-05-06/
teenager-alleged-rape-in-india-uttar-pradesh/101040022

49 Aboriginal and Torres Strait Islander Social Justice Commission, 2006.

50 Warren-Gordon, 2021: 73–4.

51 National Crime Records Bureau, 2020.

52 Nathan and Thorat, 2020.

53 CEDAW, 2014: 3. In August, 2021, a 24-year-old woman, who had accused
an MP of rape, died after setting herself on fire outside the Supreme Court
in New Delhi. The woman had alleged that she was being harassed by the
police for reporting the politician. www.indiatoday.in/india/story/alleged-
rape-victim-succumbs-to-injuries-9-days-after-self-immolating-herself-outs
ide-supreme-court-1844700-2021-08-24

54 Human Rights Watch, 2021: 323.

55 Human Rights Watch, 2021: 520.

56 CEDAW, 2020: 7.

57 Bari (2021); Human Rights Commission of Pakistan, 2019: 172.

58 Human Rights Watch, 2013: 67.

59 National Crime Records Bureau, 2019.

60 See www.bbc.com/news/stories-43262319

61 Transparency International, 2011: 4.

62 White, 2021.

63 Horton, 2020.

64 See the website 'Our Black Girls' at www.ourblackgirls.com/

65 For Commissioner Scipione's apology see, www.abc.net.au/news/2016-08-
11/andrew-scipione-apologises-to-families-of-bowraville-children/7721492.
Also see First Nations filmmaker and academic, Larissa Behrendt (2013)
documentary made with the Bowraville families.

66 Porter and Whittaker, 2019. See also the National Justice Project, www.just
ice.org.au/families-seek-closure-in-case-of-man-who-molested-dying-girl/

67 See www.justice.org.au/mona-and-cindy-32-years-a-lonely-road-to-just
ice-for-bourke-teens/

68 Porter and Whittaker, 2019. See, for example, Northern Territory Coroner
Greg Cavanagh's scathing comments in 2018 about substandard investigations
carried out by the police into First Nations deaths. www.abc.net.au/news/
2018-06-23/indigenous-murder-cases-go-cold-as-coroner-lashes-nt-police/
9899946

69 See www.aph.gov.au/Parliamentary_Business/Committees/Senate/Legal_
and_Constitutional_Affairs/FirstNationswomenchildren

70 Amnesty International Canada, 2004: 19.

71 Human Rights Watch, 2013.

72 RCMP, 2014: 7.

73 CERD, 2012: 5; CEDAW, 2015: 51.

74 NIMMIWG, 2019b: 648–51.

75 NIMMIWG, 2019b: 630. See generally vol 1(a): 621–719.

76 NIMMIWG, 2019b: 690.

77 NIMMIWG, 2019a: 4.

[78] Terwiel, 2020: 422.
[79] For example, Tapia Tapia, 2016, 2021.
[80] ATSISJC, 2004: 21.
[81] Goodmark, 2018.
[82] Goodmark, 2018: 3.
[83] See, for example, Terwiel, 2020: 423. 'Critiques of "carceral feminism" have not only drawn much-needed attention to feminist complicity with the American prison state, they have also implied a binary choice between carceral and non-carceral feminism. I suggest that envisioning a spectrum of decarceration could ground a more expansive feminist abolitionist politics'.
[84] Nancarrow, 2021.
[85] Davis and Buxton-Namisnyk, 2021; Smee, 2021.
[86] Deslandes et al, 2022.
[87] Jassal, 2020.
[88] Cited in Way (2021).

Chapter 7

[1] Myanmar Federation of Persons with Disabilities (2021); video at https://www.facebook.com/Poemgrapher/videos/10157471006821923/
[2] There are many others. See www.theguardian.com/commentisfree/2020/jun/09/sandra-bland-eric-garner-freddie-gray-the-toll-of-police-violence-on-disabled-americans
[3] The Royal Commission into Victoria's Mental Health System (2021) and the Australian Royal Commission into Violence, Abuse, Neglect and Exploitation of People with Disability (commonly known as the 'Disability Royal Commission'). Database: 'Deaths Inside: Indigenous Australian deaths in custody'. https://www.theguardian.com/australia-news/ng-interactive/2018/aug/28/deaths-inside-indigenous-australian-deaths-in-custody
[4] See www.hrw.org/topic/disability-rights
[5] Human Rights Watch, 2020d: 3.
[6] Some writers and organisations also use the terms 'psychosocial disabilities' (mental ill-health), 'neuro-disabilities' (cognitive disability), or 'learning disabilities' (cognitive disability).
[7] Rowe et al, 2017: 10–11. Like Rowe and Dowse (2021) I use the single term, not to paper over important distinctions, but to draw attention to the understanding of disability as a phenomenon which is constructed across historical and social terrains.
[8] 'The slow wearing down of populations'. Puar, 2017: xiii–iv.
[9] Appleman, 2018: 419; McNamara, 2021.
[10] Human Rights Watch, 2014a.
[11] Dowse et al, 2021: 10–11.
[12] Russell and Stewart, 2001.
[13] Connell, 2011; Erevelles, 2014.
[14] Royal Commission into Victoria's Mental Health System (2021: vol 3, 360–6) and Australian Royal Commission into Violence, Abuse, Neglect

and Exploitation of People with Disability – which is commonly referred to as the 'Disability Royal Commission'.

[15] Ritchie, 2017: 93.
[16] See https://www.change.org/p/please-give-people-with-cognitive-disability-a-fair-go-in-the-justice-system
[17] Cited in Huey et al, 2021: 19.
[18] Independent Police Complaints Commission, 2010: 53–4.
[19] Mental Health Act (2014); Royal Commission into Victoria's Mental Health System, 2021: vol 4, 371.
[20] Vallas, 2016: 5.
[21] NSW Law Reform Commission, 2012: 59; Huey et al, 2021: 17. In Victoria, Australia, mental health related 'attendances' by police grew by an average of 13 per cent each year between 2014 and 2018 (Royal Commission into Victoria's Mental Health System, 2021: vol 1, 514).
[22] For reference to the literature see Dowse et al, 2021: 21–22; also VEOHRC, 2014: 20–25.
[23] Police Accountability Project, 2019a: 14–15.
[24] Perry and Carter-Long, 2016; Law Council of Australia, 2018: 18–25; Dowse et al, 2021.
[25] See https://www.theguardian.com/us-news/2021/may/16/north-carolina-jury-awards-75m-to-brothers-wrongly-convicted-of-1983
[26] Appleman, 2018: 463.
[27] Appleman, 2018: 465.
[28] AIHW, 2018.
[29] Appleman, 2018: 464.
[30] Human Rights Watch, 2014b: 8.
[31] Human Rights Watch, 2014b: 8.
[32] Human Rights Watch, 2020d: 45.
[33] National Disability Network and National Committee on the Rights of Persons with Disability, 2017: para 49.
[34] Human Rights Watch, 2014a.
[35] See www.washingtonpost.com/graphics/investigations/police-shootings-database/?itid=lk_interstitial_manual_10 as at 22 September 2021.
[36] Perry and Carter-Long, 2016: 1; Vallas, 2016.
[37] For discussion of the US and international data, see Fuller et al, 2015.
[38] See https://newsinteractives.cbc.ca/fatalpoliceencounters/
[39] Morgan, 2021: 4–5; Civilian Complaint Review Board, 2019: 7.
[40] Police Accountability Project, 2019a: 5.
[41] For example, Perry and Carter-Long, 2016; Harriet Tubman Collective, 2017.
[42] Runnymede Trust, 2021: 21. See, for example, the death of Sean Rigg, https://www.inquest.org.uk/sean-rigg-inquest-opens
[43] Huey et al, 2021: 20–21.
[44] See https://www.theguardian.com/australia-news/ng-interactive/2018/aug/28/deaths-inside-indigenous-australian-deaths-in-custody
[45] AHRC, 2014; VEOHRC, 2014; Police Accountability Project, 2019a: 5.
[46] Sobsey, 2000; Bowman et al, 2010; Australian Bureau of Statistics, 2021.

[47] Jordan, 2004: 37; Murray and Heenan, 2012: 280.

[48] Human Rights Watch, 2018: 33–8.

[49] Armstrong, 2020.

[50] Keilty and Connelly, 2001: 280; Human Rights Watch, 2018: 26–9. For a discussion of the literature on low reporting rates, and why many people with disability who are victims of crime do not believe that the police will protect them and are reluctant to seek help or protection from the police, see AHRC, 2014; VEOHRC, 2014: 50; Dowse et al, 2021: 12–18.

[51] Ritchie, 2017: 88–103.

[52] See www.crikey.com.au/2021/10/25/death-in-geraldton-how-joyce-clarke-became-another-indigenous-statistic/ For a video of the police killing see www.watoday.com.au/national/western-australia/wa-police-officer-acquit ted-of-murder-over-shooting-of-geraldton-woman-20211022-p592g3.html

[53] Dowse et al, 2021: 5–6.

[54] Thomas, 2021.

[55] Thompson, 2021b.

[56] Angiolini, 2017; Karakulak and Kurmelovs, 2021.

[57] Her Majesty's Inspectorate of Constabulary, 2018: 12.

[58] Huey et al, 2021: 20.

[59] Consortium for Citizens with Disabilities, 2020.

[60] Canadian Mental Health Association, 2020. See www.cmha.ca/news/statem ent-on-police-and-wellness-checks

[61] See also *The Guardian* database 'Deaths Inside: Indigenous Australian deaths in custody': https://www.theguardian.com/australia-news/ng-interactive/ 2018/aug/28/deaths-inside-indigenous-australian-deaths-in-custody

[62] Dowse et al, 2021. For examples caught on video of police violence, intimidation and arrest when making a welfare check see: www.theage.com. au/national/victoria/four-police-officers-involved-in-brutality-claims-suspen ded-20180406-p4z875.html, and www.dailymail.co.uk/news/article-5632 205/Senior-constable-swears-man-called-ambulance-help-suicidal-friend.html

[63] There are many examples. See for instance in the UK, Her Majesty's Inspectorate of Constabulary (2018b: 3, 8); in Australia, the Royal Commission into Victoria's Mental Health System (2021: 24, 48) and the Police Accountability Project (2019: 10); in Canada, the Canadian Mental Health Association (2020), the Centre for Addiction and Mental Health (2020) and groups such as Doctors for Defunding the Police; and in the US, the Consortium for Citizens with Disabilities (2020) and Abolition and Disability Justice Coalition (2021).

[64] For example, the Royal Commission into Victoria's Mental Health System (2021: vol 3, 358) disapprovingly compared the $1.8 billion funding for expanded prison capacity in the State's budget to the much smaller allocations for community-based mental health services or diversion, rehabilitation, and reintegration programmes. Police themselves acknowledged to the Royal Commission the impact of inadequate investment in community-based mental health services compared to police investment over decades with an almost exclusive focus on increasing the number of police.

[65] Kim et al, 2021.

[66] We might also add the role of police violence and discrimination during the public health responses to COVID-19. In addition to the violent policing of COVID-19 public health regulations already referred to in the book, one might add the racially discriminatory aspects of policing. In the UK, police use of force increased against Black and racially minoritised communities during the COVID-19 pandemic, even while crime rates were dropping (Harris et al, 2022).

[67] Alang et al, 2017; Jablonski, 2021.

[68] Alang et al, 2017: 662–5.

[69] Alang et al, 2017; Police Accountability Project, 2019; Thompson, 2021. See also Chapter 5 reference to NCAT (India) and INQUEST (UK) who identify individuals who have committed suicide as a result of the trauma caused by police abuse and torture.

[70] Deivanayagam et al, 2021: 2.

[71] APHA, 2018.

[72] APHA, 2018.

[73] APHA, 2021.

Chapter 8

[1] See Diphoorn et al, 2021 and associated articles in *Policing*, vol 15, no 1.

[2] Sivanandan, 1990: 134.

[3] Stuart Hall, 1999: 189–90.

[4] Hall, 1999: 196.

[5] Lammy, 2017.

[6] Deloitte, 2018; see *The Guardian* database, www.theguardian.com/austra lia-news/series/deaths-inside.

[7] Worden and McLean, 2017: 4–5.

[8] Schrader, 2019: 4–5, 196–7.

[9] Independent Commission on the Los Angeles Police Department, 1991. See also Human Rights Watch, www.hrw.org/legacy/reports98/police/uspo74. htm#TopOfPage

[10] President's Task Force on 21st Century Policing, 2015: iii.

[11] Kaba, 2021: 16; Maher, 2021: 79.

[12] Schrader, 2015.

[13] Kelley, 2020.

[14] See www.whitehouse.gov/state-of-the-union-2022/

[15] Levine 1994; Jassal, 2020: 1035–1036.

[16] Borwankar (2019).

[17] Common Cause and CSDS, 2019: 32–33; Borwankar (2019).

[18] Common Cause and CSDS, 2019: 32–33; Borwankar (2019).

[19] Varghese, 2018. Also for Pakistan see Waseem (forthcoming).

[20] Productivity Commission, 2022, Table 6A.2. This is likely an over-estimate of their representation because it includes *both* sworn police officers and other staff.

[21] Cunneen, 2001: 145–6; Gorrie, 2021.

22 Vitale, 2017: 12.
23 Vitale, 2017: 12–13.
24 Vitale, 2017: 8.
25 Human Rights Watch, 2020c: 88.
26 Human Rights Watch, 2020c: 88.
27 Worden et al, 2020.
28 Vitale, 2017: 15.
29 Maher, 2021: 84.
30 Human Rights Watch, 2020c: 91.
31 Vitale, 2017: 10–11; also Schrader, 2019a, 2020; Maher, 2021.
32 Bucci, 2022.
33 Weichbaum et al, 2017.
34 Morin and Mercer, 2017.
35 Weichbaum et al, 2017; Gonzalez et al, 2019.
36 Consortium for Citizens with Disabilities, 2020.
37 Dowse et al, 2021.
38 Police Accountability Project, 2019: 8.
39 Police Accountability Project, 2019: 9.
40 Viljoen et al, 2017.
41 Viljoen et al, 2017; Simplican, 2021: 390.
42 Murray and Heenan, 2012; McCulloch et al, 2021.
43 Nancarrow et al, 2020.
44 National Institute of Justice, 2009: 35.
45 Goodmark, 2015: 1228–9.
46 Goodmark, 2015: 1233.
47 Correia and Wall (2018: 17–18) cite Amnesty International research indicating that between 2001 and 2012 more than 500 people had been killed in Canada and the US after being tasered – nearly all were unarmed.
48 Lum et al, 2020.
49 For discussion of the research literature see Vitale, 2017: 23–4 and Maher, 2021: 81–3.
50 Maher, 2021: 82; also Schrader, 2015.
51 www.washingtonpost.com/graphics/investigations/police-shootings-datab ase/?itid=lk_interstitial_manual_10 as at 22 September 2021.
52 Human Rights Watch, 2020c: 87.
53 Piza and Welsh, 2022.
54 Koziarski and Huey, 2021.
55 Betts, 2022: 9.
56 Ulbrick, 2021: 23.
57 Ulbrick, 2021.
58 Ugwudike, 2020: 483; 2021.
59 Castelvecchi, 2020.
60 AI Now Institute (2021).
61 See the ShotSpotter website, www.shotspotter.com/cities/
62 Doucette et al, 2021.
63 Cunneen, 2001: 205–10.

64 Hall, 1999.
65 Human Rights Watch, 2020c: 86.
66 Cunneen, 2001: 205–10; Vitale, 2017: 16–17.
67 Runnymede Trust, 2021: 21.
68 IPID, 2021: 38; Knoetze (2020).
69 Human Rights Watch, 2021: 390.
70 Tankebe, 2008: 82.
71 Human Rights Watch, 2014c.
72 Human Rights Council, 2019: para 43.
73 Mahtani, 2020.
74 The remaining 23 states and all union territories are non-compliant; Commonwealth Human Rights Initiative, 2021.
75 President's Task Force on 21st Century Policing, 2015: 26.
76 Human Rights Watch, 2020c: 7.
77 NIMMIWG, 2019b: 690.
78 Hopkins, 2010: 6–11; the Police Ombudsman of Northern Ireland is often mentioned as a relatively successful model, but still with limitations. Also see on police reform generally, Vitale, 2017: 17–22; Correia and Wall, 2018: 159–71.
79 For example, in the US, qualified immunity protects police from civil lawsuits; current Australian laws provide for immunity from criminal liability for police, corrections staff, and other law enforcement officers for actions carried out in the course of their duties; in India, section 197 of the Code of Criminal Procedure requires State or Central government approval before a public official can be charged with criminal offences while acting in the discharge of their duties.
80 McCulloch, 2017.
81 For example, Vitale, 2017; Kaba, 2021; Maher, 2021; Davis et al, 2022.
82 Cited in Emerge, n.d.
83 Kaba, 2021: 93–8.
84 Kaba, 2021: 96.

Chapter 9

1   Ruth Wilson Gilmore interviewed in Kushner (2019).
2   Cullors, interviewed in Heatherton (2016): 37.
3   Ruth Wilson Gilmore, www.twitter.com/rwgilmoregirls/; www.instagram.com/p/CZBNZSmskdF/ and also Ruth Gilmore Wilson, 17 April 2019, Lannan Foundation. Available at: www.youtube.com/watch?v=YeOY9Z3r Z94&list=WL&index=10
4   Davis and Martinez, 1994; Davis, 2005: 52.
5   Spade, 2020: 15. He cites the example of working with homeless people which reveals that 'racism, colonialism, immigration enforcement, ableism, police violence, the foster care system, the healthcare system, transphobia, and more are all causes of homelessness or cause further harm to homeless people'.
6   Kaba, 2021: 64.

[7] Ray, 2020. Andrew Coyle connects this approach to justice reinvestment (JR). He writes,

> the intellectual case for a new approach based on community safety and security has been constructed gradually. Initially spurred on by urban geographers and other social scientists it has been picked up at a practical level in a variety of disparate settings and is generally described as JR. Very broadly, this has involved assessing the total resources, financial and other, that are expended on the criminal justice system; evaluating what benefit members of the public and taxpayers get from this expenditure; and considering whether there might be other ways of distributing these considerable resources at local levels to provide a better return on this substantial public investment. (Coyle, 2022)

[8] Davis, 2005; McLeod, 2019; Terwiel, 2020: 423–4.

[9] Spade, 2020: 9–20.

[10] Mignolo, 2017: 16.

[11] Davis et al, 2022: 22.

[12] Davis, 2003: 106–7.

[13] There is a preference for 'options' rather than 'alternatives' because the idea of alternatives already accepts the centrality of police and policing as the point of reference.

[14] Kaba, 2021: 13.

[15] Ajadi et al, n.d.; INCITE!, n.d. b; Vitale, 2017; Beck et al, 2020; Critical Resistance, 2020; Irwin and Pearl, 2020; Pearl, 2020; Kaba, 2021: 13, 70–71; Kim et al, 2021; Maher, 2021; Davis et al, 2022: 185–91; One Million Experiments at http://www.millionexperiments.com/; #8 to Abolition at www.8toabolition.com; Don't Call the Police at www.dontcallthepolice.com/

[16] INCITE!, n.d. b; Vitale, 2017; Beck et al, 2020; Critical Resistance, 2020; Irwin and Pearl, 2020; Pearl, 2020; Kaba, 2021: 13, 70–1; Kim et al, 2021; Maher, 2021; Davis et al, 2022: 185–91. One Million Experiments at http://www.millionexperiments.com/; #8 to Abolition at www.8toabolition.com; Don't Call the Police at www.dontcallthepolice.com/.

[17] Discussed previously; see also Abolitionist Futures, UK (www.abolitionistfutures.com/defund-the-police); and Reimagining Justice in South Africa Beyond Policing (www.drive.google.com/file/d/1krNcg_saPFABqjuFk QvtVKUpIjivd8Es/view).

[18] See www.accountablenow.com/

[19] See www.cpdp.co/

[20] See www.capstat.nyc/

[21] See www.washingtonpost.com/investigations/interactive/2022/police-misconduct-repeated-settlements/

[22] Gandel, 2021.

[23] See for example, the American Friends Service Committee, https://investig ate.afsc.org/

[24] Human Rights Watch, 2020d.

[25] For a useful summary of the programme and other references, see Dowse et al, 2021: 152–5.

[26] Beck et al, 2020; White Bird Clinic, 2020; Kim et al, 2021: 32.

[27] Irwin and Pearl, 2020: 9; Kim et al, 2021: 33.

[28] Beck et al, 2020; Irwin and Pearl, 2020: 9; Kim et al, 2021: 19.

[29] White Bird Clinic, 2020: 1–4.

[30] Kim et al, 2021: 23, 34.

[31] Irwin and Pearl, 2020: 10.

[32] Irwin and Pearl, 2020: 7–10.

[33] Irwin and Pearl, 2020: 10–12.

[34] Irwin and Pearl, 2020.

[35] Pearl, 2020: 7–8.

[36] Pearl, 2020.

[37] Gruber, 2020b.

[38] For example, INCITE!, n.d. b; INCITE! Women of Color Against Violence and Critical Resistance, 2001; Goodmark, 2015, 2018; Blagg et al, 2018.

[39] Goodmark, 2018: 34–51.

[40] Goodmark, 2018: 52–74.

[41] Niolon et al, 2017.

[42] INCITE! Women of Color Against Violence and Critical Resistance, 2001.

[43] See Sisters Inside (www.sistersinside.com.au). A community defence initiative organised by Sisters Inside is the #FreeHer campaign which works in conjunction with families of incarcerated women and girls in Western Australia – where around 50 per cent of women in prison are First Nations and they are imprisoned at a rate 22 times greater than non-Indigenous women. The campaign focused on releasing incarcerated women who were imprisoned because they could not pay their fines. It raised hundreds of thousands of dollars, released hundreds of women from prison, and was largely responsible for a change in legislation.

[44] See Sisters Uncut (www.sistersuncut.org)

[45] Taylor, 2018: 42.

[46] See www.wscadv.org/news/moment-of-truth-statement-of-commitm ent-to-black-lives/

[47] Deer, 2015.

[48] Blagg et al, 2018: 7.

[49] Blagg et al, 2018: 6–8; Blagg et al, 2021: 1.

[50] ATSISJC, 2004: 21.

[51] Blagg, 2008: 91.

[52] Porter and Cunneen, 2020: 407–9.

[53] Mutongwizo and Mutongwizo, forthcoming.

[54] Blagg, 2016; Cunneen, 2021.

[55] Blagg, 2008: 114.

[56] Porter, 2016.

57 Porter, 2016.
58 Cunneen and Tauri, 2017: 128.
59 See the Justice Reinvestment Network Australia (www.justicereinvestment. net.au).
60 Carvalho, 2020.
61 Global Commission on Drug Policy, 2011: 9.
62 Metaal and Youngers, 2011: 8.
63 Tonry, 1995.
64 UN figures cited in Fernandez and Nougier, 2021: 4.
65 Global Commission on Drug Policy, 2011: 15.
66 Harm Reduction International, 2021: 3.
67 Schenwar and Law, 2020.
68 Hughes and Stevens, 2010.
69 Placing intoxicated people in community facilities can reduce deaths in police custody, see for example, Aasebø et al (2015).
70 Jelsma, 2018: 23. See also the European Drug Policy Network, 2015.
71 Metaal and Youngers, 2011: 22.
72 McMichael, 2016.
73 Neocleous, 2021a: 13.
74 Editorial, 2021: 1195.
75 See Doherty and Sullivan, 2021; GBD 2019 Police Violence US Subnational Collaborators, 2021, and www.prisonpolicy.org/blog/2020/06/05/policek illings/
76 Jumbunna Research (2022). See also www.abc.net.au/news/2022-03-11/ community-calls-for-no-more-guns-in-rural-regions./13792898.
77 Jumbunna Research (2022). See also www.abc.net.au/news/2022-03-11/ we-are-divided-by-racism-says-walkers-legal-team/13792930.
78 Editorial, 2021: 1195.

References

Aasebø, W., Orskaug, G., and Erikssen, J. (2015) 'Can deaths in police cells be prevented? Experience from Norway and death rates in other countries', *Journal of Forensic and Legal Medicine*, 37: 61–5.

ABC News (2016) 'Bowraville murders: NSW police chief says victims' families were let down' [online] 11 August, Available from: www.abc.net.au/news/2016-08-11/andrew-scipione-apo logises-to-families-of-bowraville-children/7721492

Abolition and Disability Justice Coalition (2021) *Guiding Principles Based in Disability Justice*, [online], Available from: www.abolit ionanddisabilityjustice.com/guiding-principles/

Aboriginal and Torres Strait Islander Social Justice Commissioner [ATSISJC] (2004) *Social Justice Report 2004*, Sydney: Human Rights and Equal Opportunity Commission.

Aboriginal and Torres Strait Islander Social Justice Commission [ATSISJC] (2006) *Social Justice Report 2006*, Sydney: Australian Human Rights Commission.

Aboriginal and Torres Strait Islander Women's Task Force on Violence (1999) *The Aboriginal and Torres Strait Islander Women's Task Force on Violence Report*, Brisbane: State of Queensland.

Aborisade, R.A. and Gbahabo, D.D. (2021) 'Policing the lockdown: accounts of police officers' aggression and extortion of frontline health workers in Nigeria', *Policing & Society*, DOI: 10.1080/10439463.2021.1903461.

AI Now Institute (2021) 'A new AI lexicon: surveillance: the ghosts of white supremacy in AI reform', Medium.com [online] 9 September, Available from: www.medium.com/a-new-ai-lexi con/a-new-ai-lexicon-surveillance-8a4231ef8359

Ajadi, T., Critchley, H., Jones, E., and Rodgers, J. (n.d.) *Defunding the Police: Defining the Way Forward for HRM*, Halifax (Nova Scotia): Report to the Halifax Board of Police Commissioners.

Alang, S., McAlpine, D., McCreedy, E., and Hardeman, R. (2017) 'Police brutality and black health: setting the agenda for public health scholars', *American Journal of Public Health*, 17(5): 662–5.

Alexander, M. (2010) *The New Jim Crow*, New York: The New Press.

Allam, L., Wahlquist, C., and Evershed, N. (2020) 'Aboriginal deaths in custody: 434 have died since 1991, new data shows', *The Guardian*, [online] 6 June, Available from: www.theguard ian.com/australia-news/2020/jun/06/aboriginal-deaths-in-cust ody-434-have-died-since-1991-new-data-shows

Allard, T. and Prenzler, T. (2009) 'A summary analysis of police deaths in Australia: implications for prevention', *International Journal of Comparative and Applied Criminal Justice*, 33(1): 61–82.

American Civil Liberties Union [ACLU] (2014) *War Comes Home. The Excessive Militarization of American Policing*, New York: ACLU.

American Public Health Association [APHA] (2018) *Addressing Law Enforcement Violence as a Public Health Issue*, Policy No. 201811, Washington, DC: APHA.

American Public Health Association [APHA] (2021) *Advancing Public Health Interventions to Address the Harms of the Carceral System*, Policy No. 202117, Washington, DC: APHA.

Amnesty International (1993) *A Criminal Justice System Weighted Against Aboriginal People*, London: International Secretariat.

Amnesty International (1997) *Australia. Deaths in Custody: How Many More?* London: International Secretariat.

Amnesty International (2020) 'Nigeria: killing of #EndSARS protesters by the military must be investigated', Amnesty.org, [online] 21 October, Available from: www.amnesty.org/en/lat est/news/2020/10/killing-of-endsars-protesters-by-the-milit ary-must-be-investigated/

Amnesty International Canada (2004) 'Stolen sisters: a human rights response to discrimination and violence against Indigenous women in Canada', Amnesty.ca, [online] 20 March, Available from: www.amnesty.ca/sites/default/files/amr200032004enst olensisters.pdf

Anders, R. (2021) 'Facing tear gas, Thailand's child protesters find safety in protection team', *Southeast Asia Globe*, [online] 24 March, Available from: https://southeastasiaglobe.com/thaila nds-youth-protestors/

Anderson, D.M. and Killingray, D. (eds) (1991) *Policing the Empire: Government, Authority and Control 1830–1940*, Manchester: Manchester University Press.

Anderson, D.M. and Killingray, D. (eds) (1992) *Policing and Decolonisation: Nationalism, Politics and the Police 1917–1965*, Manchester: Manchester University Press.

Angiolini, E. (2017) *Report of the Independent Review of Deaths and Serious Incidents in Police Custody*, London: Home Office.

Anti-Security Collective (2021) 'Introduction to the special issue: a critical theory of police power in the twenty-first century', *Social Justice*, 47(3–4): 1–7.

Appleman, L. (2018) 'Deviancy, dependency, and disability: the forgotten history of eugenics and mass incarceration', *Duke Law Journal*, 68(3): 417–78.

Armstrong, D. (2020) 'Statement of Dorothy Armstrong', Royal Commission into Violence, Abuse, Neglect and Exploitation of People with Disability, STAT.0090.0001.0001 [online], Available from: www.disability.royalcommission.gov.au/publications/exhibit-11-02101-stat009000010001-written-statement-dorothy-armstrong

Arnold, D. (1992) 'Police power and the demise of British rule in India, 1930–47', in D.M. Anderson and D. Killingray (eds) *Policing and Decolonisation: Nationalism, Politics and the Police 1917–1965*, Manchester: Manchester University Press, pp 42–61.

Asher, J. and Horwitz, B. (2020) 'How do police actually spend their time?' *New York Times*, [online] 19 June, Available from: https://www.nytimes.com/2020/06/19/upshot/unrest-police-time-violent-crime.html

Attwood, B. (2003) *Rights for Aborigines*, St Leonards: Allen and Unwin.

Attwood, B. and Markus, A. (1999) *The Struggle for Aboriginal Rights*, St Leonards: Allen and Unwin.

Australian Bureau of Statistics [ABS] (2021) 'Disability and violence – in focus: crime and justice statistics' [online], Available from: www.abs.gov.au/statistics/people/crime-and-justice/focus-crime-and-justice-statistics/april-2021

Australian Human Rights Commission [AHRC] (2014) *Equal Before the Law: Towards Disability Justice Services*, Sydney: AHRC.

Australian Institute of Health and Welfare [AIHW] (2018) *The Health of Australia's Prisoners*, Canberra: AIHW.

Australian Institute of Health and Welfare [AIHW] (2020) *Sexual Assault in Australia*, Canberra: AIHW.

Australian Law Reform Commission [ALRC] (2010) *Family Violence – A National Legal Response*, Sydney: ALRC.

Baldry, E. and Cunneen, C. (2014) 'Imprisoned Indigenous women and the shadow of colonial patriarchy', *Australian and New Zealand Journal of Criminology*, 47(2): 276–98.

Bari, M. (2021) 'Pakistan: backlash grows against PM Imran Khan's "sexist comments"', *Deutsche Welle*, [online] 29 June, Available from: www.dw.com/en/pakistan-backlash-grows-agai nst-pm-imran-khans-sexist-comments/a-58094002

Barker, K., Baker, M., and Watkins, A. (2021) 'In city after city, police mishandled Black Lives Matter protests', *New York Times*, [online] 20 March, Available from: https://www.nytimes.com/ 2021/03/20/us/protests-policing-george-floyd.html

Bassett, M.T. (2019) 'No justice, no health: The Black Panthers party's fight for health in Boston and beyond', *Journal of African American Studies*, 23: 352–63.

BBC (2014) 'Police not recording a fifth of crimes, watchdog report suggests', [online] 1 May, Available from: www.bbc.com/ news/uk-27226110

BBC (2021), 'Columbia protests: rights body criticizes "disproportionate" response', [online] 8 July, Available from: www.bbc.com/news/world-latin-america-57733541

Beck, J., Reuland, M., and Pope, L. (2020) 'Case study: CAHOOTS', Vera Behavioural Health Crisis Alternatives [online], Available from: www.vera.org/behavioral-health-cri sis-alternatives/cahoots

Behrendt, L. (2013) *Innocence Betrayed,* Lavarch Productions, Sydney.

Ben-Moshe, L. (2020) *Decarcerating Disability: Deinstitutionalization and Prison Abolition*, Minneapolis: University of Minnesota Press.

Betts, P.R. (2022) 'Governing the silence: the institutionalisation of evidence-based policing in modern Britain', *Justice, Power and Resistance*, 5(1): 9–27.

Blagg, H. (2008) *Crime, Aboriginality and the Decolonisation of Justice*, Annandale: Federation Press.

Blagg, H. (2016) *Crime, Aboriginality and the Decolonisation of Justice* (2nd edn), Annandale: Federation Press.

Blagg, H., Williams, E., Cummings, E., Hovane, V., Torres, M., and Woodley, K.N. (2018) *Innovative Models in Addressing Violence Against Indigenous Women: Final Report*, Sydney: ANROWS.

Blagg, H., Hovane, V., Tulich, T., Raye, D., May, S., and Worrigal, T. (2021) 'Law, culture and decolonisation: the perspectives of Aboriginal Elders on family violence in Australia', *Social & Legal Studies*, DOI: 10.1177/09646639211046134.

Blanchard E. (2014) 'French colonial police', in G. Bruinsma and D. Weisburd (eds) *Encyclopedia of Criminology and Criminal Justice*, New York: Springer, pp 1836–46.

Bloembergen, M. and Klinkers, E. (2014) 'Dutch colonial police', in G. Bruinsma and D. Weisburd (eds) *Encyclopedia of Criminology and Criminal Justice*, New York: Springer, pp 1201–11.

Bobin, F. (forthcoming) 'Policing and imperialism in France and the French empire', in C. Cunneen, A. Deckert, A. Porter, J. Tauri, and R. Webb (eds) *Routledge Handbook on Decolonizing Justice*, Abingdon: Routledge.

Borwankar, M. (2019) 'A case for diversity in police force', *Hindustan Times*, [online] 11 November, Available from: www.hindustantimes.com/india-news/a-case-for-diversity-in-police-force/story-YP0kgeVWBvARdkzaOl2KwO.html

Bowman, R., Scott, J., and Morris, T. (2010) 'Sexual abuse prevention: a training program for developmental disabilities service providers', *Journal of Child Sexual Abuse*, 19(2): 119–27.

Bricknell, S. and Doherty, L. (2021) *Homicide in Australia 2018–19*, Canberra: Australian Institute of Criminology.

Bridges, L. (2015) *The Met Gangs Matrix: Institutional Racism in Action*, London: Institute of Race Relations.

Brogden, M. (1981) '"All police are conning bastards" – policing and the problem of consent', in B. Fryer, A. Hunt, D. McBarnett, and B. Moorehouse (eds) *Law, State and Society*, London: Croom Helm.

Brogden, M. (1982) *The Police: Autonomy and Consent*, London: Academic Press.

Brown, M., Martinez, K., and Swayne, V. (2021) 'The 911 call as a horizon of abolition', Imagining Abolition: Beyond Prisons, Wars and Borders. A Virtual Gathering, 14–17 April [online], Available from: www.sites.google.com/view/imagining-abolit ion/home

Bucci, N. (2022) 'Zachary Rolfe was allegedly violent during arrests of four Aboriginal males before Kumanjayi Walker shooting', *The Guardian*, [online] 19 March, Available from: www.theguardian.com/australia-news/2022/mar/19/ zachary-rolfe-was-allegedly-violent-during-arrests-of-four-abo riginal-males-before-kumanjayi-walker-shooting

Burger, J. (1988) *Aborigines Today. Land Justice*, Report No 5, Indigenous Peoples and Development Series, London: Anti-Slavery Society.

Burrowes, N. (2018) 'Building the world we want to see: a herstory of SistaIISista and the struggle against state and interpersonal violence', *Souls*, 20(4): 375–98.

Cain, M. (1993) 'Review: Some go backward, some go forward: police work in comparative perspective', *Contemporary Sociology*, 22(3): 319–24.

Canadian Mental Health Association (2020) 'Statement on police and wellness checks' [online], Available from: www.cmha.ca/ news/statement-on-police-and-wellness-checks

Carvalho, B. (2020) 'Latin America is ready for its Black Lives Matter reckoning', *New York Times*, 29 June.

Castelvecchi, D. (2020) 'Mathematicians urge colleagues to boycott police work in the wake of killings', *Nature*, [online] 19 June, Available from: www.nature.com/articles/d41 586-020-01874-9

Cavanagh, G. (2010) *Inquest into the Death of Gottlieb Rubuntja [2010] NTMC 048*, Alice Springs: Coroner's Court of the Northern Territory [online], Available from: https://justice. nt.gov.au/__data/assets/pdf_file/0008/208772/a00122009-gottlieb-rubuntja.pdf

Centre for Addiction and Mental Health, Canada (2020) 'CAMH statement on police interactions with people in mental health crisis' [online], Available from: www.camh.ca/en/camh-news-and-stories/camh-statement-on-police-interactions-with-peo ple-in-mental-health-crisis

Centro de Estudios Legales y Sociales (2018) *The Internal War: How the Fight Against Drugs is Militarizing Latin America*, Buenos Aires: Centro de Estudios Legales y Sociales.

Centro de Investigación y Docencia Económicas (2019) *Monitor del Uso de la Fuerza Letal en América Latina: Un Estudio Comparativo de Brasil, Colombia, El Salvador, México y Venezuela, 2019*, Aguascalientes, Mexico: Centro de Investigación y Docencia Económicas.

Chartrand, V. (2019) 'Unsettled times: Indigenous incarceration and the links between colonialism and the penitentiary in Canada', *Canadian Journal of Criminology and Criminal Justice*, 61(3): 67–89.

Chaudhary, V. (2019) 'Forty years on, Southall demands justice for killing of Blair Peach', *The Guardian*, [online] 21 April, Available from: https://www.theguardian.com/uk-news/2019/apr/21/southall-demands-justice-killing-of-blair-peach-1979

Civilian Complaint Review Board [CCRB] (2019) *Taser Use in CCRB Complaints 2014–2017*, New York: CCRB.

Committee on the Elimination of Discrimination Against Women [CEDAW] (2014) 'Concluding observations on the combined fourth and fifth periodic reports of India', CEDAW/C/IND/CO/4-5, Geneva: United Nations.

Committee on the Elimination of Discrimination Against Women [CEDAW] (2015), 'Report of the inquiry concerning Canada of the Committee on the Elimination of Discrimination Against Women', CEDAW/C/OP.8/CAN/1, Geneva: United Nations.

Committee on the Elimination of Discrimination Against Women [CEDAW] (2020), 'Concluding observations on the fifth periodic report of Pakistan', CEDAW/C/PAK/CO/5, Geneva: United Nations.

Committee on the Elimination of Racial Discrimination [CERD] (2012) 'Concluding observations of the Committee on the Elimination of Racial Discrimination: Canada, Eightieth Session', CERD/C/CAN/CO/19-20, Geneva: United Nations.

Committee Against Torture [CAT] (2019) 'Concluding observations on the Initial Report of Bangladesh', CAT/C/BGD/CO/1, Geneva: United Nations.

Common Cause and CSDS (2019) *Status of Policing in India Report 2019*, New Delhi: Common Cause and Lokniti (CSDS).

Commonwealth Human Rights Initiative (2021) *Government Compliance with Supreme Court Directives on Police Reforms: An Assessment*, New Delhi: Commonwealth Human Rights Initiative.

Connell, R. (2011) 'Southern bodies and disability: rethinking concepts', *Third World Quarterly*, 32(8): 1369–81.

Consortium for Citizens with Disabilities (2020) 'Statement on reducing police responses to people with disabilities' [online], Available from: www.c-c-d.org/fichiers/Policing-statement-9-14-20.pdf

Coroners Court of New South Wales (2021) 'Inquest into the deaths of John, Jack and Jennifer Edwards' [online] 7 April, Available from: www.coroners.nsw.gov.au/coroners-court/coronial-findings-search.html

Correia, D. and Wall, T. (2018) *Police: A Field Guide*, London: Verso.

Corruption and Crime Commission, Western Australia (2012) 'Charges to be considered over tasering of Kevin Spratt: media release', Perth: Corruption and Crime Commission.

Country Reports on Human Rights Practices (2020) 'Pakistan', Washington: Bureau of Democracy, Human Rights and Labor, United States Department of State.

Cowell, D., Jones, T., and Young, J. (eds) (1982) *Policing the Riots*, London: Junction Books.

Coyle, A. (2022) 'Towards a better way', Centre for Crime and Justice Studies [online], Available from: www.crimeandjustice.org.uk/resources/towards-better-way

Crenshaw, K. (2020) 'Fear of a Black uprising: confronting the white pathologies that shape racist policing', *The New Republic*, 13 August, pp 12–15.

Crime and Misconduct Commission, Queensland (2005) *Oleoresin Capsicum (OC) Spray Use by Queensland Police*, Brisbane: Crime and Misconduct Commission.

Critical Resistance (2020) 'Our communities, our solutions: an organiser's toolkit for developing campaigns to abolish policing' [online], Available from: https://criticalresistance.org/updates/check-out-our-new-organizers-toolkit-to-abolish-policing/

Cunneen, C. (2001) *Conflict, Politics and Crime: Aboriginal Communities and the Police*, Abingdon: Routledge.

Cunneen, C. (2003) 'Zero-tolerance policing and the experience of New York City', in S.H. Decker, L.F. Alarid, and C. Katz (eds) *Controversies in Criminal Justice: Contemporary Readings*, Los Angeles: Roxbury Publishing Company, pp 144–57.

Cunneen, C. (2007) 'Riot, resistance and moral panic: demonising the colonial other', in S. Poynting and G. Morgan (eds) *Outrageous! Moral Panics in Australia*, Hobart: ACYS Publishing, pp 20–9.

Cunneen, C. (2009) 'Law, policing and public order: the aftermath of Cronulla', in G. Noble (ed) *Lines in the Sand. The Cronulla Riots, Multiculturalism and National Belonging*, Sydney: Institute of Criminology Press, pp 220–31.

Cunneen, C. (2021) 'Cartographies of place: being, country and Indigenous justice', in A. Harkness and R. White (eds) *Crossroads of Rural Crime*, Bingley: Emerald Publishing, pp 31–44.

Cunneen, C. and McDonald, D. (1997) *Keeping Aboriginal and Torres Strait Islander People Out of Custody*, Canberra: Aboriginal and Torres Strait Islander Commission.

Cunneen, C. and Rowe, S. (2015) 'Decolonising Indigenous victimisation', in D. Wilson and S. Ross (eds) *Crime, Victims and Policy*, Basingstoke: Palgrave Macmillan, pp 10–32.

Cunneen, C. and Tauri, J. (2017) *Indigenous Criminology*, Bristol: Policy Press.

Cunneen, C., White, R., and Richards, K. (2015) *Juvenile Justice*, 5th edn, Melbourne: Oxford University Press.

Cunneen, C., Baldry, E., Brown, D., Brown, M., Schwartz, M., and Steel, A. (2013) *Penal Culture and Hyperincarceration*, Farnham: Ashgate.

Cunningham, D. (2022) 'Policing white supremacy: asymmetry and inequality in protest control', *Social Problems*, DOI: 10.1093/socpro/spac010.

Dahir, A.L., Maclean, R. and Chutel, L. (2020) 'George Floyd's killing prompts Africans to call for police reform at home', *New York Times*, [online] 8 July, Available from: https://www.nytimes.com/2020/07/03/world/africa/george-floyd-protests-police-africa.html

Davis, A.Y. (1982) *Women, Race and Class*, London: The Women's Press.

Davis, A.Y. (1998) 'Racialised punishment and prison abolition', in J. James (ed) *The Angela Y Davis Reader*, Oxford: Blackwell, pp 96–107.

Davis, A.Y. (2003) *Are Prisons Obsolete*, New York: Seven Stories Press.

Davis, A.Y. (2005) *Abolition Democracy*, New York: Seven Stories Press.

Davis, A.Y. and Martinez, E. (1994) 'Coalition building among people of color', *Inscriptions*, 7, Santa Cruz: Center for Cultural Studies, UC.

Davis, A.Y., Dent, G., Meiners, E., and Richie, B. (2022) *Abolition. Feminism. Now.*, Dublin: Penguin Random House.

Davis, A.Y., Davis, M., Gilmore, R.W., and Taylor, K.-Y. (2021) 'Abolition, Cultural Freedom and Liberation: Lannan Readings and Conversations and Haymarket Books' [video], [online] 5 October, Available from: https://www.youtube.com/watch?v= WLO0UuSnPzU

Davis, M. and Buxton-Namisnyk, E. (2021) 'Coercive control law could harm the women it's meant to protect', *Sydney Morning Herald*, [online] 2 July, Available from: www.smh.com.au/natio nal/nsw/coercive-control-law-could-harm-the-women-it-s-meant-to-protect-20210701-p5861e.html

de Carvalho Silva, L. and Langeani, B. (2019) 'Low impact, wrong direction: why São Paulo state drug policy is inefficient and ineffective', *Journal of Illicit Economies and Development*, 1(2): 204–19.

Deer, S. (2015) *The Beginning and End of Rape: Confronting Sexual Violence in Native America*, Minneapolis: University of Minnesota Press.

Deivanayagam, T., Lasoye, S., Smith, J., and Selvarajah, S. (2021) 'Policing is a threat to public health and human rights', *BMJ Global Health*, DOI:10.1136/bmjgh-2020-004582.

Deloitte (2018) 'Review of the Implementation of the Recommendations of the Royal Commission into Aboriginal Deaths in Custody' [online], Available from: www.niaa.gov.au/sites/default/files/publications/rciadic-review-report.pdf

Desai, S. (2020) 'Defund the police means defund the police', *briarpatch*, July/August [online], Available from: www.briarpa tchmagazine.com/articles/view/defund-the-police-means-def und-the-police

Deslandes, A., Longbottom, M., McKinnnon, C., and Porter, A. (2022) 'White feminism and carceral industries: strange bedfellows or partners in crime and criminology?', *Decolonization of Criminology and Justice*, 4(2): 5–33.

Dickinson, E. (2021) 'Pandemic gloom and police violence leave Columbia in turmoil', The Crisis Group, [online] 6 May, Available from: www.crisisgroup.org/latin-america-caribbean/ andes/colombia/pandemic-gloom-and-police-violence-leave- colombia-turmoil

Diphoorn, T., Leyh, B.M., and Slooter, L. (2021) 'Transforming police reform: global experiences through a multidisciplinary lens', *Policing*, 15(1): 340–7.

Doherty, L. and Sullivan, T. (2021) *Deaths in Custody Australia 2019–20*, Canberra: Australian Institute of Criminology.

Doucette, M., Green, C., Dineen, J., Shapiro, D., and Raissian, K.M. (2021) 'Impact of ShotSpotter technology on firearm homicides and arrests among large metropolitan counties: a longitudinal analysis, 1999–2016', *Journal of Urban Health*, 98(5): 609–21.

Douglas, H. and Fitzgerald, R. (2018) 'The domestic violence protection order system as entry to the criminal justice system for Aboriginal and Torres Strait Islander People', *International Journal for Crime, Justice and Social Democracy*, 7(3): 41–57.

Dowse, L., Rowe, S., Baldry, E., and Baker, M. (2021) *Police Responses to People with Disability*, Sydney: Royal Commission into Violence, Abuse, Neglect and Exploitation of People with Disability.

Dunbar-Ortiz, R. (2014) *An Indigenous Peoples' History of the United States*, Boston: Beacon Press.

Eastwood, N., Shiner, M., and Bear, D. (2013) *The Numbers in Black and White: Ethnic Disparities in the Policing and Prosecution of Drug Offences in England and Wales*, London: Release.

Editorial (2021) 'Fatal police violence in the USA: a public health issue', *The Lancet*, 398: 1195.

Egwu, P. (2020) 'As the world marches for American victims, police brutality in Africa goes unnoticed', *Foreign Policy*, [online] 17 June, Available from: www.foreignpolicy.com/2020/06/17/black-lives-matter-protests-africa-police-brutality/

Elliott-Cooper, A. (2021) *Black Resistance to British Policing*, Manchester: Manchester University Press.

Emerge (nd) 'The abolitionist horizon: building a world without police or prisons' [online], Available from: www.dsaemerge.org/the-abolitionist-horizon-building-a-world-without-police-or-prisons/

Equality and Human Rights Commission UK (2010) *Stop and Think. A Critical Review of the Use of Stop and Search Powers in England Wales*, London: Equality and Human Rights Commission.

Erevelles, N. (2014) 'Crippin' Jim Crow: disability, dis-Location and the school-to-prison pipeline', in L. Ben-Moshe, C. Chapman, and A. Carey (eds) *Disability Incarcerated. Imprisonment and Disability in the United States and Canada*, New York: Palgrave Macmillan, pp 81–100.

European Drug Police Network (2015) *Alternative Development: Providing Viable Alternatives to Illicit Drug Cultivation*, Brussels: European Drug Police Network.

Evans, J. (2021) 'Penal nationalism in the settler colony: on the construction and maintenance of "National Whiteness" in settler Canada', *Punishment and Society*, DOI: 10.1177/14624745211023455.

Fanon, F. (1967) *The Wretched of the Earth*, Harmondsworth: Penguin.

Farmer, C. and Evans, R. (2020) 'Primed and ready: does arming police increase safety? Preliminary findings', *Violence and Gender*, 7(2): 47–56.

Fassin, D. (2013) *Enforcing Order. An Ethnography of Urban Policing*, Cambridge: Polity Press.

Federal Bureau of Investigation (2021) 'FBI releases 2020 statistics on law enforcement officers killed in the line of duty' [press release], [online] 21 May, Available from: https://www.fbi.gov/news/pressrel/press-releases/fbi-releases-2020-statistics-on-law-enforcement-officers-killed-in-the-line-of-duty

Fernandez, A.C. and Nougier, M. (2021) 'Punitive drug laws: 10 years undermining the Bangkok Rules, International Drug Policy Consortium Briefing Paper' [online], Available from: www.penalreform.org/resource/punitive-drug-laws-10-years-undermining-the-bangkok/

Findlay, M. (2004) *Introducing Policing*, Melbourne: Oxford University Press.

Fleetwood, J. and Lea, J. (2020) 'De-funding the police in the UK', *British Society of Criminology Newsletter*, No 85 [online], Available from: https://www.britsoccrim.org/wp-content/uploads/2020/08/BSCN85-Fleetwood-Lea.pdf

Foley, G. (2001) *Black Power in Redfern 1968–1972* [online], Available from: http://gooriweb.org/history/233.pdf

Fuller, D., Lamb, R., Biasotti, M., and Snook, J. (2015) *Overlooked in the Undercounted: The Role of Mental Illness in Fatal Law Enforcement Encounters*, Arlington: Treatment Advocacy Center.

Gallagher, A., Raffle, E., and Maulana, Z. (2020) 'Failing to fulfil the responsibility to protect: the war on drugs as crimes against humanity in the Philippines', *Pacific Review*, 33(2): 247–77.

Gandel, S. (2021) '"Fiscal Justice Ratings" fight police brutality with finance', *The New York Times*, [online] 16 October, www.nytimes.com/2021/10/16/business/dealbook/fiscal-justice-ratings.html

Garton, S. (1987) 'Policing the dangerous lunatic: lunacy incarceration in New South Wales 1843–1914', in M. Finnane (ed), *Policing in Australia. Historical Perspectives*, Kensington: New South Wales University Press.

GBD 2019 Police Violence US Subnational Collaborators (2021) 'Fatal police violence by race and state in the USA, 1980–2019: a network meta-regression', *The Lancet*, 398: 1239–55.

Geary, R. (1985) *Policing Industrial Disputes 1983 to 1985*, London: Methuen.

Gilroy, P. (1987 [1982]) 'The myth of Black criminality' in P. Scraton (ed) *Law, Order and the Authoritarian State*, Milton Keynes: Open University Press, pp 107–20.

Global Commission on Drug Policy (2011) *War on Drugs. Report of the Global Commission on Drug Policy* [online], Available from: www.globalcommissionondrugs.org/wp-content/themes/gcdp_v1/pdf/Global_Commission_Report_English.pdf

Go, J. (2020) 'The imperial origins of American Policing: militarization and imperial feedback in the early 20th century', *American Journal of Sociology*, 125(5): 1193–254

Goldson, B., Cunneen, C., Russell, S., Brown, D., Baldry, E., Schwartz, M., and Briggs, D. (2021) *Youth Justice and Penality in Comparative Context*, London: Routledge.

Gonzalez, J.M.R., Bishopp, S., Jetelina, K.K., Gabriel, K.P., and Cannell, M.B. (2019) 'Does military veteran status and deployment history impact officer involved shootings? A case–control study', *Journal of Public Health*, 41(3): e245–e52

Goodall, H. (1996) *Invasion to Embassy: Land in Aboriginal Politics in New South Wales, 1770–1972*, St Leonards: Allen and Unwin.

Goodmark, L. (2015) 'Hands up at home: militarized masculinity and police officers who commit intimate partner abuse', *Brigham Young University Law Review*, 5: 1183–246.

Goodmark, L. (2018) *Decriminalizing Domestic Violence: A Balanced Approach to Intimate Partner Violence*, Oakland: University of California Press.

Gordon, P. (1985) '"If they come in the morning …": the police, the miners and Black people', in B. Fine and R. Millar (eds) *Policing The Miners' Strike*, London: Lawrence and Wisehart.

Gorrie, R. (2021) *Black and Blue: A Memoir of Racism and Resilience*, Melbourne: Scribe.

Gramlich, J. (2017) 'Most violent and property crimes in the U.S. go unsolved', Pew Research Centre, [online] 1 March, Available from: https://www.pewresearch.org/fact-tank/2017/03/01/most-violent-and-property-crimes-in-the-u-s-go-unsolved/

Gramlich, J. (2020) 'What the crime data says (and doesn't say) about crime in the United States', Pew Research Centre, [online] 20 November, Available from: https://www.pewresearch.org/fact-tank/2020/11/20/facts-about-crime-in-the-u-s/

Green, E. and Mora, D. (2021) 'US-trained cops in Mexico killed migrants, set them on fire, say prosecutors', Vice World News, [online] 5 August, Available from: https://www.vice.com/en/article/93y847/us-trained-cops-in-mexico-killed-migrants-set-them-on-fire-say-prosecutors

Gruber, A. (2020a) *The Feminist War on Crime*, Oakland: University of California Press.

Gruber, A. (2020b) 'How police became the go-to response to domestic violence', Slate, [online] 7 July, Available from: www.slate.com/news-and-politics/2020/07/policing-domestic-violence-history.html

Gruber, A. (forthcoming) 'Colonial carceral feminism', in C. Cunneen, A. Deckert, A. Porter, J. Tauri, and R. Webb (eds) *Routledge Handbook on Decolonizing Justice*, Abingdon: Routledge.

Hall, S. (1980) 'Drifting into a law and order society', in J. Muncie, E. McLaughlin, and M. Langan (eds) *Criminological Perspectives: A Reader*, London: Sage, pp 257–70.

Hall, S. (1999) 'From Scarman to Stephen Lawrence', *History Workshop Journal*, 48: 187–97.

Hall, S., Critcher, C., Jefferson, T., Clarke, J., and Roberts, B. (1978) *Policing the Crisis*, London: Macmillan Publishers.

Harcourt, B (2018) *The Counterrevolution: How Our Government Went to War Against Its Own Citizens*, New York: Basic Books.

Harm Reduction International (2021) 'The harms of incarceration' [online], Available from: www.hri.global/files/2021/06/14/HRI_Briefing_Prisons_June2021_Final1.pdf

Harriet Tubman Collective (2017) 'Disability solidarity: completing the "vision for black lives"', *Harvard Kennedy School Journal of African American Public Policy*, 69–72.

Harring, S. (1983) *Policing a Class Society*, New Brunswick: Rutgers University Press.

Harris, D. (2020) 'Racial profiling: past, present and future?' *American Bar Association* [online], Available from: www.americanbar.org/groups/criminal_justice/publications/criminal-justice-magazine/2020/winter/racial-profiling-past-present-and-future/

Harris, S., Joseph-Salisbury, R., Williams, P., and White, L. (2022) 'Notes on policing, racism and the Covid-19 pandemic in the UK', *Race and Class*, 63(2): 92–102.

Hayes, C. (2018) *A Colony in a Nation*, New York: W.W. Norton.

Heatherton, C. (2016) '#BlackLivesMatter and global visions of abolition: an interview with Patrisse Cullors', in J.T. Camp and C. Heatherton (eds) *Policing the Planet*, London: Verso, pp 35–40.

Her Majesty's Inspectorate of Constabulary and Fire & Rescue Services, UK (2018a) *Understanding the Difference: The Initial Police Response to Hate Crime*, London: HMICFRS.

Her Majesty's Inspectorate of Constabulary and Fire & Rescue Services, UK (2018b) *Policing and Mental Health: Picking up the Pieces*, London: HMICFRS.

Her Majesty's Inspectorate of Constabulary and Fire & Rescue Services, UK (2021) *Disproportionate Use of Police Powers. A Spotlight on Stop and Search and the Use of Force*, London: HMICFRS.

Hine, K. (2020) 'Road crashes, assaults and being spat on: the dangers facing Australian police in the line of duty', *The Conversation*, 1 May, Available from: https://theconversation. com/road-crashes-assaults-and-being-spat-on-the-dangers-fac ing-australian-police-in-the-line-of-duty-137594

House of Representatives Standing Committee on Aboriginal and Torres Strait Islander Affairs, Australia (1994) *Justice Under Scrutiny*, Canberra: AGPS.

Holmes, J. and Fitzgerald, J. (2017) *Trends in NSW Police Clear-Up Rates*, Sydney: NSW Bureau of Crime Statistics and Research.

Hönke, J. and Müller, M.M. (eds) (2016) *The Global Making of Policing*, Abingdon: Routledge.

Hope, R. (2021) 'Myanmar: girl, 7, reported shot dead in brutal crackdown on anti-coup protesters in Myanmar', *Sky News*, [online] 23 March, Available from: https://news.sky.com/story/ myanmar-girl-7-reported-shot-dead-in-brutal-crackdown-on-anti-coup-protesters-in-myanmar-12254593

Hopkins, T. (2010) *An Effective System for Investigating Complaints Against Police*, Victoria Law Foundation, Available from: https:// www.parliament.vic.gov.au/images/Submission_4-1_Hopkin s_Tamar.pdf

Horton, T. (2020) 'When Black children go missing why isn't this breaking news?' *Chicago Defender*, [online] 10 September, Available from: www.chicagodefender.com/when-black-child ren-go-missing-why-isnt-this-breaking-news/

Howell, E. (2014) 'Black Power – by any means possible', in G. Foley, A. Schapp, and E. Howell (eds) *The Aboriginal Tent Embassy*, Abingdon: Routledge, pp 67–83.

Huey, L., Ferguson, L., and Vaughan, A. (2021) *The Limits of Our Knowledge: Tracking the Size and Scope of Police Involvement with Persons with Mental Illness*, Ottawa: Royal Society of Canada.

Hughes, C. and Stevens, A. (2010) 'What can we learn from the Portuguese decriminalization of illicit drugs?', *British Journal of Criminology*, 50(6): 999–1022.

Human Rights and Equal Opportunity Commission [HREOC], Australia (1991) *Racist Violence: Report of the National Inquiry into Racist Violence*, Canberra: AGPS.

Human Rights Commission of Pakistan (2019) *State of Human Rights in 2018*, Lahore: Human Rights Commission of Pakistan.

Human Rights Council (2019) *Human Rights in the Administration of Justice. Report of the United Nations High Commissioner for Human Rights*, Human Rights Council, Forty-Second Session, A/HRC/42/20.

Human Rights Watch (2013) '"Those who take us away". Abusive policing and failures in protection of Indigenous women and girls in Northern British Columbia, Canada' [online], Available from: www.hrw.org/sites/default/files/reports/canada0213 webwcover_0.pdf

Human Rights Watch (2014a) *'Treated Worse than Animals': Abuses Against Women and Girls with Psychosocial and Intellectual Disabilities in Institutions in India*, New York: Human Rights Watch.

Human Rights Watch (2014b) *One Billion Forgotten: Protecting the Human Rights of Persons with Disabilities*, New York: Human Rights Watch.

Human Rights Watch (2014c) *'No Answers, No Apology': Police Abuses and Accountability in Malaysia*, New York: Human Rights Watch.

Human Rights Watch (2016a) *'Bound by Brotherhood': India's Failure to End Killings in Police Custody*, New York: Human Rights Watch.

Human Rights Watch (2016b) *'This Crooked System': Police Abuse and Reform in Pakistan*, New York: Human Rights Watch.

Human Rights Watch (2018) *Invisible Victims of Sexual Violence: Access to Justice for Women and Girls with Disabilities in India*, New York: Human Rights Watch.

Human Rights Watch (2020a) 'Kenya: police brutality during curfew', [online] 22 April, Available from: www.hrw.org/news/2020/04/22/kenya-police-brutality-during-curfew

Human Rights Watch (2020b) *World Report 2020: Events of 2019*, New York: Human Rights Watch.

Human Rights Watch (2020c) *'Kettling' Protesters in the Bronx: Systemic Police Brutality and Its Costs in the United States*, New York: Human Rights Watch.

Human Rights Watch (2020d) *Living in Chains: Shackling of Peoples with Psychosocial Disabilities*, New York: Human Rights Watch.

Human Rights Watch (2021) *World Report 2021: Events of 2020*, New York: Human Rights Watch.

Ifill, S.A. (2007) *On The Courthouse Lawn: Confronting the Legacy of Lynching in the Twenty First Century*, Boston: Beacon Press.

INCITE! (n.d. a) 'Policing sex work' [online], Available from: www.incite-national.org/policing-sex-work/

INCITE! (n.d. b) 'Law enforcement violence against women of color and trans people of color. An organizer's resource and toolkit' [online], Available from: www.incite-national.org/wp-content/uploads/2018/08/TOOLKIT-FINAL.pdf

INCITE! (2001) 'Statement on gender violence and the prison industrial complex' [online], Available from: www.incite-natio nal.org/incite-critical-resistance-statement/

Independent Commission on the Los Angeles Police Department (1991) *Report of the Independent Commission on the Los Angeles Police Department* [online], Available from: www.michellawy ers.com/wp-content/uploads/2010/06/Report-of-the-Inde pendent-Commission-on-the-LAPD-re-Rodney-King_Redu ced.pdf

Independent Police Complaints Commission, UK (2010) *Deaths In or Following Police Custody: An Examination of the Cases 1998/ 99 – 2008/09*, London: IPCC.

Independent Police Conduct Authority (2012) *Thematic Report: Deaths in Custody – A Ten Year Review*, Wellington: Independent Police Conduct Authority.

Independent Police Investigative Directorate (2021) *Annual Report 2020/2021 Financial Year*, Pretoria: IPID.

International Criminal Court [ICC] (2021) Decision on the Prosecutor's request for Authorisation of an Investigation Pursuant to Article 15(3) of the Statute, Situation in the Republic of the Philippines, Pre-Trial Chamber 1, 15 September 2021, No. ICC-01/21.

Irwin, A. and Pearl, B. (2020) *The Community Responder Model: How Cities Can Send the Right Responder to Every 911 Call*, Washington, DC: Center for American Progress.

Iyengar, R. (2007) 'Does the certainty of arrest reduce domestic violence? Evidence from mandatory and recommended arrest laws', National Bureau of Economic Research Working Paper Series No. 13186, Cambridge, MA: National Bureau of Economic Research.

Jablonski, N. (2021) 'Racism has a physical impact in the body – here's how', *The Conversation*, 31 January.

Jack, S.P., Petrosky, E., Lyons, B.H., Blair, J.M., Ertl, A.M., Sheats, K.J., and Betz, C.J. (2018) 'Surveillance for violent deaths: National Violent Death Reporting System, 27 States, 2015', *Surveillance Summaries*, 67(11): 1–32.

Jacobs, L.A., Kim, M.E., Whitfield, D.L., Gartner, R.E., Panichelli, M., Kattari, S.K., Downey, M.M., McQueen, S.S., and Mountz, S.E. (2021) 'Defund the police: moving towards an anti-carceral social work', *Journal of Progressive Human Services*, 32(1): 37–62.

James, S.E., Herman, J.L., Rankin, S., Keisling, M., Mottet, L., and Anafi, M. (2016) *The Report of the 2015 U.S. Transgender Survey*, Washington, DC: National Centre for Transgender Equality.

Jannetta, J. (2020) 'It wasn't enough: The limits of police-community trust-building reform in Minneapolis', Urban Wire [The blog of the Urban Institute], 4 June.

Jassal, N. (2020) 'Gender, law enforcement, and access to justice: evidence from all-women police stations in India', *American Political Science Review*, 114(4): 1035–54.

Jelsma, M. (2018) 'Human rights, illicit cultivation and alternative development: connecting the dots' [Discussion paper], Transnational Institute [online], Available from: www.ohchr.org/Documents/HRBodies/HRCouncil/DrugProblem/HRC39/TransnationalInstitute.pdf

Johnston, E. (1991) *National Report*, Canberra: Royal Commission into Aboriginal Deaths in Custody.

Johnson, H., Ollus, N., and Nevalla, S. (2008) *Violence Against Women: An International Perspective*, New York: Springer.

Johnson, V. (2021) 'Capital siege raises questions over extent of white supremacist infiltration of US police', *The Conversation*, [online] 15 January, Available from: www.theconversation.com/capitol-siege-raises-questions-over-extent-of-white-supremacist-infiltration-of-us-police-153145

Jones, D. (1982) *Crime, Protest, Community and Police in Nineteenth Century Britain*, London: Routledge.

Jordan, J. (2004) 'Beyond belief? Police, rape and women's credibility', *Criminal Justice*, 4(1): 29–59.

Jumbunna Research (2022) 'Walker Family & Yuendumu Elders condemn Rolfe not guilty verdict', Jumbunna Institute, [online] 11 March, Available from: www.jumbunna.institute/2022/03/11/walker-family-yuendumu-elders-condemn-rolfe-not-guilty-verdict/

Kaba, M. (2021) *We Do this Till We Free Us*, Chicago: Haymarket Books.

Kalhan, A., Singh, S., and Moghe, K. (2020) 'Locked down, trapped and abandoned migrant workers in Pune City', *Economic and Political Weekly*, 27 June.

Karakulak, H. and Kurmelovs, R. (2021) '"Excited delirium" used by police', *The Saturday Paper*, No. 363, [online] 21 August, Available from: www.thesaturdaypaper.com.au/news/politics/2021/08/21/excited-delirium-used-police/162946800012314

Keilty, J. and Connelly, G. (2001) 'Making a statement: an exploratory study of barriers facing women with an intellectual disability when making a statement about sexual assault to police', *Disability & Society*, 16(2): 273–91.

Kelley, R.D.G. (2020) 'What abolition looks like, from the Panthers to the people', Level, [online] 26 October, Available from: https://level.medium.com/what-abolition-looks-like-from-the-panthers-to-the-people-6c2e537eac71

Killingray, D. (1991) 'Guarding the extended frontier: policing the Gold Coast, 1865–1913', in D.M. Anderson and D. Killingray (eds) *Policing the Empire: Government, Authority and Control 1830–1940*, Manchester: Manchester University Press, pp 106–25.

Kim, M., Chung, M., Hassan, S., and Ritchie, A. (2021) *Defund the Police – Invest in Community Care: A Guide to Alternative Mental Health Responses*, Interrupting Criminalization [online], Available from: www.interruptingcriminalization.com/s/Crisis-Response-Guide.pdf

Knoetze, D. (2020) 'Police are not being held accountable for child killings, watchdog records reveal', *Daily Maverick*, [online] 8 September, Available from: www.dailymaverick.co.za/article/2020-09-08-police-are-not-being-held-accountable-for-child-killings-watchdog-records-reveal/

Knutsson, J. and Noree, A. (2010) 'Police use of firearms in the Nordic countries: a comparison', in J.B. Kuhns and J. Knutsson (eds) *Police Use of Force: A Global Perspective*, Oxford: Praeger, pp 115–23.

Kolsky, E. (2010) *Colonial Justice in British India: White Violence and the Rule of Law*, New Delhi: Cambridge University Press.

Koziarski, J. and Huey, L. (2021) '#Defund or #Re-Fund? Re-examining Bayley's blueprint for police reform', *International Journal of Comparative and Applied Criminal Justice*, 45(3): 269–84.

Kraska, P. (2007) 'Militarization and policing: its relevance to 21st century police', *Policing*, 1(4): 501–13.

Kraska, P. and Williams, S. (2019) 'The material reality of state violence: the case of police militarization', in W.S. DeKeseredy, C.M. Rennison, and A.K. Hall-Sanchez (eds) *The Routledge International Handbook of Violence Studies*, Abingdon: Routledge, pp 145–59.

Kushner, R. (2019) 'Is prison necessary? Ruth Wilson Gilmore might change your mind', *New York Times Magazine*, [online] 17 April, Available from: www.nytimes.com/2019/04/17/magazine/prison-abolition-ruth-wilson-gilmore.html

La Vigne, N., Fontaine, J., and Dwivedi, A. (2017) *How Do People in High-Crime, Low-Income Communities View the Police?* Washington, DC: Urban Institute.

Lammy, D. (2017) *The Lammy Review: An Independent Review Into the Treatment of, and Outcomes for, Black, Asian and Minority Ethnic Individuals in the Criminal Justice System*, London: UK Government Publishing Service.

Law Council of Australia (2018) *People with Disability: Final Report* [online], Available from: www.lawcouncil.asn.au/justice-project/final-report

Levine, P. (1994) 'Walking the streets the way no decent woman should: women police in World War 1', *The Journal of Modern History*, 66(1): 34–78.

Levinson, J., Wilson, C., Doubek, J., and Nuyen, S. (2020) 'Federal officers use unmarked vehicles to grab people in Portland, DHS confirms', *All Things Considered*, National Public Radio, [online] 17 July, Available from: https://www.npr.org/2020/07/17/892277592/federal-officers-use-unmarked-vehicles-to-grab-protesters-in-portland

Liem, M., Suonpää, K., Lehti, M., Kivivuori, J., Granath, S., Walser, S., and Killias, M. (2019) 'Homicide clearance in Western Europe', *European Journal of Criminology*, 16(1): 81–101.

Lindon, G. and Roe, R. (2017) *Deaths in Police Custody: A Review of the International Literature*, London: Home Office.

Lothian, K. (2005) 'Seizing the time: Australian Aborigines and the influence of the Black Panther Party, 1969–1972', *Journal of Black Studies*, 35(4): 179–200.

Lum, C., Koper, C.S., Wilson, D.B., Stoltz, M., Goodier, M., Eggins, E., Higginson, A., and Mazerolle, L. (2020) 'Body worn cameras' effects on police officers and citizen behaviour: a systematic review', *Campbell Systematic Review*, 16(3): 1–40.

Macpherson, W. (1999) *The Stephen Lawrence Inquiry*, CM 4262–1. London: The Stationery Office.

Maher, G. (2021) *A World Without Police: How Strong Communities Make Cops Obsolete*, London: Verso.

Mahtani, S. (2020) 'While U.S. tackles police brutality, Hong Kong is in denial', *The Washington Post*, [online] 19 June, Available from: www.washingtonpost.com/world/asia_pacific/hong-kong-police-brutality-black-lives-matter-george-floyd-protests/2020/06/18/911454a4-aeee-11ea-98b5-279a6479a1e4_story.html

Maynard, R. (2017) *Policing Black Lives: State Violence in Canada from Slavery to the Present*, Halifax: Fernwood Publishing.

McCulloch, J. (2017) 'Police, crime and human rights', in L. Weber, E. Fishwick, and M. Mamo (eds) *The Routledge International Handbook of Criminology and Human Rights*, Abingdon: Routledge, pp 323–32.

McCulloch, J., Maher, J., Walklate, S., and McGowan, J. (2021) 'Justice perspectives of women with disability: an Australian story', *International Review of Criminology*, 27(2): 196–210.

McLeod, A. (2019) 'Envisioning abolition democracy', *Harvard Law Review*, 132: 1613–49.

McManus, H., Shafer, J., and Graham, A. (2019) 'Race and the procedural justice model of policing', in J. Unnever, S. Gabbidon, and C. Chouhy (eds) *Building A Black Criminology*, New York: Routledge, pp 317–43.

McMichael, C. (2016) 'Police wars and state repression in South Africa', *Journal of Asian and African Studies*, 51(1): 3016.

McNamara, D. (2021) 'Policing in the age of the asylum: early legislative interventions in the lives of persons with disabilities', *Disability Studies Quarterly*, 41(2): 1–18.

Mental Health Act (2014), [online] s351(1), Available from: https://content.legislation.vic.gov.au/sites/default/files/2022-08/14-26aa024%20authorised.pdf

Metaal, P. and Youngers, C. (2011) *Systems Overload: Drug Laws and Prisons in Latin America*, Amsterdam/Washington: Transnational Institute and Washington Office on Latin America.

Mignolo, W. (2017) 'Interview with Walter Mignolo', in M. Woons and S. Weier (eds) *Critical Epistemologies of Global Politics*, Bristol: E-International Relations Publishing, pp 11–25.

Miki, Y. (2021) 'Black and Indigenous histories of Brazil's race mixture', *NACLA – Report on the Americas*, 53(3): 304–9.

Miles-Johnson, T. (2013) 'LGBTI variations in crime reporting: how sexual identity influences decisions to call the cops', *Sage Open*, 3(2), DOI: 10.1177/2158244013490707.

Millie, A. (2014) 'What are the police for? Re-thinking policing post-austerity', in J.M. Brown (ed), *The Future of Policing*, Abingdon: Routledge, pp 52–63.

Morgan, J. (2021) 'Policing under disability law', *Stanley Law Review*, 73: 1–64.

Morin, R. and Mercer, A. (2017) 'A closer look at police officers who have fired their weapon on duty', Pew Research Center, [online] 8 February, Available from: www.pewresearch.org/fact-tank/2017/02/08/a-closer-look-at-police-officers-who-have-fired-their-weapon-on-duty/

Moses, D. (2000) 'An antipodean genocide? The origins of the genocidal moment in the colonisation of Australia', *Journal of Genocide Research*, 2(1): 89–106.

Movement for Black Lives [M4BL] (2020) '#DEFUNDPOLICE, #FUNDTHEPEOPLE, #DEFENDBLACKLIVES: concrete steps toward divestment from policing and investment in community safety' [#DefundPolice Public Downloads/Defund Toolkit.pdf], [online], Available from: www.drive.google.com/drive/folders/1gZz_k20UY0JQADf2UKblS5ivMqo-53Rx

Murray, S. and Heenan, M. (2012) 'Reported rapes in Victoria: police responses to victims with a psychiatric disability or mental health issue', *Current Issues in Criminal Justice*, 23(3): 353–68.

Mutongwizo, T. and Mutongwizo, N. (forthcoming) 'Inherited structures and indigenised policing in Africa: Insights from South Africa and Zimbabwe', in C. Cunneen, A. Deckert, A. Porter, J. Tauri, and R. Webb (eds) *Routledge Handbook on Decolonizing Justice*, Abingdon: Routledge.

Myanmar Federation of Persons with Disabilities (2021) 'Press statement, 18 February, 2021' [online] 23 February, Available from: www.arsvi.com/2021/20210218e.htm

Nancarrow, H. (2021) 'Domestic violence law: when good intentions go awry in practice', in R. Vijeyarasa (ed) *International Women's Rights Law and Gender Equality: Making the Law Work for Women*, London: Routledge.

Nancarrow, H., Thomas, K., Riongland, V., and Modini, T. (2020) *Accurately Identifying the 'Person Most in Need of Protection' in Domestic and Family Violence Law*, Sydney: ANROWS.

Nathan, R. and Thorat, V. (2020) 'Atrocities against Dalit girls and women in UP', *Economic and Political Weekly*, 3 October.

National Campaign Against Torture [NCAT] (2020) *India: National Report on Torture 2019*, New Delhi: National Campaign Against Torture.

National Campaign Against Torture [NCAT] (2021) *India: National Report on Torture 2020*, New Delhi: National Campaign Against Torture.

National Commission on Human Rights [NCHR], Pakistan (2019) *Report on Enforced Disappearances*, Islamabad: NCHR.

National Crime Records Bureau (2019) *Report on Missing Women and Children in India*, New Delhi: Indian Government.

National Crime Records Bureau (2020) *Crime in India: Statistics. Volume 1*, New Delhi: Indian Government.

National Disability Network and National Committee on the Rights of Persons with Disability (2017) *Parallel Report of India on the Convention on the Rights of Persons with Disabilities (CRPD)* [online] 31 March, Available from: www.ncpedp.org/sites/all/themes/marinelli/documents/DRAFT%20CRPD%20India%20Parallel%20Report%20(31st%20March%202017).pdf

National Human Rights Commission, India (2018) *Annual Report 2017–2018* [online], Available from: www.nhrc.nic.in/annual reports/2017-2018

National Human Rights Commission, Nigeria (2020) 'Press release', [online] 15 April, Available from: www.nigeriarights.gov.ng/nhrc-media/press-release/100-national-human-rights-commission-press-release-on-covid-19-enforcement-so-far-report-on-incidents-of-violation-of-human-rights.html

National Inquiry into Missing and Murdered Indigenous Women and Girls [NIMMIWG] (Canada) (2019a) *Reclaiming Power and Place: The Final Report of the National Inquiry into Missing and Murdered Indigenous Women and Girls. Executive Summary* [online], Available from: www.mmiwg-ffada.ca/final-report/

National Inquiry into Missing and Murdered Indigenous Women and Girls [NIMMIWG] (Canada) (2019b) *Reclaiming Power and Place: The Final Report of the National Inquiry into Missing and Murdered Indigenous Women and Girls*, Volume 1(a) [online], Available from: www.mmiwg-ffada.ca/final-report/

National Institute of Justice (2009) *Practical Implications Around Domestic Violence Research: For Law Enforcement, Prosecutors and Judges*, Washington DC: U.S. Department of Justice.

National Law Enforcement Officers Memorial Fund (2020) *Law Enforcement Officers Fatalities Report*, Washington DC: National Law Enforcement Officers Memorial Fund.

Naudé, C.M.B., Prinsloo, J.H., and Ladikos A. (2006) *Experiences of Crime in Thirteen African Countries: Results from the International Crime Victim Survey*, Turin: UNICRI-UNODC.

Nembhard, S. and Robin, L. (2021) *Racial and Ethnic Disparities Throughout the Criminal Justice System*, Washington DC: Urban Institute.

Neocleous, M. (2021a) '"Original, absolute, indefeasible": or, what we talk about when we talk about police power', *Social Justice*, 47(3–4): 9–32.

Neocleous, M. (2021b) 'Kettle logic', *Critical Criminology*, 29: 183–97.

Newton, H.P. (1973) *Revolutionary Suicide*, London: Penguin.

Niolon, P.H., Kearns, M., Dills, J., Rambo, K., Irving, S., Armstead, T.L., and Gilbert, L. (2017) *Preventing Intimate Partner Violence Across the Lifespan: A Technical Package of Programs, Policies, and Practices*, Atlanta, GA: Centers for Disease Control and Prevention.

Noor, P. (2018) 'Met police use tasers and restraints more often against black people', *The Guardian*, [online] 5 December, Available from: www.theguardian.com/uk-news/2018/dec/05/met-police-use-tasers-and-restraints-more-often-against-black-people

NSW Law Reform Commission (2012) *People With Cognitive and Mental Health Impairments in the Criminal Justice System: Diversion*, Sydney: NSW Law Reform Commmission, Report 135.

NSW Legislative Council Standing Committee on Social Issues (2021) *Gay and Transgender Hate Crimes between 1970 and 2010*, Sydney: NSW Parliament, Report No 58.

NSW Ombudsman (2012) *How are Taser weapons used by the NSW Police Force?* Sydney: New South Wales Ombudsman.

Office for National Statistics (2021) *Homicide in England and Wales: Year Ending March 2020*, London: Office for National Statistics.

Office of the Aboriginal and Torres Strait Islander Social Justice Commissioner (1996) *Indigenous Deaths in Custody 1989–1996*, Sydney: HREOC.

Oklahoma Commission to Study the Tulsa Race Riot of 1921 (2001) *Tulsa Race Riot: A Report by the Oklahoma Commission to Study the Tulsa Race Riot of 1921*, Oklahoma, [online] 28 February, Available from: www.okhistory.org/research/forms/freport.pdf

Onuoha, F.C., Ezirim, G.E., and Onuh, P.A. (2021) 'Extortionate policing and the futility of COVID-19 pandemic nationwide lockdown in Nigeria: insights from the South East Zone', *African Security Review*, DOI: 10.1080/10246029.2021.1969961.

Oppenheim, M. (2021) 'Women being arrested and criminalised after reporting violence and abuse, says MPs', *The Independent*, [online] 18 May, Available from: www.independent.co.uk/news/uk/home-news/women-pointless-arrests-criminal-justice-system-b1848981.html

Owen, C. (2016) *'Every Mother's Son is Guilty': Policing the Kimberley Frontier of Western Australia 1882–1905*, Crawley: University of Western Australia Publishing.

Pearl, B. (2020) *Beyond Policing: Investing in Offices of Neighborhood Safety*, Washington, DC: Centre for American Progress.

Perry, D. and Carter-Long, L. (2016) *The Ruderman White Paper on Media Coverage of Law Enforcement Use of Force and Disability*, Boston: Ruderman Family Foundation.

Petre, A. (2021) 'Racism, police brutality and online hate: why Romania's Roma are no nearer their Black Lives Matter moment', BIRN, [online] 31 March, Available from: www.balkaninsight.com/2021/03/31/racism-police-brutality-and-online-hate-why-romanias-roma-are-no-nearer-their-black-lives-matter-moment/

Piza, E. and Welsh, B. (eds) (2022) *The Globalization of Evidence Based Policing*, London: Routledge.

Police Accountability Project (2019) *First Submission to the Royal Commission into Victoria's Mental Health System*, Victoria: Flemington Kensington Community Legal Centre.

Porter, A. (2016) 'Decolonising policing: Indigenous night patrols, counter-policing and safety', *Theoretical Criminology*, 20(4): 548–65.

Porter, A. (2020) 'Sugar, slavery and the birth of preventive policing: the Thames River Police 1789-present' [Working Paper], Melbourne Law School Research Seminar Series, Melbourne Law School, Paper on file with the author, 17 August, Available from: www.academia.edu/49103403/Sugar_Slavery_and_the_Birth_of_Preventive_Policing_The_Thames_River_Police

Porter, A. and Cunneen, C. (2020) 'Policing settler colonial societies', in P. Birch, M. Kennedy, and E. Kruger (eds) *Australian Policing*, London: Routledge, pp 397–411.

Porter, A. and Whittaker, A. (2019) 'Missing and murdered Aboriginal children: apologies offer little in the face of systemic police failures', *The Guardian*, [online] 20 August, Available from: www.theguardian.com/commentisfree/2019/aug/20/missing-and-murdered-aboriginal-children-apologies-offer-lit tle-in-the-face-of-systemic-police-failures

President's Task Force on 21st Century Policing (2015) *Final Report of the President's Task Force on 21st Century Policing*, Washington DC: Office of Community Oriented Policing Services.

Prison Police Initiative (2019) 'Policing women: race and gender disparities in police stops, searches, and use of force' [blog], [online] 14 May, Available from: www.prisonpolicy.org/blog/2019/05/14/policingwomen/

Productivity Commission (2022) Report on Government Services, Part C, Available from: https://www.pc.gov.au/ongo ing/report-on-government-services/2022

Puar, J. (2017) *The Right to Maim*, Durham: Duke University Press.

Ransby, B. (2018) *Making All Black Lives Matter*, Oakland: University of California Press.

Ravi, P. (2020) 'The unnamed George Floyds of India – episodic police brutality in 2019–2020', *Feminism in India*, [online] 17 June, Available from: www.feminisminindia.com/2020/06/17/unnamed-george-floyds-india-episodic-police-brutal ity-2019-20/

Ray, R. (2020) 'What does defund the police mean?', Brookings Institute, [online] 19 June, Available from: https://www.brooki ngs.edu/blog/fixgov/2020/06/19/what-does-defund-the-pol ice-mean-and-does-it-have-merit/

Reiner, R. (1985) *The Politics of the Police*, Brighton: Wheatsheaf Books.

Reiner, R. (2010) *The Politics of the Police* (4th edn), London: Routledge.

Richie, B.E. (2012) *Arrested Justice: Black Women, Violence and America's Prison Nation*, New York: New York University Press.

Ritchie, A.J. (2006) 'Law enforcement violence against women of color', in INCITE! Women of Color Against Violence (eds), *Color of Violence: The Incite! Anthology*, Cambridge MA: South End Press, pp 138–56.

Ritchie, A.J. (2017) *Invisible No More: Police Violence Against Black Women and Women of Color*, Boston: Beacon Press.

Ritchie, A.J. and Jones-Brown, D. (2017) 'Policing race, gender, and sex: a review of law enforcement policies', *Women & Criminal Justice*, 27(1): 21–50.

Roberts, T. (2005) *Frontier Justice: A History of the Gulf Country to 1990*, St Lucia: University of Queensland Press.

Rodríguez, D. (forthcoming) 'The obsolescence of "police brutality": counterinsurgency in a moment of police reform' in C. Cunneen, A. Deckert, A. Porter, J. Tauri, and R. Webb (eds) *Routledge Handbook on Decolonizing Justice*, Abingdon: Routledge.

Ronan, W. (2020) 'New FBI hate crime report shows increase in LGBTQ attacks' [press release], Human Rights Campaign, [online] 17 November, Available from: www.hrc.org/press-relea ses/new-fbi-hate-crimes-report-shows-increases-in-anti-lgbtq-attacks

Roslin, A. (2016) 'The secret epidemic of police domestic violence: how it affects us all', *Family & Intimate Partner Violence Quarterly*, 8(4): 319–29.

Rowe, S. and Dowse, L. (2021) 'Enabling penal abolition: the need for a reciprocal dialogue between critical disability studies and penal abolitionism', in M.J. Coyle and D. Scott (eds) *The Routledge International Handbook on Penal Abolition*, London: Routledge, pp 206–16.

Rowe, S., Simpson, J., Baldry, E., and McGee, P. (2017) *The Provision of Services Under the NDIS for People with Disabilities who are in Contact with the Criminal Justice System*, Melbourne: Australians for Disability Justice.

Royal Canadian Mounted Police [RCMP] (2014) *Missing and Murdered Aboriginal Women: A National Operational Overview*, RCMP [online], Available from: https://www.rcmp-grc.gc.ca/en/missing-and-murdered-aboriginal-women-national-oper ational-overview

Royal Commission into Victoria's Mental Health System (2021) *Final Report. Executive Summary*, Volumes 1–5, Melbourne: State of Victoria.

Royal Commission on Aboriginal Peoples (1996) *Report of the Royal Commission on Aboriginal Peoples*, Volume 1, Ottawa: Minister of Supply and Services Canada.

Runnymede Trust (2021) *England Civil Society Submission to the United Nations Committee on the Elimination of Racial Discrimination*, London: Runnymede Trust.

Russell, M. and Stewart, J. (2001) 'Disablement, prison, and historical segregation', *Monthly Review*, 5(3): 61–75.

Sälter, G. (2014) 'Early modern police and policing', in G. Bruinsma and D. Weisburd (eds) *Encyclopedia of Criminology and Criminal Justice*, New York: Springer, pp 1243–56.

Santos, B. de Sousa (2021) 'On Israel's colonial occupation of Palestine: the final solution without end', *Critical Legal Thinking*, [online] 17 June, Available from: www.criticallegalthinking.com/2021/06/17/on-israels-colonial-occupation-of-palestine-the-final-solution-without-end/

Schenwar, M. and Law, V. (2020) *Prison by Any Other Name*, New York: The New Press.

Schrader, S. (2015) 'The liberal solution to police violence: ensuring trust will ensure more obedience', *The Indypendent*, [online] 30 June, Available from: www.indypendent.org/2015/06/the-liberal-solution-to-police-violence-restoring-trust-will-ensure-more-obedience/

Schrader, S. (2019a) *Badges Without Borders: How Global Counterinsurgency Transformed American Policing*, Berkeley: University of California Press.

Schrader, S. (2019b) 'Book review: *The Counterrevolution: How Our Government Went to War Against its Own Citizens*', *Social Justice*, 46(2/3): 167–72.

Schrader, S. (2020) 'Defund the global policeman', *N+1*, 38, [online], Available from: https://nplusonemag.com/issue-38/politics/defund-the-global-policeman/

Schrader, S. (2021) 'The lies cops tell and the lies we tell about cops', *The New Republic*, [online] 27 May, Available from: www.newrepublic.com/article/162510/cops-lie-public-safety-defund-the-police

Seale, B. (1967) 'The coming long hot summer', *The Black Panther*, 20 June, 1(3): 4–7, [online], Available from: www.marxists.org/history/usa/pubs/black-panther/index.htm

Segrave, M., Wickes, R., and Keel, C. (2021) *Migrant and Refugee Women in Australia: The Safety and Security Study*, Clayton: Monash University.

Sekhri, A. (2020) 'The Criminal Law Review Committee', *The India Forum*, 6 November, [online], Available from: https://www.theindiaforum.in/issues/november-6-2020

Sentencing Project (2018) *Report to the UN Special Rapporteur on Contemporary Forms of Racism, Racial Discrimination, Xenophobia, and Related Intolerance Regarding Racial Disparities in the United States Criminal Justice System*, Washington DC: The Sentencing Project.

Sim, J., Scraton, P., and Gordon, P. (1987) 'Introduction: crime, the state and critical analysis', in P. Scraton (ed) *Law, Order and the Authoritarian State*, Milton Keynes: Open University Press, pp 1–70.

Simon, J. (2007) *Governing Through Crime: How the War On Crime Transformed American Democracy and Created a Culture of Fear*, New York: Oxford University Press.

Simplican, S.C. (2021) 'Politicizing disability in political science, COVID-19, and police violence', *Politics, Groups, and Identities*, 9(2): 387–94.

Sinclair, G. (2006) *At the End of the Line: Colonial Policing and the Imperial Endgame*, Manchester: Manchester University Press.

Sinclair, G. (2008) 'The "Irish" policeman and the Empire: influencing the policing of the British Empire–Commonwealth', *Irish Historical Studies*, 36(142): 173–87.

Sinclair, G. and Williams, C. (2007) '"Home and Away": the cross-fertilisation between "Colonial" and "British" policing, 1921–85', *The Journal of Imperial and Commonwealth History*, 35(2): 221–38.

Sivanandan, A. (1990) *Communities of Resistance: Writings on Black Struggles for Socialism*, London: Verso.

Smee, B. (2021) 'Racist: coercive control laws could harm Indigenous women in Queensland, advocates warn', *The Guardian*, [online] 18 May, Available from: www.theguardian.com/australia-news/2021/may/18/racist-coercive-control-laws-could-harm-indigenous-women-in-queensland-advocates-warn

Smith, A. (2005) *Conquest: Sexual Violence and American Indian Genocide*, Brooklyn: South End Press.

Sobsey, D. (2000) 'Faces of violence against women with developmental disabilities', *Impact*, 13(3), [online], Available from: www.ici.umn.edu/products/impact/133/default.html

Spade, D. (2020) *Mutual Aid: Building Solidarity During this Crisis and the Next*, London: Verso Books.

Stannard, D. (1992) *American Holocaust*, New York: Oxford University Press.

Stenson, K. (2000), '"Some day our prince will come": zero tolerance policing in Britain', in T. Hope and R. Sparks (eds) *Crime, Risk and Insecurity*, London: Routledge.

Stockwell, A. (1992) 'Policing during the Malayan emergency, 1948–60: communism, communalism and decolonisation', in D.M. Anderson and D. Killingray (eds) *Policing and Decolonisation: Nationalism, Politics and the Police 1917–1965*, Manchester: Manchester University Press, pp 105–27.

Strong, K. (2018) 'Do African lives matter to Black Lives Matter? Youth uprisings and the borders of solidarity', *Urban Education*, 53(2): 265–85.

Sultana, R. and Dey, S.R. (2020) 'Children of the Tongi Child Development Centre (CDC): their experiences before detention', *Social Sciences Review* [Dhaka University Studies, Part-D], 37(1): 255–75.

Tankebe, J. (2008) 'Colonialism, legitimation and policing in Ghana', *International Journal of Law, Crime and Justice*, 36: 67–84.

Tapia Tapia, S. (2016) 'Sumak Kawsay, coloniality and the criminalisation of violence against women in Ecuador', *Feminist Theory*, 17(2): 141–56.

Tapia Tapia, S. (2021) 'A decolonial feminist critique of penality', *Critical Legal Thinking*, [online] 29 March, Available from: www.criticallegalthinking.com/2021/03/29/a-decolonial-feminist-critique-of-penality/

Tatour, A. and Tatour, L. (forthcoming) 'Settler colonialism and the criminalization of Palestinian resistance', in C. Cunneen, A. Deckert, A. Porter, J. Tauri, and R. Webb (eds) *Routledge Handbook on Decolonizing Justice*, Abingdon: Routledge.

Taylor, C. (2018) 'Anti-carceral feminism and sexual assault – a defense', *Social Philosophy Today*, 34: 29–49.

Terwiel, A. (2020) 'What is carceral feminism?', *Political Theory*, 48(4): 421–42.

Thom, K. and Quince, K. (2020) 'Black Lives Matter outrage must drive police reform in Aotearoa-New Zealand too', *The Conversation*, 9 June.

Thomas, G. (2021) 'Statement of Geoffrey Thomas', Royal Commission into Violence, Abuse, Neglect and Exploitation of People with Disability, STAT.0279.0001.0001 [online], Available from: www.disability.royalcommission.gov.au/publications/exhi bit-11-02801-stat027900010001-written-statement-statement-geoffrey-thomas-0

Thompson, C. (2021) 'Fatal police shootings of unarmed black people reveal troubling patterns', National Public Radio, [online] 25 January, Available from: www.npr.org/2021/01/25/956177 021/fatal-police-shootings-of-unarmed-black-people-reveal-troubling-patterns

Thompson, V. (2021a) 'Policing in postcolonial continental Europe' [video], YouTube [online], Available from: www.yout ube.com/watch?v=ZFw0XULKjDM

Thompson, V. (2021b) 'Understanding the policing of black, disabled bodies', Centre for American Progress [online], Available from: www.americanprogress.org/issues/disability/ news/2021/02/10/495668/understanding-policing-black-disab led-bodies/

Tomsen, S. (2002) *Hatred, Murder and Male Honour: Anti-Homosexual Homicides in New South Wales 1980–2000*, Canberra: Australia Institute of Criminology.

Tomsen, S. and Kirchengast, T. (2019) 'Victimhood, truth and criminal justice failure in relation to anti-homosexual violence and killings in New South Wales', *Current Issues in Criminal Justice*, 31(2): 181–93.

Tonry, M. (1995) *Malign Neglect*, New York: Oxford University Press.

Transparency International (2011) 'Corruption and human trafficking' [Working Paper No 3], [online], Available from: www.transparency.org/en/publications/working-paper-corruption-and-human-trafficking

Tribune (1986) 'Interview: Arthur Scargill – "You fight for your class"', *Tribune*, 26 February, p 16.

Uddin, M.K. (2020) 'Abductions and disappearances in Bangladeshi policing', *Policing*, 14(3): 643–56.

Ugwudike, P. (2020) 'Digital prediction technologies in the justice system: the implications of a "race-neutral" agenda', *Theoretical Criminology*, 24(3): 482–501.

Ugwudike, P. (2021) 'AI audits for assessing design logics and building ethical systems: the case of predictive policing algorithms', *AI and Ethics*, DOI: 10.1007/s43681-021-00117-5.

Ulbrick, A. (2021) *Predictive Policing and Young People*, Melbourne: Police Accountability Project.

UN Office on Drugs and Crime (2019) *Global Study on Homicide: Homicide Trends, Patterns and Criminal Justice Responses*, Vienna: UN Office on Drugs and Crime.

US Department of Justice (2016) *Investigation of the Baltimore City Police Department*, Washington DC: US Department of Justice, Civil Rights Division.

Vallas, R. (2016) *Disabled Behind Bars: The Mass Incarceration of People With Disabilities in America's Jails and Prisons*, Washington DC: Center for American Progress.

van Dijk, J., van Kesteren, J., and Smit, P. (2007) *Criminal Victimisation in International Perspective*, Den Haag: WODC.

Varghese, A. (2018) 'Abolishing the orderly system: colonial relic feeds off hierarchies of caste and class within police rank and file', The Leaflet, [online] 3 September, Available from: www.theleaflet.in/abolishing-the-orderly-system-colonial-relic-feeds-off-hierarchies-of-caste-and-class-within-police-rank-and-file/

Victorian Equal Opportunity and Human Rights Commission [VEOHRC] (2014) *Beyond Doubt: The Experiences of People with a Disability Reporting Crime*, Melbourne: VEOHRC.

Viljoen, E., Bornman, J., Wiles, L., and Tonsing, K. (2017) 'Police officer disability sensitivity training: a systematic review', *Police Journal: Theory, Practice and Principles*, 90(2): 143–59.

Vitale, A. (2017) *The End of Policing*, London: Verso.

Warren-Gordon, K. (2021) 'Decolonizing approach to understanding intimate partner violence in Belize', *Decolonization of Criminology and Justice*, 3(1): 63–81.

Waseem, Z. (forthcoming) 'A postcolonial condition of policing? Exploring policing and social movements in Pakistan and Nigeria' in A. Aliverti, H. Carvalho, A. Chamberlen, and M. Sozzo (eds) *Decolonising the Colonial Question: Colonial Legacies, Contemporary Problems*, Oxford: Oxford University Press.

Way, K. (2021) 'The solution of violence against women will never be more police', *Vice*, [online] 19 March, Available from: www.vice.com/en/article/qjp7db/the-solution-to-violence-against-women-will-never-be-more-police-atlanta-shooting

Weichbaum, S., Schwartzapfel, B., and Meagher, T. (2017) 'When warriors put on the badge', The Marshall Project [online], Available from: www.themarshallproject.org/2017/03/30/when-warriors-put-on-the-badge

Weichselbaum, S., Seville, L.R., Siegel, E., Neff, J., and Vansickle, A. (2021) 'Violent encounters with police send thousands of people to the ER every year', The Marshall Project [online] Available from: www.themarshallproject.org/2021/06/23/violent-encounters-with-police-send-thousands-of-people-to-the-er-every-year#

West, B. and Gandi, S. (2006) 'Reporting abuse: a study of people with disabilities', *Disability Studies Quarterly*, 26(1), [online] Available from: https://dsq-sds.org/article/view/650/827

White, N. (2021) 'Black people go missing in vast numbers – but campaigners say their cases are being ignored', *The Independent*, [online] 8 April, Available from: www.independent.co.uk/news/uk/home-news/black-people-missing-b1827530.html

White Bird Clinic (2020) *Crisis Assistance Helping out on the Streets: Media Guide*, Eugene, Oregon: White Bird Clinic.

Whitlock, C. (2019) 'Unguarded nation: Afghan security forces, despite years of training, were dogged by incompetence and corruption', *The Washington Post*, [online] 9 December, Available from: www.washingtonpost.com/graphics/2019/investigations/afghanistan-papers/afghanistan-war-army-police/

Wilson, J.Q. and Kelling, G.L. (1982) 'Broken Windows', *The Atlantic Monthly*, 249(3): 29–38.

Wootten, H. (1991) *Regional Report of Inquiry in New South Wales, Victoria and Tasmania, Royal Commission into Aboriginal Deaths in Custody*, Canberra: AGPS.

Worden, R.E. and McLean, S. (2017) *Mirage of Police Reform: Procedural Justice and Police Legitimacy*, Oakland: University of California Press.

Worden, R.E., McLean, S., Engel, R., Cochran, H., Corsaro, N., Reynolds, D. et al (2020) 'The impacts of implicit bias awareness training in the NYPD', University of Cincinnati Center for Police Research and Policy, [online] Available at: https://www1.nyc.gov/assets/nypd/downloads/pdf/analys is_and_planning/impacts-of-implicit-bias-awareness-training-in-%20the-nypd.pdf

World Health Organisation (2021) *Violence Against Women* [Fact Sheet], [online] 21 March, Available from: www.who.int/news-room/fact-sheets/detail/violence-against-women

Wright, D. (2004) *Report of the Commission of Inquiry into Matters Relating to the Death of Neil Stonechild*, Regina: Ministry of Justice.

Index

References to figures appear in *italic* type. References to endnotes show both the page number and the note number (231n3).

mental health-related deaths in
  custody 139
non-crime related incidents 44
police clear-up rates 47
prosecutions of police officers 163
removing to a 'place of safety' 135
stop and search powers 103
violence against Blacks 102
young peoples' experiences of
  policing 57
Equality and Human Rights
  Commission (UK) 104
equality before the law 29
ESMAD riot police (Columbia) 10
Europe 11, 47, 49
Everard, Sarah 111–12
evidence-based policing
  (EBP) 159–60
Excess Property Program (US
  Department of Defense) 106–7
'excited delirium syndrome' 142
ex-military recruits 156
Ezekwe, Tina 7

F

families 76, 77, 138
Fanon, Frantz 26–7, 53, 64, 65
Fatal Force database (*The Washington
  Post*) 88
fatal shootings
  Australia 90, 130–1, 141, 187
  Canada 139–40
  Latin America 9–10
  United States (US) 46, 88, 90
favelas (Brazil) 91, 98
Federal Bureau of Investigation
  (FBI) 46, 60, 66, 86, 88
Federal Race Discrimination
  Commissioner (Australia) 79
Félix, Ágatha 98
Female and male Elders 180–2
feminist abolitionism 127, 128
feminist activism 113–14
financial costs for misconduct 174–5
First Nations
  abolitionists 180
  colonial dispossession 13
  community safety patrols 183
  deaths by law enforcement 89
  deaths in police custody 89
  legal and medical services 67, 69
  movements for self-
    determination 64, 69

policing 29–32
rape and sexual violence 113
tasers 102–3
and use of OC spray 103
women 113, 120, 126
Floyd, George 6, 9, 55–6, 107,
  142, 155
Foley, Gary 68–9
Foucault, M. 21–2
France 23, 28, 40, 103
Francis, Peter 74–5
French Empire and colonies 26, 27, 28
French Indochina 28

G

Gangs violence matrix database 57, 160
Garner, Eric 98, 155
Gately, Kevin 71
Gay Pride 59
gendarmeries 23, 26, 28
gender inequality 122
Germany 11
Ghana 26, 28, 54, 163
Gilmore, Ruth Wilson 4, 166, 168
Gilroy, Paul 71, 73
Global Commission on Drug
  Policy 184
Global Gender Gap Report 122
global north/south divide 5
'global' policing 35
global protests 11–12
Globe and Mail 11
Goodmark, Leigh 107, 118–19,
  157, 178
Gordon, P. 70
Green, Dixon 76
Greenup, Evelyn 124
Greenwood, Tulsa, Oklahoma 34
Gruber, Aya 114, 178
Guardia Civil 23
The Guardian 89, 100, 131, 140
Guatemala 36
Guiliani, Rudolph 82–3
Gundy, David 78

H

Haiti 35
Hall, Stuart 70, 71–2, 149,
  154, 162
Hampton, Fred 66
Handsworth riots (Birmingham)
  72, 73
Harcourt, Bernard 18, 35, 106

O

Oaxaca State, Mexico 9–10
OC spray 101, 102–3
Oklahoma Commission of
Inquiry 34
Ontario, Canada 136
open-source databases 174
Osagie, Osaze 143
oversight and accountability 165

P

Pakistan 95–7, 121–2
Palestine Mandate 35
Palestinians 13, 97
Palm Island, Queensland 80
Papua, Indonesia 8
paramilitary police 70, 78–9
Paris model 23
Pashtun Tahafuz Movement
(PTM) 96
Pat, John 76, 99
Peach, Blair 71, 74
Peel, Robert 22, 42
Pennsylvania State Police 29
people with disabilities 130–46
criminalisation 134
custodial sentences 136–8
demanding to end policing 175–7
institutionalising 133
marginalisation and police
violence 139
medicalisation and police
violence 142
non-state violence 140
police disability awareness
training 156–7
police killing Black Americans 130
police resisting acknowledging 136
poverty and disadvantage 134
public health concerns 145
reporting offences 50–1
repressive management 131
welfare/wellness checks 143–4
see also mental ill-health
Pew Research Centre 52
Philadelphia 2
Philippine Constabulary 29
Philippines 8, 28, 29, 90–1
Pinto, Joao Pedro Mattos 98
police
administration proposals 172–3
as appropriate responders 136

as 'carers' of last resort 133
brutality 6, 9
culture 55
deaths 45–6
defining by end goals 43
democratic institution 14
detention 101
exploitation and control 189–90
historical role 39–41
killings 9, 90–9
legitimacy 43, 151, 159
powers 24, 57, 154, 189
practical options to reduce 171–5
recruiting marginalised groups 153
repression 6, 110
sexual violence 119–20
stations as a place of safety 135
Police Accountability Project
(Australia) 156–7
Police Against Black People (Institute
of Race Relations) 71
Police Support Units (PSUs, UK) 70
police violence
causing disabilities and mental
ill-health 145
and colonialism 27, 64
and community-based
organisations 85
First Nations women and
girls 120
global movement against 6–11
legal authority for violence and
coercion 43
nature and intensity of 96–7
'non-fatal' forms 101–3
official data for 101–2, 109
and the poor and marginalised 109
and racism 8
sex workers 119
unpunished 12
see also violence against women
policing
colonial settings 25–9
and community health 144
controlling populations 133
and criminalisation 132–3, 145
foreign policy objectives 35
institutional frameworks of
repression 4–5
legitimacy and acceptability 61–2
maintaining systemic
inequalities 58–9
as a sociohistorical process 21

rule of law 26
Runnymede Trust 139

S

'Safe Outside the System' (SOS) 179
Salazar, Victoria 10
Saskatoon 'freezing deaths'
    (Canada) 98
Scargill, Arthur 72–3
Scarman Inquiry 148–9, 162
Schrader, S. 19, 36, 43, 50, 106
Seale, Bobby 64
self-immolation 121n53
self-reports of justifiable
    homicides 88
settler colonial states 29–32, 97, 183
sexual misconduct 118
sexual violence 39, 113–14
sex workers 119
Sheik Jarrah, Israel 13
ShotSpotter 161
Sim, J 74
Simon, Jonathan 18
Sinclair, Georgina 35
Sista II Sista 81, 82, 179
Sistas Liberated Ground 82
Sisters Inside (Australia) 179
Sisters Uncut (UK) 179
'sit-at-home' strikes (Nigeria) 7
Sivanandan, A. 70, 73, 85, 149
slavery 12, 32–3
Smallman, Mina 111
Smallman, Nicole 112
Smith, Cindy Rose 124–5
Smith, Mona Lisa 124–5
social control 23–4
social divisions 48
social services 3, 53, 174, 176
solving crimes 43–4, 46–8
South Africa 7, 25–6, 148, 163,
    183, 186–7
South Carolina 32
South Sudan 137
Spade, Dean 169
Spain 23
Special Anti-Robbery Squad (SARS,
    Nigeria) 7
'Special Branch' police 35
'Special Demonstration Squad' (UK) 74
Special Patrol Group (SPG) 70–1
Speedy-Duroux, Clinton 124
Spratt, Kevin 103n66

state police 23, 182–3
state repression 4–5, 6, 186
state violence 88, 97
Stephen Lawrence Campaign 74–5,
    76, 99
Stephen Lawrence Day 75
stop and search 103–5
Stop LAPD Spying Coalition 161
'street-level bureaucracies' 55
Survived and Punished 179
SWAT teams 107
Sydney, Australia 79–80, 136
Sykes, Roberta 68
systemic racism *see* racism

T

Tactical Response Group (TRG) 78
Taiwan 8
Tamil Nadu, India 9
Tankebe, Justice 26, 38, 54
Tanzania 49
tasers 102–3, 139, 158
Taylor, Breona 107
technical fixes 158–61
Texas 2
Texas Rangers 30
Thailand 13
Thames River Police 23, 25
Third World movement 65
Thomas, Geoffrey 142
Thomas, Justen 134–5
Thorat, V. 121
Tonry, Michael 185
Toronto 10–11, 59, 81
torture 9–10, 92–5, 109, 120, 164
Tottenham, London 73, 74
Toxteth riots (Liverpool) 25, 72
Trail of Broken Treaties march
    (US) 67
training 44, 106, 154–8
Traoré, Adama 98
Trump, Donald J. 108–9
trust and legitimacy 151
Truth and Reconciliation
    Commission (South
    Africa) 148
Tulsa Riots 34
Turkey 59

U

Uganda 49, 137–8
Ugwudike, P. 160

prisoners having mental ill-health 132, 137
racial murders 34
reporting and recording crime 48–9, 50
State Department 36, 95–6
struggle against police and state violence 64
systemic racism 104–5
Transgender Survey 59
Violence Against Women Act 127
'war on drugs' and 'war on terror' 110
unresolved trauma 141–2
Urban Institute 52
US-centric discourses 169n7
Uttar Pradesh police 121

V

vagrancy 33
Venezuela 90n16
Victoria, Australia 118, 135, 139, 156–7
Vietnam War 64
The View 112
violence against women 111–29
  demands for safety and protection 111–12
  options for responding to 178–82
  partner violence 113, 140
  by police 119–20
  police being problematic 115–18
  policing being the answer 112–15
  reporting violence 115–18, 120–1
  see also intimate partner violence; police violence; women
violence and welfare 144
violence interrupters 178
violence of neglect 99–101, 110
Virginia, US 2
Vitale, A. 30, 154, 155, 158
Voice for Baloch Missing Persons (VBMP) 95
Volmer, August 28

W

Walker-Craig, Colleen 124
Walker, Kumanjayi 156, 187–8
Walker, Robert 76
war on drugs 90–2, 184–5
war on terror 81, 106, 107, 110, 119

'war power' (Neocleous) 106
Waseem, Zoha 96
The Washington Post 88, 139, 159, 174–5
Wazir, Arif 96
We Are Invisible (The View) 112
welfare/wellness checks 143–4
Western Australia 29–30, 31–2, 78, 103n66
West India Committee 23
West Papua, Indonesia 8
White colonisers 30
Whiteness of democratic rights 33
White police killings 89
White Supremacy Extremism 86
White violence 33–4
Williams, S. 107
Wilson, J.Q. 83
Winnipeg 11
women
  blamed for being raped 121–2
  criminalisation and incarceration 115
  gendered stigmas 141
  imprisonment for drug offences 185
  in Indian police 153
  missing or murdered 122–6
  needless arrests 117
  'non-voluntary' contact with police 119
  racism in the justice system 112
  revictimisation 116
  and sexual violence 93
  see also intimate partner violence; violence against women
women-led police stations 128
working-class communities and families 24–5
World Health Organisation 113

Y

Yawaru people 77
Yellowhead Highway (BC, Canada) 122
youth justice 58

Z

zero tolerance policing (ZTP) 43, 82–6, 119, 159
Zimbabwe 183